Studies in Romance Languages: 44

John E. Keller, Editor

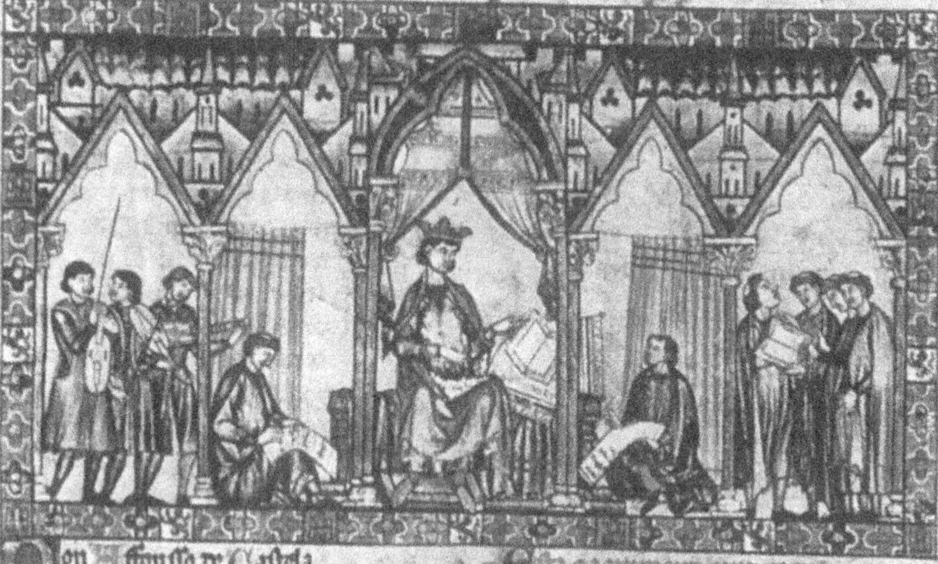

Don Affonsso de Castela,
de Toledo, de Leon
Rey e ben des Conpostela
ta o Reyno d'Aragon,
e de Cordova, de Jahen
de Sevilla outrossy,
e de Murça u gran bé-
lle fez Deus com' aprendi,
e Algarve que gãou
de mouros e nossa fe
meteu y. E ar poblou
Badalouz que Reyno é
muit' antigu' que tolleu
a mouros, Neul', Xerez,
Beger, Medina prender
e Alcalá foran vez.
Que os Romãos Rey
e por dereit' e Sennor
este Livro com' achei
fez. A onrr' e a loor
da virgen santa Maria,
que est madre de Deus,
en que ele muito fia,
Por en dos miragres seus
fez cantares e sões
saborosos de cantar,
todos de sennas razões,
com' y podedes achar.

Esta é a primeira cantiga de loor de Santa Maria, ementando os VII goyos que ouve de seu fillo.

Des oge mais quer' eu
trobar pola Sennor
onrrada, en que Deus quis carne fillar, beeyta
e sagrada, por nos dar gran soldada.
no seu reyno e nos erdar, por seu
de sa mesnada, de vida perlongada. sen

Daily Life Depicted
in the
Cantigas de Santa Maria

John Esten Keller and Annette Grant Cash

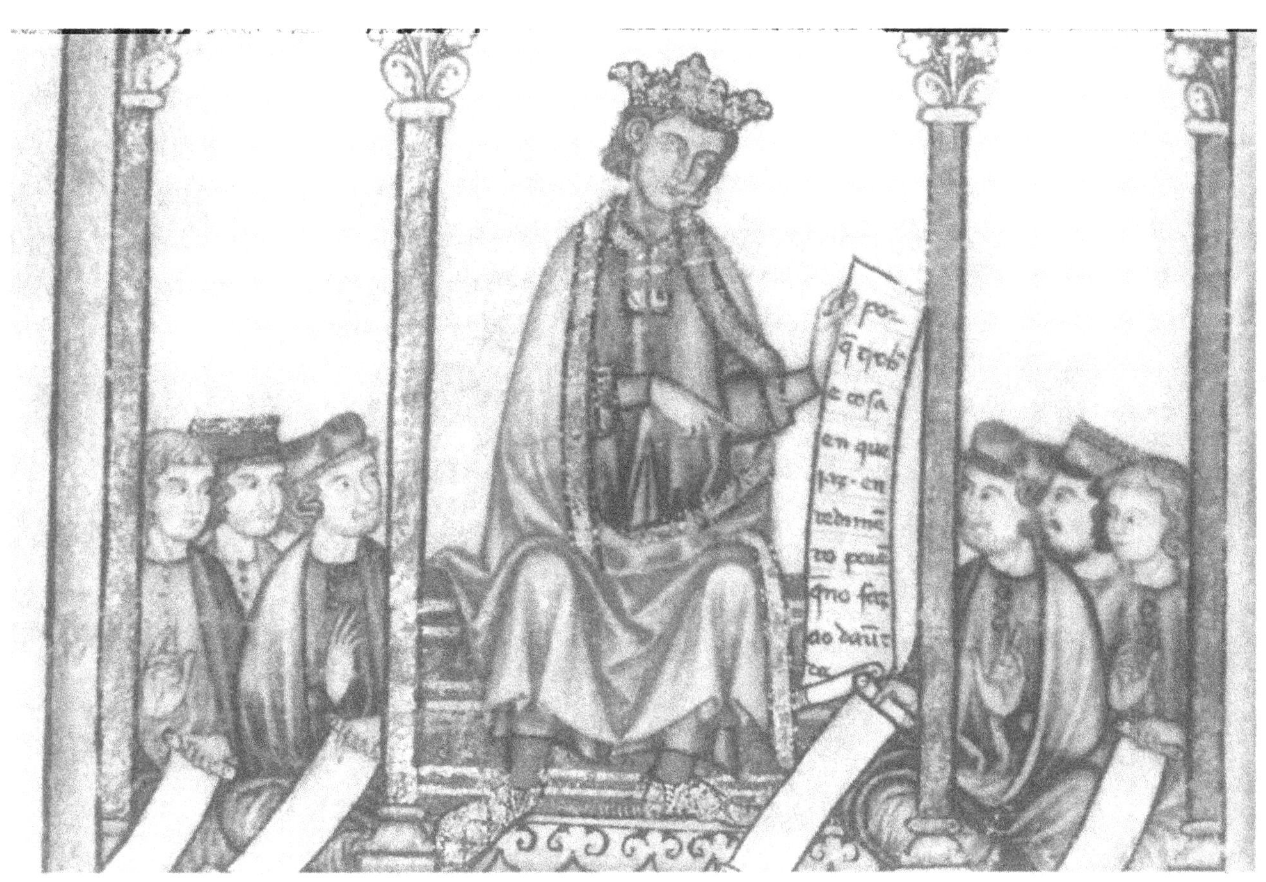

THE UNIVERSITY PRESS OF KENTUCKY

Publication of this volume was made possible in part
by grants from the Program for Cultural Cooperation
between Spain's Ministry of Education and Culture
and United States' Universities,
the Samuel H. Kress Foundation, and
the National Endowment for the Humanities.

Editorial and Sales Offices: The University Press of Kentucky
663 South Limestone Street, Lexington, Kentucky 40508-4008

02 01 00 99 98   1 2 3 4 5

Frontispiece: Alfonso with his scribes and musicians in
the prologue of the *Cantigas de Santa Maria.* MS TI.1.
Authorized by the Patrimonio Nacional and Edilán

Library of Congress Cataloging-in-Publication Data

Keller, John Esten.
  Daily life depicted in the Cantigas de Santa Maria / John Esten
Keller and Annette Grant Cash.
     p. cm. — (Studies in Romance languages ; 44)
  Includes bibliographical references and index.
  ISBN 0-8131-2050-0 (cloth : alk. paper)
  1. Alfonso X, King of Castile and Leon, 1221-1284. Cantigas de
Santa María. 2. Alfonso X, King of Castile and Leon, 1221-1284.
Cantigas de Santa Maria—Illustrations. 3. Manners and customs in
literature. 4. Manners and customs in art. 5. Middle Ages in
literature. 6. Middle ages in art. 7. Spain—Social life and
customs. 8. Spain—Civilization—711-1516. 9. Illumination of
books and manuscripts, Medieval—Spain. 10. Illumination of books
and manuscripts, Spanish. 11. Códice de Florencia. I. Cash,
Annette Grant, 1943- . II. Title. III. Series: Studies in
Romance languages (Lexington, Ky.) ; 44.
PQ9189.A44C335 1998
861'.1—dc21   98-17601

For Dinsmore and Claude,
without whose support and patience
we could not have completed this book

Contents

Illustrations follow page 52

Foreword

The *Cantigas de Santa Maria* is a book about miracles and a miraculous book. Inspired by King Alfonso's devotion to the Virgin Mary, it extols her virtues through art, music, and poetry, which convey a rich composite of the life, culture, and thought of thirteenth-century Iberia. Encomiums abound when the *Cantigas* are mentioned—the variety of its versifications, the richness of its musical repertoire, the vast collection of miracle tales, the lavishness of the miniatures—an awesome and overwhelming abundance. Yet underlying the exquisite artistry is a disarming simplicity. The language of the poems is straightforward and colloquial, with passages of natural dialogue. The miniatures provide an animated and faithful panorama of daily life. The miraculous is expressed in terms of the real so that all may understand the message of the Virgin's mercy and redemption. This realism, wherein all elements of the populace could recognize themselves, their activities, and their joys and tribulations, was meant to instruct as well as to entertain *(enseñar y deleitar)*. It has continued to do so throughout succeeding ages.

The pictorial record of the *Cantigas* is extremely vivid. Folk wisdom has it that "seeing is believing"—that is, the visual is the most immediately accessible to child and adult alike, and one need not be literate or educated to capture the sense. Such was the intent of the miniatures. Holy Mary intervenes directly in the concerns of humankind and the miracles take place in a recognizable context. We can indeed believe the illustrations of the *Cantigas*. While obeying certain esthetic conventions to serve the narrative, didactic, and spiritual purposes of the stories, the artists mime the world around them without intent to distort or embellish. They chronicle the lyrical of the

mundane, with a fascination for detail and a passion for accuracy. In visualizing the episode to be illustrated, they supply the costumes, scenery, utensils, furnishings, and other items that would or should have been there. Imagination seeks expression within the bounds of verisimilitude. In *Cantiga* 23 (panel 3) a meal is offered to a king on a table set with cloth, bowls, knives, goblets, and bread, as in a typical upper-class home. In 148 (panel 5) (pl. 23) spear-bearing men seek help for their knight in a village, which is shown complete with tile-roofed cottages, chickens, doves, geese, and a sow with piglets. To illustrate the theme that all creatures should honor Holy Mary, the artists have chosen graceful, exotic animals and birds, including a giraffe, an elephant, a zebra, and a camel, which they must have seen in the king's zoo (*Cantiga* 29, panel 5 [pl. 29]). Even the supernatural—divine and demonic beings, heaven and hell—are envisioned in terms of the known: a soul enters heaven, which is a walled garden with date palms and other trees and flowers (41, 6); angels tend the sick (81, 2) just as human nurses do (67, 1 [pl. 58]); a lifelike devil grimaces and rubs tears from his eyes when the lustful knight becomes virtuous (137, 5). These few examples are the merest hint of the visual record of thirteenth-century life in over two thousand paintings contained in the Escorial Codex T.I.1 *(Códice Rico)* and the Florence Codex.

Those familiar with the *Cantigas* have long been aware of the scope and detail of the miniatures and their potential for the understanding of many facets of the European Middle Ages. Partial studies have been done, but nothing with the scope of the present book has heretofore been undertaken. Obstacles to more comprehensive investigations were the breadth and versatility of background knowledge required, the rarity of the manuscripts and other documents, and the sheer magnitude of the task. Thus, for many scholars, teachers, students, and curious readers of diverse interests and pursuits, the miniatures have remained little known and not readily accessible.

Because of the efforts of two learned and diligent scholars, the panorama of daily living as seen in the *Cantigas* can now unfold before a larger audience. Through scrupulous research combined with a sense of wonder and the excitement of discovery, the authors have endeavored to promote the understanding of the *Cantigas* by placing this priceless array within reach of all who might have occasion to consult it. This is truly in accord with the spirit and intent of the wise king himself, who strove to collect, preserve, and disseminate knowledge and beauty. Although offering coherent codification and a wealth of information, insights, and illustrations, this study does not preclude nor conclude. Rather, it is a beginning, an invitation to others to enjoy and probe more deeply into the world of the *Cantigas de Santa Maria.*

Kathleen Kulp-Hill

Acknowledgments

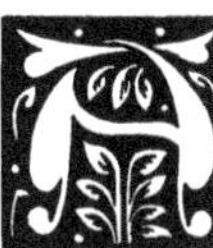 project as detailed and as comprehensive as *Daily Life Depicted in the* Cantigas de Santa Maria could not have been completed without the interest and assistance of many people and the assistance of various institutions. We thank fellow *cantigueiros* for their advice and suggestions: Maricel Presilla for her insights concerning the role of death in the *Cantigas* and for constant support; Connie Scarborough for treatment of the Virgin's role in the miniatures and her expert coeditorship of the *Bulletin of the Cantigueiros;* the late Dorothy Clotelle Clarke Shadi for her definitive study of the poetry of the *Cantigas* and for her support and invaluable suggestions for our book; Kathleen Kulp-Hill for her expertise in clothing and especially for her invaluable translation of the entire corpus of the *Cantigas de Santa Maria* and for the captions in T.I.1; Walter Mettmann for his invaluable definitive edition of the *Cantigas;* the late Charles L. Nelson for his expertise in the artistic composition of the miniatures; Israel J. Katz for his expertise in the music of the *Cantigas* and for his leadership in the conference in New York and the publication of its papers; Joseph F. O'Callaghan for his historic studies of Alfonso X and Spain during Alfonso's reign and his research into the shrine of Santiago de Compostela; Anthony J. Cárdenas for his *Alfonsine Newsletter;* Samuel Armistead for his ever valuable counsel; Robert I. Burns for his sagacious ideas for improvement; and the many scholars whom we fondly call fellow cantigueiros, too numerous to list but whose works have aided us greatly.

We express deep gratitude to Don Federico Manuel Gómez González de Pablos, president of Spain's Patrimonio Nacional, to the Biblioteca Nazionale Centrale of Florence, and to Don Francisco Requena Sánchez and Don Agustín Santiago Luque of Edilán for permission to use illustrations for our book.

We greatly appreciate our families, whose steadfast support and help enabled us to work unencumbered by daily chores and provided the many hours of uninterrupted concentration necessary for us to complete this work, envisioned many years ago.

Introduction

cross millennia patrons of learning ordered artists to record elements of daily life in order to perpetuate these practices. The Caves of Altamira, with the millennia-old cave paintings, the frescoes of Ancient Egypt, and the *Très Riches Heures* of Jean, Duke of Berry are excellent examples. Their reasons for such patronage are probably numerous, and Alfonso X, known as El Sabio (the Learned) (ruled 1252-84) had his own reasons to create a record of the daily life of his subjects on a scale never equaled in Europe before his time, during it, or even until the present day. This record he caused to be visualized in one of the most personal and remarkable series of manuscripts, known collectively as the *Cantigas de Santa María.* Two of the four manuscripts of the *Cantigas* are illustrated with upwards of two thousand miniatures, and one of these, known today as the *Códice Rico* (Escorial T.I.1) is lavishly illuminated. The other, Banco Rari 20, generally designated as F (Florentine) contains many complete pages of illustration, but also many incomplete folios. A third manuscript with a hundred *cantigas,* known as the *Códice de Toledo* (To), is not illustrated. A fourth, j.b.2 (Escorial E) contains 427 songs, virtually all the *Cantigas de Santa María* found in the other three, and some not found in those three. It is decorated with illuminated capitals, and each tenth miracle is illustrated by a depiction of one or more musicians playing instruments. Walter Mettmann, the acknowledged authority concerning the four manuscripts, offers a remarkably detailed description of each manuscript in his monumental four-volume study and critical edition (1959-72), as well as synoptic tables showing the correspondence between the manuscripts' miracles and other songs (1:xvi-xix).

When Prince Alfonso, to be crowned as Alfonso X in 1252, chose the Blessed Virgin as his patron and protectress, he conceived the most important ex-voto imaginable. This was possible because he was a researcher and planner par excellence as he initiated and produced his many books. When one turns the pages of his volumes of the *Cantigas de Santa María,* one can almost believe, as did he, that he was divinely inspired and under heavenly protection. Did he realize that this remarkable work, begun while he was a prince (we suspect) and continued until almost the year of his death in 1284, would record and preserve all that it has? Scholars still busily researching the *Cantigas* know that Alfonso's favorite book, his great tribute to Saint Mary, his ex-voto par excellence, in the longest codex (E) contains 427 miracles interspersed with songs of praise *(cantigas de loor)* and, at the end of E, contains hymns of other varieties to be discussed subsequently.

The miracles in T.I.1 and F that we treat are the basis of our study of daily life and need no further identification; however, the songs of praise require considerable treatment. These *cantigas* are of deep religious significance. The miniatures of the *loores* in T.I.1 and F depict, for the most part, Alfonso's responses to and explanations of Saint Mary's virtues and powers. Since each tenth *cantiga* was planned to be a *loor,* and since T.I.1 contains 194 *cantigas,* there should be nineteen *loores;* there are only seventeen, though, because numbers 40 and 150 are missing. In all but two of the *loores,* 60 and 180, from which he is absent, Alfonso appears as *auctor* or lecturer as he explains the contents to various audiences.

In F, which is far less orderly than T.I.1, each *loor* is not a tenth *cantiga.* Instead, the *loores,* of which there are nine out of the 104 *cantigas,* should be numbered 27 (240)

30 (310), 40 (320), 56 (270), 64, (230), 76 (250), 86 (409), 91 (360), and 96 (210) (the numbers in parentheses refer to MS E), because only a few of the *cantigas* in F are numbered. Only *Loores* 30, 40, and 96 are illustrated and form part of our study. Alfonso appears only in 30 and 96. Of all seventeen *loores* in T.I.1 and three in F, only a small portion offer what can be regarded as revealing elements of daily life. In T.I.1 50, in which is portrayed the flagellation of Jesus, we see the bonds binding him to a pillar and the three-branched scourge, as well as the flogger's short tunic; in 120, panel 1, musicians; in 130, 3, a suitor attempting to seduce a woman; and in 140, 6, gamblers and people kissing amorously.

As to plants in the *loores,* we record stylized lilies in pots, which Ana Domínguez Rodríguez (1987, 73) thinks may be stage settings for dramatizations of hymns in 140, 3 and 160, 3; date palms in 60, 1 and 100, 6; and the apple in the Garden of Eden in 60, 1. Aside from these, most hymns depict the public of both sexes (nobles, commoners, clerics) listening to Alfonso's explications.

All personages, even those in the life of Jesus, wear thirteenth-century clothes. In short, the *loores* provide little information about daily living, aside from clothing.

In the other *loores* of T.I.1 and F appear devils, angels, hell depicted as an open-mouthed dragon, the Tree of Jesse, Jesus, Mary and Joseph, and Adam and Eve, and these are recorded in the pertinent categories seen in the table of contents.

The concept that the *Cantigas de Santa María* is, strictly speaking, a book composed of miracles with each tenth *cantiga* a song of praise *(cantiga de loor)* is incorrect. Number 401 is a petition that Alfonso directed to the Virgin; 403 sings of her seven sorrows; 406 is a *maya* (a song for May), a truly lovely lyric in the tradition of the pan-European May songs; 410 is a prologue to five *festas* or feast days of Saint Mary; 411 deals with Saint Mary's birth and her parentage; 412 is a feast day and song of praise; 413 is about her virginity and about the feast day of the Immaculate Conception, and how Saint Ildefonso changes its date; 414 deals with the Trinity of Saint Mary, describing her three kinds of virginity; 415 treats the Annunciation when Gabriel visits the young Virgin Mary; 416 is one of the usual songs of praise; in 417 we read that she takes the boy Jesus to Simeon in the temple; 418 is one of the typical songs of praise; 419 tells of her ascension; 420 treats the procession in heaven when she ascends; 421 is about Judgment Day; in 422 she beseeches her Son to have mercy on humanity; 423 deals with the Creation; 424 sings of the visit of the Magi to the newborn Christ Child; 425 recounts Jesus' resurrection and 426 his ascension; and 427 narrates how the Holy Spirit

descends upon the apostles. Of course, these varieties of song are not illustrated and are not basic to our description of daily life, but even so, we believe that readers interested in the *Cantigas* in toto will find these remarks pertinent. Our study adds considerably to materials associated with the life of Alfonso, since his actions in the miniatures and their texts are only rarely found in actual histories.

The *Cantigas* preserved every verse form then known in Spain before the Golden Age except the sonnet. Dorothy Clotelle Clarke's undisputed and probably definitive article reveals that Alfonso and his poets included meters thought to have arisen much later than the *Cantigas de Santa María,* for example, the *romance* (ballad) meter and, even more surprisingly, *arte mayor* (Clarke 1955, 94). We should regard this accomplishment alone as a most significant contribution to poetic art. And, since *cantigas* are songs (poems set to music), musicologists, notably Higinio Anglés and his former student, the distinguished musicologist José María Lloréns Cisteró, regard the *Cantigas de Santa María* as the most complete repository of medieval Spanish music. It is therefore reasonable to suspect that Alfonso, prince and monarch, realized all this and, indeed, even planned to record and preserve these many verse forms and musical notations of his time for posterity.

A third harvesting of his kingdom's culture was the technique of relating the Virgin's miracles in the form of brief narratives. Each miracle utilized the age-old narrative techniques, which contained the nine elements best suited to the writing of stories—plot, characterization, setting, mood or tone, effect, point of view, conflict, theme, and style (Keller 1979b, ix). Let us be bold enough to call the Alfonsine miracles short stories, for that is what they really are. And let us be even bolder to agree with the well-known art historian Ana Domínguez Rodríguez that some of the *cantigas de loor* are dramatizations (1987, 66).

It appears that the pious Alfonso sent collectors of miracles and scribes to study existing anthologies of miracles, past and present, in Spain and beyond its borders, in order to assemble the vast repository making up his *Cantigas.* Included were the miraculous tales penned by his contemporary Gil de Zamora in Latin, and others from the copious anthologies compiled in France, both in Latin and in the vernacular. Miracles from Italian collections (Mettmann 1988) also were included, as well as some belonging to the Church's eastern repositories. Nor should we omit Gonzalo de Berceo's *Milagros de Nuestra Señora,* a collection also contemporary with the *Cantigas* and containing some of the same miracles. The fifteenth-century *Libro de los exenplos por abc,* in prose, contains many of these same Alfonsine stories. We cannot, of course, be certain that Clemente

Sánchez, archdeacon of Valderas in León, knew the *Cantigas,* but the possibility exists (Keller et al. 1992). Alfonso, then, in addition to recording and preserving his nation's culture, verse forms, and music, preserved most of the known miracles of the Virgin and preserved as well the elements needed in their telling.

Very unusual and extremely contributive to present-day studies are the Alfonsine miracles not found in standard collections. These were what we feel must be classified as miracles told by the Spanish folk that were not a part of literary tradition. Without the *Cantigas* scores of miracles of popular origin would not have survived. Therefore we have considered Alfonso as a collector of the folklore of his people (Keller 1965). And we have reason to regard him as an early folklorist, since he states that when he heard of a popular miracle, he sometimes traveled to the miracle site so as to learn it from people who witnessed it, as seen in *Cantiga* 18, panel 6 (pl. 3).

Surely across the years, as the *Cantigas* increased in number and as Alfonso caused them to be illustrated in medieval Spain's finest volumes of medieval illuminations, he was consciously recording and preserving the daily life of his many-faceted peoples.

The Parameters of Daily Life

Too often, studies on medieval daily life have centered on clothing, castles, housing, agriculture, and food. Daily life means a great deal more: it involves many factors—milieu and how people moved in and through locales. It treats what people thought; what entertainment they enjoyed; what sins they committed; how and where they traveled on land and water; their superstitions; their homes and furniture; the violent acts they committed; the place of women, of children, of men, of the clergy, of the law; and, since we are studying Spain's daily life, the same areas in Muslim and Jewish life, as well as the effect of history and fauna and flora—in short most of what life contained.

Joseph F. O'Callaghan's recent book *The Learned King* (1993), we believe, is the most up-to-date and authoritative study of Alfonso's life and therefore, to a great extent, of his role in the daily political life of his times. We refer our readers to his most valuable study, which treats the political and historical facets of daily life that we rarely find in the miniatures. One of the two American authorities on Alfonso X's reign, Joseph O'Callaghan is a professional historian; we hope that we, as students of literature and related areas—for example, folklore and comparative literature—can also contribute somewhat to social and even factual history based upon what Alfonso reveals in his *cantigas* miniatures.

We agree with O'Callaghan when he points out that "[m]any of the stories were taken from a common European repertoire and do not necessarily reflect situations in Castile" (1993, 99-100). We must add that the settings and actions in a goodly number of *cantigas* are based on history much older than the thirteenth century, for example, the life of Saint John of Damascus in F 22 (265), who died in 754. But even such stories are illustrated by miniatures in which personages from earlier times are depicted in thirteenth-century garb and in settings contemporary with Alfonso. Of course in these illustrations appear facets of daily life of thirteenth-century Spain often not taken into account by scholars. Medieval miniaturists did not study the costumes and settings of previous ages. Therefore, we see in *Cantiga* 5A (pl. 43) the Emperor Julian (died 363) wearing the clothes of monarchs contemporary with Alfonso.

As for the details of dress seen in the miniatures, we have relied greatly upon the discussion of attire by Kathleen Kulp-Hill. The point of view of this truly expert scholar adds greatly to the understanding of dress in the *Cantigas.* We refer also to the detailed descriptions of clothing and the line drawings illustrating Christian, Jewish, and Muslim masculine and feminine attire, weaponry, and armor that Guerrero-Lovillo reproduces from the miniatures.

Concerning castles and the homes and their furnishings of both nobles and commoners—Christian, Jewish, and Muslim—they are illustrated in the miniatures of both T.I.1 and F, sometimes in detail, at other times only suggesting their complete appearance, and occasionally in what seems to be exaggerated or fanciful presentations. Some, according to Guerrero-Lovillo (1949, 227ff.), are identifiable.

Alfonso X of Castile and León was the patron of more books than any other medieval monarch. Our investigation of his interest in the daily life of his subjects offers, we believe, the first comprehensive and detailed account of how people lived in his realm. Earlier we investigated certain of the elements of daily life (Keller 1958), but not until now has so complete a study of daily life based upon actual illustration of it been undertaken and published.

We have based our research for the current volume primarily upon T.I.1, the *Códice Rico* of the *Cantigas de Santa María,* and to a lesser extent upon F, the Florentine manuscript—this because of the latter's unfinished miniatures. In our opinion Alfonso, who envisaged his *Cantigas* while still a prince, later realized how his ex-voto to Saint Mary, his patron saint, would become a veritable encyclopedia of pictorial art, musical notation, poetics, brief narrative, familial anecdotes, and daily life. However, once he became ruler, possessed of funds for favorite projects, he surely began to comprehend what a great contribution to culture his favorite work would be. Encyclopedic is the most proper term for the *Cantigas de Santa María.*

The *Cantigas* present a world, and its exploration continues to uncover unexpected facts. Apparently Alfonso wanted to reveal the locale for most of the miracles. We were surprised to learn how many locales were listed by name. T.I.1 and F list some ninety cities, villages, monasteries and convents, shrines, chapels, rivers, springs, and forests. Although admittedly few can be identified in the miniatures, some have been, we believe; but since they are named in the texts of the *Cantigas,* we felt obliged to include their names as found in T.I.1 and F.

Many locales have vanished from present-day Spanish and other European and eastern geographies, or the medieval names have been changed. Walter Mettmann has identified many in notes to his critical editions. The identification of some may never be reliably made.

The proper names of people appear with frequency in T.I.1 and F and, of course, in E. Identifications of many of these are scattered through volume 4 of Mettmann's Coimbra edition (1959-72) and in footnotes throughout the Castalia edition (1986-89); Agapito Rey 1927 is also pertinent. Scholars concerned with the historical and social aspects seen in the miniatures in T.I.1 and F should study personages in both codices. And there is need for a scholarly edition of F since differences appear in its texts, compared with those for miniatures in T.I.1. Indeed, there are some differences between the texts of T.I.1 and F on the one hand and the same *cantiga* texts in E, on the other. Even the titles in T.I.1 contain slightly different wording from those in E, as do the few captions in F.

We are certain that when Guerrero-Lovillo (1949, 34) pointed to the handiwork of three different artists, he was referring only to T.I.1 and not to F, since in F can be seen the work of artists not represented in T.I.1.

Visual Narrative Techniques of the Miracles

For any reader not familiar with the presentation of the visualized incidents of the miracles, we have chosen for illustrative purposes *Cantiga* 64 of Codex T.I.1 (pl. 1) because its story is especially interesting, because its characters are strongly portrayed (one of them is an early version of the famous Celestina), and because the miniatures reveal the technique of depicting two or more actions in one panel by the use of "dramatic arches"; furthermore, few pages of miniatures are more beautiful or of better artistic quality. If the reader will follow our description while viewing the color plate of this miracle, he or she should arrive at a clear understanding of the visualization of the *Cantiga.* The caption above each panel fairly well describes what appears in it, and the six captions together narrate the main events of the miracle. As on all pages of miniatures, the panels are to be viewed from left to right, beginning at the top. The order of calligraphy in blue and red alternates frequently in the pages of miniatures. The upper left panel under study is headed by azure rubrics, whereas the panel at its right is headed by brilliant scarlet letters. In the second set of panels the color of the rubrics is reversed, the scarlet at the left, the blue at the right. And in the last band of panels the same rule of opposites is maintained: blue, red, red, blue. At each corner of each panel, one of the two symbols of Alfonso's realm appears. At the left of the first panel is the golden three-towered castle representing Castile, and at the right corner the lion rampant of León. For the following four panels the rule of opposites continues: lion-castle, castle-lion. The symmetrical reversal of symbols, like that of the colored captions, makes for an esthetic whole.

The action in each panel allows the viewer to participate in the miracle. Panel 1, according to the caption, "How a knight married a very beautiful damsel," is divided by three golden arches, under each of which can be seen three aspects of the overall action. In the left-hand arch, we see the wedding party with the bride's and groom's parents; in the center arch kneel the young couple before the priest and an acolyte; the right-hand arch reveals the altar, upon which stands a golden monstrance.

Panel 2, "How his master sent to tell him in his letter that he was to go to serve him," shows the couple seated under the left-hand arch as the messenger in the right-hand arch hands the knight a letter. We see the husband's hand projecting into the right-hand arch to receive it. The seal on the letter is clearly visible. The knight wears the typical *bonete,* which Guerrero-Lovillo (1949, 208) reveals in a line drawing in the second band of *bonetes* and last in the line. His robes are elegant, and from beneath them one foot projects, enabling the viewer to see that he is wearing the pointed type of shoes sketched by Guerrero-Lovillo (223), probably like the one seen in band two of his sketch—the shoe at the right of the band. The young wife wears a *toca* resembling Guerrero-Lovillo's sketch in the middle of his second band of such headgear (210).

Panel 3, "How the knight commended his wife to Saint Mary so that she might guard her from dishonor," in the left-hand arch shows the couple as the knight points into the second arch, in which is seen an altar on which is a statue of Saint Mary seated and holding the Christ Child on her lap. The tiles of the altars are in bright colors; this is true of all altars in all miniatures.

Panel 4, "How a gentleman begged a go-between to enable him to possess that lady," is divided into three arches. In the first one we see him discussing the matter with an old woman, the typical *alcahueta* or female pimp. She and the gentleman clasp hands as though to seal the bargain. He wears a different *birrete,* as seen in Guerrero-Lovillo 1949, 208. They are standing in the street. The second division of this panel has two arches. We see the go-between kneeling under one arch as she tries to persuade the wife to accept a gift from her would-be seducer and to agree to admit him to her house. The wife, in the second arch at the far right, with her right hand seems to gesture a negative reply.

Panel 5, "How the lady could neither put on or take off the shoe which the go-between gave her," shows her in the left-hand arch struggling with the shoe, while the go-between strives from the right-hand arch to help her, reaching into the arch occupied by the lady.

Panel 6, "How her husband came from the army and removed the shoe," contains a very large left-hand arch. In it we see that they are in their bedroom. She is seated on the four-poster bed while he, half-seated, with both hands removes the shoe. The wife, in the narrow right-hand arch, reaches into his arch, into which her foot projects, and, having raised her skirt, helps him take off the shoe. Such is the construction or presentation of all the *cantigas* that are miracles, but not for the *loores* or songs of praise.

Fortunately, various biographical studies concerning Alfonso are available. Some are lengthy and comprehensive (Ballesteros y Beretta 1963; O'Callaghan 1993) and others more concise (Procter 1951; Keller 1967). Therefore, we have not included anything like a biography of Alfonso; however, since the miniatures of the *Cantigas* contain unexpected visualized vignettes concerning incidents in his life and of his family and relatives, we are able to record what historians often have overlooked.

No study of daily life in medieval Spain should fail to consider the high regard with which the "noble Moor" was held. In the *Cantigas* the "noble Moor" is represented, but in much earlier works, *The Poem of Mío Cid,* for example, nobility was a part of Moorish character. The "noble Moor" is present in Spanish letters across the centuries: in the novella *El Abencerraje,* in a play by Lope de Vega based on the novella, and in *Don Quixote* when the *Caballero de la triste figura* believes he *is* the noble Abindarráez. For a complete treatment of the "noble Moor," see Francisco López Estrada and John E. Keller, *El Abencerraje* (1964), which treats the "noble Moor" into modern Spanish literature.

Jews in the *Cantigas* fare less attractively. Noble Moors were knights and warriors, but Jews did not appear in such a noble guise. There existed an unfortunate but nonetheless real disregard for them, even a hatred, which is reflected in the *Cantigas.* The persecution of Jews was prevalent because Christians were taught to scorn, vilify, and even kill Jews, so we could not avoid this aspect of thirteenth-century daily life. Jewish people who appear in the *Cantigas* are not always vilified, but even so, most Jewish people are considered inimical to the Christian faith. For treatment of the Jewish problem in the *Cantigas,* see studies by Albert I. Bagby (1971) and Dwayne Carpenter (1986).

Many scholars have treated daily life in the Middle Ages. At least two of these deal with life in Spain: the late Kenneth Scholberg's *Spanish Life in the Late Middle Ages* (1965) deals with the fifteenth century and therefore does not refer to the *Cantigas;* Marcelin Defourneaux's book under the title, in translation by Newton Branch, *Daily Life in Spain in the Golden Age* (1971) obviously did not draw information from the *Cantigas;* the study of greatest value is Guerrero-Lovillos's *Las Cantigas: Estudio arqueológico* (1949). It discusses many aspects of the Alfonsine work, especially as regards clothing, but it does not discuss all the facets seen in the miniatures. Other studies on clothing are Michèle Beaulieu, *Le costume antique et médiéval* (1951), and Carmen Bernis Madrazo, *Indumentaria medieval española* (1956). We list in the bibliography other studies of daily life: António H. de Oliveira Marques's *Daily Life in Portugal in the Late Middle Ages* deals with the twelfth through the fifteenth centuries, but inexplicably he does not include the *Cantigas* in his investigation. See also the works by Joseph and Frances Gies, Louis F. Salzman's book (1929) on English daily life, Urban T. Holmes Jr.'s excellent study (1952) of life in twelfth-century France, and Amparo García Cuadrado's *Las Cantigas: El Códice de Florencia* (1993), which treats elements of daily life illustrated by line drawings.

Methodology

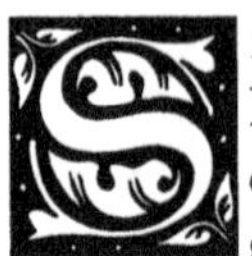

Since the *Códice Rico,* archived at the Escorial Palace, where Philip II placed it in the sixteenth century, is the primary source of our investigation of daily life in the *Cantigas de Santa Maria,* Keller studied codex T.I.1 there. However, given the difficulties involved, we have been able to use, thanks to permission, the excellent facsimile edition of T.I.1 published by Edilán in 1979. We have never encountered a more perfect facsimile of any Spanish manuscript. The same does not hold true for F, the manuscript archived in Florence, but only as regards the original. Edilán's facsimile of F is again meticulously reproduced.

We scrutinized carefully each page of miniatures in T.I.1 and F, numbering about two thousand individual panels or divisions of the six-paneled pages, in search of everything revealing elements of daily life. As we worked, we found it necessary to establish some twenty-seven categories and additional subcategories, for example, occupations, religion, health, and fauna and flora, which are listed in the contents. We include sieges, battlefields, travel, hunting and fishing, pilgrimages, games—indeed, possibly most of the elements of daily life among all the masses and classes. Whenever we treat the activities of individuals or groups of people or their possessions—swords, altarpieces, sconces, shoes, for example—we indicate the number and panel of the *cantiga* in which they are depicted; for example, 8, 2 refers to the second panel of *Cantiga* 8. This provides a means for quick reference to the illustrations of each category we list. In some cases we include color plates of entire pages; in others of individual panels. Frequently, when describing single panels, we refer to the full-page color illustration that contains the single panel.

Mention must be made here concerning the volumes that accompany both of Edilán's facsimiles, T.I.1 (Alfonso

X el Sabio 1979) and Banco Rari, the so-called Florentine manuscript (Alfonso X el Sabio 1989). Both facsimiles and their accompanying volumes can be found in many libraries around the world, since Edilán printed 2,200 copies of the former and 1,100 of the latter. Also available is Guerrero-Lovillo's black and white facsimile of T.I.1 and his studies of it in the same volume (1949).

When referring to the Florentine manuscript, we use F to indicate it. For example, F 4, 2 stands for panel 2 of *cantiga* number 4. The absence of much pagination in this manuscript led us to paginate from the miniatures as they occurred. T.I.1's accompanying volume contains Filgueira Valverde's transcription of the original, his translation of it into modern Spanish prose, commentaries (often including sources), transcriptions of the captions appearing above the six panels of the pages of miniatures, labeled *rótulos,* and musical transcriptions in modern notation prepared by Lloréns Cisteró. The accompanying volume of Banco Rari's facsimile edition matches the format of T.I.1. This manuscript contains no musical notation. Surprisingly, in both manuscripts there are variations from statements in the captions and the events visualized in the illustrations, and even variations between the text and the pictured events. Such changes, of course, do not diminish or alter the evidences of daily life as depicted. Connie Scarborough in her doctoral dissertation (1982) treats the variations between text and miniatures in T.I.1.

Filgueira Valverde's shorter edition, *Cantigas de Santa Maria* (1985), offers the translation into modern Spanish of all 194 *cantigas* in T.I.1, plus the modernization of the prosification in Old Spanish of *cantigas* 2-25, found in the lower margin of each of these *cantigas.* His commentaries are scholarly, although he omits the transcription of the captions and of the music. This paperback volume was published by Editorial Castalia in *Odres Nuevos* in 1985. James Chatham (1976), John Keller and Robert Linker (1974), and Anthony Cárdenas (1988-89) have treated the prosifications of *cantigas* 2-25.

We have found invaluable the translation into English of the *Cantigas* by Kathleen Kulp-Hill, not yet published. She has generously allowed us to include her translations when needed.

Our plan was not to cover every element of daily life preserved in all medieval Spanish texts. We know that a multitude of elements might be covered by studying medieval law, in particular Alfonso el Sabio's *Siete Partidas,* and by taking into consideration medieval Spanish literature and religious tracts—in short, the entire scope of what was written. Our plan, even though it cannot be comprehensive, can and indeed does cover a remarkably rich visualization of aspects of daily life. We believe firmly that the artists who produced the miniatures painted what they saw concerning elements of daily life, including details, and that they represent authentic recordings of how people lived, worked, traveled, fought, played, ate, slept, married, made love, gave birth, died, and so on almost ad infinitum. Words can describe these matters, but pictures contribute so much more.

We mentioned earlier that when Alfonso commissioned the *Cantigas,* as stories written down in verse, illustrated, and set to music, he seems to have kept in mind, as did his helpers, many of the nine elements of the "classic design." Of the nine elements of narration, setting reveals the most about daily life, but other of the nine elements often contribute as well.

The *Códice Rico,* T.I.1., caused few problems as we took from it examples of daily life. It is an almost perfect manuscript; all of its pages of miniatures are complete, except for a few that lack captions. The Florentine codex posed greater problems. This manuscript, carefully described by Solalinde (1918, 150-63) and more fully by Mettmann (1959, 1:vii-xxiv), contains numerous pages of incomplete illustrations. In some cases there are only the frames designed to surround the miniatures; most pages of miniatures lack the explanatory captions. Even more confusing (and not well documented by anyone) are the miniatures that are separated from their verbal accounts and therefore misnumbered by various scholars. There is still much work to be done to unravel all these confusing elements, but this we must leave for other scholars, since here we are primarily concerned with what the miniatures reveal as regards daily life.

After each *cantiga* in F appears the corresponding number in MS E, which contains 427 *cantigas.* For a correspondence between all MSS of the *Cantigas,* see Mettmann's synoptic table (1959, 1:xvi-xix).

In T.I.1 CXLXI, an impossible number, should be numbered CXLVI, and indeed it is followed by CXLVII. T.I.1's 185 is 186 in E, 186 in T.I.1 is 187 in E, and 187 in T.I.1 is 185 in E. F 62 (233) has no illustration; F 62^1 is 247; F 65 is 232 and F 65^1 is 236; F 66 is 284; F 66^1 is 266; F 67 is listed by Mettman as 225, but F 67 has two pages of miniatures that illustrate two different miracles. Therefore we designate F 67 as 225 and F 67^1 as 258.

We repeat that scholars who research the *Cantigas* and their visualizations and verbalizations of miracles, songs of praise, and other songs, know that the miniatures contain facets of daily life not mentioned in the poetic narratives. It is not as well known that sometimes the action seen in the miniatures does not match what the written account states. This has made it necessary for us to read every *cantiga* in order to discover these variations. We have also, of course, resorted to Connie Scarborough's dissertation. In so doing we found references to where the action takes place, and often we found the names of historical persons taking part in the action. Those references, we believe, greatly enhance our study, since they reveal that miracles took place not only in many regions of Spain, but also abroad and even in times much earlier than Alfonso's. We indicate the places and personages not pictured in the miniatures with a T following the number to indicate that they appear in the text and a C to indicate that they appear in the captions. In our opinion, some careful investigation as to geographical names should be carried out as regards not only the 194 *cantigas* in T.I.1 and the 104 in F, but all of the other *cantigas* in E and To. Simply knowing how many cities, villages, monasteries, and churches are mentioned contributes considerably to *cantiga* studies and should be invaluable to geographers. We think such references indicate that many, though not all, who heard the *cantigas* sung or read were educated well enough to understand the references, revealing still another facet of daily life. Also a detailed investigation of the personages who play roles in the miracles would yield insights.

It is our fondest hope that our book will contribute to a greater appreciation of the scope of the *Cantigas,* to a better understanding of how Spaniards lived in the thirteenth century, and to the history of ideas, social history, true history, literature, folklore, comparative studies, and many more areas.

The category index in the appendix contains a comprehensive listing of items pertinent to each category. Since there are twenty-seven categories, a few with subheadings, and hundreds of elements of daily life, obviously we could not record all these in the narrative portion of our study. What we have narrated we believe provides a good representation of each category. Our index of each category complements the narrative parts of these classifications and offers many additional references.

1
Classes and Masses

Royalty and Nobility

Beginning at the top of the social hierarchy, emperors and kings and queens, we may note that no medieval books concern themselves more intimately with the lives of their patrons than did Alfonso's *Cantigas de Santa Maria.* In Codex T.I.1 the Wise King is actually depicted in a variety of royal regalia and everyday dress in many miracles and in fifteen of the seventeen *cantigas de loor* or hymns of praise. He does not appear in numbers 60 and 180. Wherever the artists depicted him in the *loores,* he seems, as we have seen, to be playing the role of *auctor* or narrator, the person who in Roman drama used to explain the content of the plays acted out by mimes, who, of course, were silent. In the songs of praise, Alfonso seems to be telling the viewer what is taking place in the miniatures. We are more convinced of this when we take into consideration that in several pages of miniatures we see musicians playing instruments and singers singing, and in at least one miniature (T.I.1 120, 1 [pl. 2]) playing, singing, and dancing. None of these activities are mentioned in the text of this *cantiga,* and since this page contains no captions, we are left to comment without any verbal assistance.

Even though histories of medieval Spanish literature argue that Alfonso's realm was bereft of drama, except for the *Auto de los reyes magos*—which it would seem was not staged—Ana Domínguez Rodríguez (1987) makes it clear that she considers that some of the hymns of praise were dramatic pieces actually sung; and John Keller (1990) agrees with her and goes further, suggesting dramatization in *cantigas* she did not treat, including miracles. Keller (1967, 92-93) suggests that miracles, as well as hymns of praise and other songs, may have been staged, basing his

supposition in part on the Virgin's images, which even in a simple page of miniatures change position for no stated reason. Perhaps a living model was used by the artists, and she grew weary. The conclusion that there was no drama in Castile and León until the fifteenth century has never seemed acceptable to us. After all, Alfonso in his *Siete Partidas,* title 6, law 34 makes it very clear that he approved of religious drama and condemned farces or *juegos de escarnio,* which latter, we argue, would not have been condemned had they not been present in his kingdom. If we are correct in our suppositions, then Alfonso sponsored staged representations, giving his subjects dramatized rituals and brief dramatic productions that, since they were set to music and sung, could indeed be regarded as operatic (Keller 1990). Surely such brief dramatizations would have played a significant part in the daily life of medieval Castile and León—indeed, in all areas of Alfonso's realm. The Waverly Consort (1972) presents some *cantigas* as though they were acted out as well as sung by different singers and played by different musicians. A good many other phonographic recordings of *cantigas* exist: Experiences Anonymes' *Music of the Middle Ages,* Pro Musica's *Spanish Medieval Music,* Decca's *Spanish Medieval Music,* the *Colección de Música Antigua Española,* I, and Trio Live Oak's *Don Alfonso the Wise, Music of Medieval Spain,* to name some of the better-known platters. Several of these now have been recorded on compact discs. Richard Kinkade (1986) supports the dramatic presentation of Berceo's *Milagros* in his article on theater in the round.

As to the miracles of T.I.1, Alfonso is depicted in 18 (pl. 3), 142 (pl. 4), and 169. In 18, 6, he stands in a church with some of his retainers and receives from two priests a *toca* or wimple. The unusual content of this miracle is so interesting and revelatory of daily life that we narrate it here. The title reads "This is how Saint Mary made the silkworms spin two veils, because the lady who kept them had promised her one and had not given it to her." In panel 1 we see the woman kneeling before the altar of the Virgin in Segovia. She holds out a shallow dish in which are many silkworms, enlarged so that the viewer can see what they are. We assume that these are dead or dying. We refer our readers to Guerrero-Lovillo's transcription of the captions (1949, 381) and to Kulp-Hill's translation (1995). In panel 2 the woman is seen again in the same church. She realizes that she has forgotten to give the statue the wimple she had promised, and she hastens home to prepare one. Panels 3 and 4 merit close attention as concerns daily life. In both we see the part of the silk-production works where the worms live. Two groups of worms in 3, all anatomically correct, can be seen on large flat shelves or trays, tilted perpendicularly so that the viewer can see them. One group of worms has all but finished weaving the length of silk that is to be the veil; the second team of worms is in the midst of weaving a second length. On the trays can be seen the fresh green mulberry leaves upon which the worms feed. Panel 5 is divided into three narrative arches, enabling the artists to visualize three elements of the story. In the arch to the left we see the altar with the Virgin's image seated on it; the center arch shows two priests waiting to receive the *tocas* (wimples) that the giver and a second woman offer them. It is in panel 6 that Alfonso appears. Its caption reads "How King Alfonso took one of them to keep in his chapel." This panel also is divided into three arches. In the one to the left is the usual altar with the seated Virgin and Child. The center arch contains three priests who are handing the wimple to Alfonso. The right-hand arch covers three of the king's attendants.

The very fact that Alfonso traveled to Segovia, once he had learned of the miracle, contributes to our conception of daily life. Keller (1984) points to a king who was a collector of miracles; one might even consider him to have been a medieval folklorist, as Keller calls him (1965). No history or chronicle relates that Alfonso traveled about gathering miracles. This *cantiga* reveals a facet of his private daily life.

Cantiga 142 (pl. 4) is very personal, since in three of its panels (1, 3, and 5) Alfonso is seen as he hawks for heron. The title reads "How Holy Mary saved from death one of the king's men who had entered a river to retrieve a heron." The viewer will see that in panel 1 Alfonso, seated on a mule (rather than a horse, since mules are less fractious), has launched a falcon at a heron. In panel 2 we see,

in three incidents in the same panel, that the hawk has struck the heron, has broken its wing, and has made it fall toward the surface of the water. In panel 3 Alfonso finds that the dogs will not enter the turbulent stream, and he asks who will. In panel 4 a man from Guadalajara goes into the river, and we see that he has grasped the heron but is being swept under the water. The fifth incident appears in panel 6 as the man comes out of the river as a result of Alfonso's prayers to the Virgin. We believe that this disorder in visualized incidents was caused so that the artists could preserve the pattern of the page. In the left-hand column of panels, 1, 3, and 5, we see the king on land, and in the right-hand column of panels, 2, 4, and 6, the scene is the river. Keller and Kinkade (1984, 27-28) treat this artistic technique extensively.

Cantiga 169 is of special interest for daily life. In panel 2 Alfonso, as prince ruling Murcia for his father, refuses a delegation of Muslims, who ask him to allow them to demolish a church in the Moorish quarter that is dedicated to Saint Mary. In panel 3 King James of Aragon, Alfonso's uncle, also refuses, and in panel 4 Alfonso, now king, finally relents and gives permission. In panel 5 the Muslim king, upon hearing of Alfonso's decision, tells another delegation of Muslims that he fears the wrath of the Virgin. The demolishers are seen in panel 6 uselessly attempting to tear down the church under the gaze of the Virgin.

One page of miniatures in T.I.1, *Cantiga* 97, "How Holy Mary saved from death the favorite of a king whom the others had slandered," does not mention Alfonso as the particular king; however, the king depicted in panels 3, 4, 5, and 6 looks exactly like all the other pictures of Alfonso in T.I.1. This *cantiga* shows the king's anger and how it changed to sympathy.

Moving from T.I.1 to F in our study of royalty, we utilize diapositives graciously prepared by the Biblioteca Nazionale in Florence, which appear in Edilán's facsimile, Alfonso X el Sabio 1989.

In F 44 (257), "How Holy Mary saved her relics from being harmed while many others were damaged," we see the king in panels 1, 2, 4, 5, and 6. His robes and his hands and feet are visible; the miniaturist has not painted his face, however, although his crown rests upon the place where his face and head should be. Other personages in the five panels also lack faces. This often happens in F, where there are also instances of entire blank panels. We assume that the making of miniatures was accomplished by various artists in an assembly line fashion and that the artist who was assigned to draw the faces had not finished his work before the pages were bound. Elements of royal daily life in F 44 (257) consist of Alfonso's reliquaries in which he stored the relics of saints and especially of Holy Mary. He left all of them in Seville and went to Castile for ten years. When he returned, all were damaged except hers.

Alfonso's illnesses are treated in F; we discuss them in chapter 10 on health.

Other miracles about the royal family contribute significant information about daily life. In T.I.1 122, which has no captions, Alfonso's mother, Queen Beatriz of Suabia in Toledo, holds her recently demised daughter, Princess Berenguela, before the Virgin's altar. Subsequent panels depict how the queen had the princess locked in the Virgin's shrine, and the lock and key are plainly visible in panel 3. As soon as Holy Mary resuscitates her daughter, Queen Beatriz sets out for Las Huelgas, the convent to which the child had been promised. Panel 5 (pl. 61) shows the queen and the princess borne on an enclosed litter carried by men and horses. It is this litter that tells us much about travel. This one has heavy curtains, and through an opening we see the queen holding her child.

More royal family members are depicted in F than in T.I.1. *Cantiga* F 7 (256) reveals in the text a facet of Alfonso's life as a small boy. He reports that he heard the story then. This miniature has no color except in the framing design of the usual rosettes. Line drawings in considerable detail outline soldiers, battlements, and tents, and in panel 4 the queen lies dying in bed. At death's door with fever and about to bear a child, she causes a metal image of Holy Mary to be forged and placed beside her. In the line drawings of panel 5, the image can be seen being carried to Beatriz by two women. In panel 6 Beatriz kneels before the image. From this page we glean a good deal about daily life—the queen's faith and the cure from a sacred image.

In F 10 (292) the deceased King Ferdinand III appears in a vision. In panel 1 we see him above the sleeping treasurer, whose vision it is, giving him certain orders. He must take a fine ring from Ferdinand's statue, which his son, Alfonso, had had sculpted in his honor, and must place it on the finger of the Virgin's statue. This is done. In panel 6 at the far right Alfonso appears. This page of miniatures reveals the belief in visions and shows the statue built for Ferdinand at his son's behest. The miniatures herein are of much poorer quality than any others in both Codices F and T.I.1. Quite obviously, an artist far less skilled than any of the others produced them. Why, we wonder, would a miniature of almost childlike quality appear in a royal manuscript? Could this page have been produced by a person of great consequence, possibly by Alfonso himself or one of his children?

In Codex E appear numerous miracles not found in T.I.1 and F that deal with Alfonso's family and retainers.

We do not include these because they are not illustrated by miniatures.

In addition to Alfonso and his family, we read about and see portrayed other royal people. Virtually all are depicted in garments worn by thirteenth-century Spanish royalty, except, of course, for Muslim kings, who wear eastern clothing. Alfonso, patron of history, read extensively about royalty in the ancient world, in the Eastern Empire, which still existed in his time, and in the Muslim world. He would have expected educated subjects to be familiar with such rulers. The less educated would at least have had some cognizance of the Roman Empire in both the eastern and western forms as indicated in *Cantiga* 15 (5 in E) of the *Códice Rico,* "How Holy Mary helped the Empress of Rome to bear the great hardships which she suffered," an adaptation and reworking of the widely disseminated Byzantine romance about an empress named Beatriz, whose husband, states the text, was not known to the writers by name. This famous tale, written as well as recited by troubadours and *juglares,* seems to have first appeared in the eighth century. It also penetrated folklore and is therefore a candidate for wide oral circulation in Spain as well as elsewhere. Since the people of Spain, both the educated and the folk, knew this story, we can regard it as a part of the entertainment element of daily life. The miniatures depict the Roman court (15A, 1 and 5, and 15B, 6), travel by land (15A, 4) and by sea (15B, 1, 2, and 3), a royal bedroom (15A, 6), the pope (15B, 5 and 6), and the empress curing lepers (15B, 4, 5, and 6). It is strange that all the personages, nobles and commoners, except the pope, are depicted as blond. The pope has a dark beard. His hair is covered by his high-peaked miter. Panels 4 and 5 of 15B show carts in which lepers ride to be cured by the empress.

Cantiga 131, "How Saint Mary protected the Emperor of Constantinople from dying under a rock which fell on him while all the others who were with him died," shows the blond emperor Alexios I (1081-1118) wearing a royal crown that differs from the crowns worn by Spanish royalty and regal garments with the same rosette design found in the framing of the page (panel 1). The eastern clergy all wear black beards (panel 3), and the Patriarch, seen in bed (panel 4), also has a dark beard. The name of the emperor is Alexios in the text and the empress is named Jordana. She beseeches the Virgin to save her husband, who lies buried underground (panels 3, 5). Her prayers go on for an entire year while the Virgin keeps the emperor safe (panel 5).

In F 22 (265), "How Saint Mary healed the hand of John the Damascene which had been cut off" (pl. 64), we see an emperor who has heard of John's abilities and demands that he be sent to him by the Persian burgher who has bought him from Muslims. We treat this miracle in more detail in the section "Commoners and Occupations," where we discuss teachers.

Additional Roman emperors appear. The Caesar who speaks to the apostles in *Cantiga* 27 might be Augustus. Elements of daily life worthy of mention are the finery of the apostles' robes and of the Jews (panel 1) and the depiction of Caesar, regally clad and seated on a throne, with a royal canopy over him. His guards are wearing the same chain mail seen in Alfonso's time (panel 2); Caesar orders the church to be locked for forty days, and we see this done (panel 3); after the twelve apostles appeal personally to Saint Mary (panel 4), Caesar orders the doors of the church opened. We see on the wall a painting of Saint Mary. In the text we read that her image was found painted on the wall before the altar (panel 5), after or where Saint Peter had swept the floor. In panel 5 we see Peter pouring water on the floor from a pitcher and sweeping with a small broom. The Jews, realizing her power, give up possessing the church. The depiction of Jews in thirteenth-century garb contributes to our knowledge of Jewish life.

Another Roman emperor, Julian the Apostate (316-61), appears in *Cantiga* 5 of the *Códice Rico,* where we read of the wickedness of Julian and how he died. We see his army on the march, with Julian at its head, and his soldiers in the chain mail of Alfonso's time. He wears a golden helmet unlike those seen on Spanish monarchs and surmounted by a golden crown. Saint Basil bows before him and offers him rye bread and is given by Julian hay in mockery. The saint wears an eastern habit, and his tonsure is clearly seen beneath his golden halo (panel 1 [pl. 43]). He and other Christians beseech the Virgin to protect them from Julian, who has threatened to return and destroy their monastery (panel 2). In a vision Basil sees the Virgin accompanied by saints (panel 3). Saint Mary then dispatches Saint Mercurio in white armor and on a white horse to slay Julian (panel 4). His armor is that of a thirteenth-century Spanish warrior. Mercurio runs his lance through Julian's abdomen in a scene of very violent action (panel 5). When Mercurio's armor is not found in his sepulchre, Basil says he will find it (panel 6).

Basil shows Mercurio's bloody lance, which tells people that he has slain Julian (5B, 1). In the remaining panels, we see the pagan philosopher Libanos, who had taught Basil and even Julian in better times (panel 2), and in panel 3 he is converted and baptized in a medieval font.

When Archbishop Ildefonso was the primate of Spain (657-67), King Recceswinth ruled as the twenty-eighth of the Visigothic kings (653-72). In *Cantiga* 2, "How Saint Mary appeared in Toledo to Saint Ildefonso and gave him

an alb which she brought from Paradise with which he might say Mass," we see this king playing a minor part in the miracle, depicted in a procession with Ildefonso, various clergy, and youthful acolytes. The king's robes are like Alfonso's and so is his crown (panel 3).

Church Hierarchy

Most of the entire hierarchy of the Church is represented, from popes and patriarchs to parish priests and nuns, as well as lay clerks. And of course there are also Islamic *alfaquíes* and Jewish wise men. Only the higher clergy are distinguished by dress, for example, the popes, mitered bishops, and eastern patriarchs. Several monastic orders are represented, both masculine and feminine—Cistercians, Dominicans, Cluniacs, Franciscans. All are distinguished by their habits, but their orders are not mentioned in the captions of the miniatures and only rarely in the text. Cardinals do not appear, but archbishops do, as well as many bishops. The interiors of churches and monasteries do not suggest particular orders, but one can see furnishings of monasteries and churches, aside from altars, arches, choir stalls, altarpieces, monstrances, communion patens and chalices, and pulpits. See chapter 20, "Structures." The artists apparently did not paint distinguishable features of church buildings, but possibly experts in painting churches were assigned these parts of the panels.

Medieval life as we know it was regulated by the Church, and even the very pace of life depended upon the canonical hours. In such an atmosphere all Christians were observers and most were religious, even though many people sinned against Christian morality. Almost all sinners revered the Blessed Virgin and the saints, and even murderers, thieves, the incestuous, and adulterers called upon the Virgin in times of peril and were often forgiven by her, as were some repentant Jews and Muslims. It was indeed an age of deep and abiding faith, especially as regards the greatness of the Virgin at the height of Marian devotion.

Many members of the hierarchy appear as sinners in the *Cantigas,* and these we have treated in some detail here, as well as in chapter 12, "Love, Lust and Marriage," and chapter 16, "Punishments." Herewith we list representative members of the hierarchy in descending order.

First of all is the pope, who, though not a Spaniard, appears in 15B, 5 and 6; 65A, 3; 115A, 5; and F 54 (206). As usual, the setting, even though it is in Rome, is characteristic of Alfonso's Spain. The pope is distinguished by his papal miter and robes.

The primate of Spain—in the *Cantigas* he is Saint Ildefonso, archbishop of Toledo—appears in the second miracle of T.I.1 in the first five panels. In panel 1 he is composing his defense of Saint Mary's virginity and is seated at a typical slanted writing desk with an armoire behind him (see Guerrero-Lovillo 1949, 302). A white dove sits on his shoulder; he is then depicted as he disputes with heretics and Jews (panel 2); then he marches in a religious procession with the Visigoth King Recceswinth, accompanied by clergy of various ranks who bear crosiers and other religious accoutrements and preceded by boy acolytes (panel 3); Saint Leocadia appears to him (panel 4); Saint Mary presents the alb made in heaven (panel 5 [pl. 52]); his successor, Archbishop Siagrio, dons the alb, which strangles him. He appears again in 12, 1 and 2, wearing his miter, and in 3 wearing the kind of hat worn by lawyers and physicians.

Bishops appear frequently. In 7, 6 (pl. 40), a bishop, not wearing the miter, examines the abbess accused of fornicating with her steward; in 19, 5, a mitered bishop judges three knights who have violated church sanctuary; then he witnesses the forging of their swords into belts to be worn in penance (panel 6); in 33, 6, a mitered bishop, saved from shipwreck in a storm, thanks Saint Mary; in 66, 1, 4, 5, and 6, the Bishop of Auvergne receives an award from Saint Mary for his devotion; in 67, 5 and 6 (pl. 58), a bishop, wearing his miter, exorcises a devil who has taken possession of a dead body in order to destroy a good man. In 101, 6, a mitered bishop takes part in a procession celebrating Saint Mary's curing a deaf-mute.

The lower orders of the clergy, both male and female, appear with great frequency—indeed in cases too numerous to treat in their totality. Among the most significant are nuns who run away with their lovers or attempt to. Such nuns appear in 55, 58, 59 (pl. 39), 94 (pl. 38), and F 28 (285). We treat these miracles in detail in chapter 12, "Love, Lust and Marriage."

Some miracles about nuns and monks, the pious and the wayward, are of special interest in that they offer very interesting facets of daily life. In the case of the pregnant abbess mentioned above, nuns report her to the bishop (7, 3) and witness the results of her divine delivery (panel 6) (pl. 40); in *Cantiga* 8 (pl. 11) a tonsured priest believes that witchcraft has caused a lighted candle to leave its holder and alight upon a jongleur's fiddle as he plays before Saint Mary's altar (panels 2 and 3); in *Cantiga* 9 (pl. 5) a monk agrees to bring an icon from the Holy Land to a lady innkeeper (panel 1); he is seen kneeling before the Holy Sepulchre (panel 2); he buys an icon, a portrait of the Virgin and Jesus the Child, from an open-air shop on the street (panel 3). On the way home he is accosted first by a lion and then by robbers, but all are defeated by the icon (panel 4); the icon, placed in the rigging of the ship on which he travels homeward bound, calms a storm

(panel 5); and he gives the icon to the lady innkeeper, who places it on the Virgin's altar (panel 6). This miracle reveals much about medieval life—the pilgrimage to Jerusalem, the shop open to the street, the dangers pilgrims might expect (lions did roam the Holy Land in those days, and robbers with hooks to capture pilgrims did likewise). In *Cantiga* 14 a monk, dying unconfessed, is attacked by demons (panel 1); the Virgin appears to Jesus and the monk is allowed to confess before he dies (panel 5); in *Cantiga* 32 an ignorant monk knows only the *Ave María,* but his devotion leads Saint Mary to excuse his ignorance (panel 2). In 48 a knight denies water from his spring to monks (panel 2); they beseech the Virgin to help them (panel 3); she moves the spring away from the knight's land (panel 4); then his water dries up (panel 5); and he cedes rights to the spring to the monks (panel 6).

In *Cantiga* 52 (pl. 6) the Virgin sends mountain goats to a monastery for the monks to milk (panels 1 and 2); the monks, dining in their refectory, have bowls of milk (panel 3); they give thanks (panel 4); a novice monk steals a kid while one of the brethren milks a goat (panel 5); the goats flee, never to return (panel 6).

In *Cantiga* 54 monks sing in a small chapel (panel 1); one monk is stricken with disease and lies dying (panel 2); thinking him dead, the brethren cover his face with a cowl (panel 3); the Virgin anoints his face with her milk (panel 4); he recovers (panel 5); the brethren kneel before her altar giving thanks (panel 6).

In number 56 a great devotee of the Virgin dies (panel 4), and when the Virgin makes the monks disinter his body, they find five roses growing from the mouth of the well-preserved corpse (panel 5 [pl. 31]).

In 61 one of the Virgin's shoes cures a man with a twisted mouth (panel 4); in 71 a nun prays every day, completing the entire book of prayers to Saint Mary; *Cantiga* 73 recounts the faith of monks whom we see singing in choirs in panels 1, 2, 3, and 4.

The motif of the monk who slept in a monastery garden for three centuries is found in *Cantiga* 103 (pl. 7): the monk demonstrates his everlasting devotion to Saint Mary (panel 1); he finds a beautiful fountain in the garden (panel 2); he listens to the song of a bird (a goldfinch?), and three hundred years pass (panel 3); he marvels upon seeing a door in the monastery that he does not recognize (panel 4); the monks do not recognize him, of course, and he tells them of his miraculous story (panel 5); all the monks praise Saint Mary (panel 6).

Cantiga 123 deals with a monk who is accepted in a monastery (panel 1); he sickens (panel 2); he is saved from devils by a candle sent by Saint Mary (panel 3); he dies (panel 4); he returns from the dead to reveal her mercy (panel 5).

Unusual, in that the miracle rejuvenates an aged monk prone to collapse and fall, is number 141: he is led before Saint Mary's altar (panel 4), is returned to the age of thirty, and is not recognized by the other monks (panel 5). In *Cantiga* 149 a priest doubts the holy sacrament, even as he conducts communion service (panel 1); the Host vanishes from his sight (panel 2), and he is frantic (panel 3); the Virgin appears and shows him the Child Jesus and tells him he is the Corpus Christi (panel 4); he then sees the Host and weeps (panel 5); he dies and angels carry him to heaven (panel 6). The lustful priest in 151, in bed with his mistress, is treated in chapter 12. A faithful prior appears in 164, 1; for the monks in 186 who lack bread and find it in their *hórreo* (granary), see plate 46 and chapter 15, "Places, Sites, and Locales."

In *Cantiga* 111, "How an ordained priest who served Holy Mary died in the river which runs through Paris, and on the third day Holy Mary revived him and brought him out of the river," an ordained priest is lustful. On the way to his mistress he drowns, but he is revived by the Virgin after lying for four days under water. We have a discrepancy here between the title ("the third day") and the text, which mentions four days.

Gluttonous and greedy monks are depicted in *Cantigas* 47, 75, and 88. In 47, "How Holy Mary saved the monk whom the devil tried to frighten in order to seize his soul" (pl. 8), a monk drinks far too much wine in the wine cellar, and on realizing his sin, he goes quickly but very unsteadily (panel 3) to the church to repent. The devil in the guise of a bull, an ugly wild man, and a lion comes to frighten him, but Holy Mary drives them away and lectures the monk to reform his ways. In 88, "How Holy Mary made a physician who had become a monk eat the viands that the other monks ate, which had a disagreeable taste to him," the physician-turned-monk detests the simple fare of the monastery because he is used to eating fish, meat, and good bread as well as drinking fine wine. He stirs up the brothers so that they begin to ask for food prohibited by their order. When the monks arise to go to the chapel to pray, the Virgin gives each one some food from a golden cup that she holds, but she refuses it to the physician/monk until he repents of his gourmandizing habits. In 75A, "How Holy Mary caused the priest to see that poverty with humility is better than ill-gotten wealth with pride and arrogance," a wealthy usurer and a poor woman are at death's door. The chaplain goes to the rich man's house in the hope of receiving a great deal of money from him by helping him to die in grace. When a messenger comes to the chaplain to ask him to hear the confession of the poor old woman and give her communion, he refuses. A gospeler in the rich man's house goes to the old woman, who lives in a thatched hut (pl. 9), and confesses her, seeing visions of Holy Mary around her bed. On returning to the rich man's house, he sees frightening devils all about. Holy Mary tells the cleric to realize that money is not always wealth.

Many virtuous members of the clergy are also represented: for example, Saint Ildefonso in *Cantiga* 2 and Saint John of Damascus in *Cantiga* F 22 (265), both mentioned previously.

Commoners and Occupations

Occupations in Spain paralleled those in the rest of Christian Europe, except for a few that were specifically Spanish. The miniaturists depicted all of these in Spanish settings, with the workers wearing Spanish clothing no matter where they lived. In our treatment, we have given the locale of each miracle that illustrates civic occupations and social classes, in order to remind our readers that to the miniaturists, a carpenter or a bishop or a farmer in a foreign land appeared as the illustrators saw them in Spain. We have not treated in detail in this section all of the incidences of classes and professions, but we have listed most of them in the appendix. The social classes are treated in descending order of rank, as the personages in the "Royalty and Nobility" and "Church Hierarchy" sections were arranged.

Both knights who were nobles and those who were not we have listed as knights. In the *Cantigas* the word *cavaleiro* needs consideration, since it means both "knight" and "gentleman." Of course, many gentlemen were knights in the full military sense of the word. Indeed, nearly all the men called *cavaleiro* in the *Cantigas* are military men who, like the Cid, were not of the nobility. We are able to identify true military knights from the captions occasionally, but they can be definitely identified in the text of the miracles and by what they are wearing in the illustrations. Gentlemen who were not knights seem to be landowners, whose occupation might be overseeing their farms or their cattle and sheep ranches, as for example in *Cantiga* 48, whose locale is Monsarraz in Catalonia. Some gentlemen probably sponsored merchants on land and sea; still others were robbers and raiders, men of the upper class who pillaged their neighbors or robbed travelers. Even men termed corsairs or pirates could have been knights. One especially beautiful miracle, in number 63 (pl. 60), deals with a knight, seen in full armor, who delays going into battle in order to hear mass. Either the Virgin or some minion of hers takes his place in battle. The locale is San Esteban de Gormaz. In chapter 12, "Love, Lust, and Marriage," various knights and gentlemen are depicted.

Men and women in various professions above day

laborers appear in many miniatures. Physicians appear frequently. An example can be seen in 157, 3 (see pl. 10), in which doctors fail to remove a kitchen knife that has punctured the mouth and jaw of a woman innkeeper who made fritters out of flour stolen from pilgrims on their way to Rocamadour. But when she goes to the shrine of the Virgin, a priest neatly withdraws the knife. In 173 doctors cannot remove a kidney stone, but the Virgin of Salas causes it to emerge and to be found in the sufferer's bed. A surgeon is depicted in 177 replacing the eyes of a man after his enemies have gouged them out. Other examples of doctors will be found in the listing of categories in the appendix.

Judges are seen frequently. A good example is the Spanish high judge in 119, 2. Another judge orders a villainous young man hanged for his evil deeds; and in 76, 2, a judge sentences a thief to die on the gallows. *Merinos* were magistrates who served as judges. In 13 a thief named Elbo is sentenced by a *merino* to be hanged.

Poets and scholars, both lay and ecclesiastical, often called troubadours or minstrels, abound, as did jongleurs (in Galician *jogrars*). One of these, a professional entertainer from Germany named Pedro de Sigrar, played his fiddle and sang to honor the Virgin at Rocamadour, seen in *Cantiga* 8 (pl. 11). A troubadour in Catalonia is seen in 194. Troubadours usually composed the songs, leaving singing and playing to jongleurs, just as today professional singers usually do not write the songs they sing.

In the *Cantigas* poets play important roles. These the miniaturists portray most often in manuscript F. Very interesting is the youthful poet in F 79 (307). (See chap. 4, "Disasters and Accidents," in which the eruption of Mount Etna in Sicily is made to subside after the Virgin asks the poet to write a song in her praise. The scenes of the volcano are remarkable [pl. 12].) In F 33 (202) a poet in Paris finds it impossible to create rhyme, so he begs Saint Mary to give him the ability, and of course she does and he presents her with a *cantiga*. In F 47 (291) we see and read about a sinful poet in Toro, who so pleases her with a song in her honor that she frees him from prison, forgiving him for the crime he has committed, which was rape. So greatly did she love those who wrote verses in her praise.

A priest, who was also a poet, in Alenquer in Portugal, *Cantiga* F85 (316), liked to write scurrilous songs of mockery known as *cantigas de escarnio*. When a church is built across the river from his church and when congregations favor it because of Saint Mary's relics found there, he burns that church and the Virgin blinds him for it. But when he rebuilds her shrine, she cures his blindness and he promises to write thereafter only songs of praise for her.

Teachers are also depicted. In 4, 1 (see pl. 13), we see a clerical teacher in Bourges instructing young boys, who sit on the floor as he teaches them. This is one of the most interesting miracles. When a Jewish lad, popular with the Christian students, sees a vision in which the Virgin gives communion to the Christian boys, he gets in line, and to him, indeed, if not to the other boys who were given communion by the abbot, the Virgin gives the holy wafer. When the lad's father, a glass maker, learns of this, he thrusts his son into his furnace. Inside it she protects the boy from the flames, and when he emerges and reports her presence, Christians put the Jewish father into the furnace, where he dies. In F 22A, 1 (265), John of Damascus, it will be recalled, is captured by Muslims and sold to a Persian burgher, who makes him the teacher of his son. John teaches the boy handwriting so much like his that no difference can be detected. The emperor of Rome demands John as a gift, and he soon becomes the emperor's counselor. When the evil Persian student forges letters and places them in the palace to incriminate John, he is sentenced to have his hand cut off (pl. 64). After they cut off his hand, John prays all night long, begging Saint Mary to restore his hand, since he is guiltless, and she restores it.

Professional sculptors and painters were not omitted by the miniaturists. Of special interest is the fresco painter in *Cantiga* 74 (pl. 14). In this valuable depiction, we see the painter on a low wooden scaffold, on which he has placed paint pots, as he paints the Virgin and the devil in all his hideousness in panels 1 and 2. In panel 3, on a high scaffold, he paints the Madonna and the Child in a lofty arch; in panel 4 the devil knocks down the scaffold, and we see the painter's stool falling along with the entire scaffolding, but the brush with which he paints the Madonna's face sticks to it and supports him aloft until they rebuild the scaffold and he is saved. In 136, 6 (pl. 70), a painter and sculptor in Foggia in Italy and in F 45 (312) the same painter and sculptor in Catalonia is seen as he paints and sculpts.

Skilled workers are well represented. A master stonemason in Castrojeriz, F 63 (252), falls from a high place. Of course Saint Mary saves him. Masons are seen repairing a church in Germany in 42, 1 (pl. 50). A carpenter in Monsarraz, Portugal, builds a coffin in F 55 (223). In 19, 6, we see a blacksmith in Sicily with his forge, and in F 42, 1 (362), a goldsmith in Chartres. A seamstress in Chartres sews in 117, 2, and another, also in Chartres, is seen in 148, 3.

Money changers in Soissons are seen in 41, 1; in 62; in 25A, 1; and in F 35B, 4 (305). There is a usurer, a Jew, in 25A, 1. Merchants play significant roles: one of the best examples can be seen in 35B, 4, where we see bales being loaded by stevedores. See the many examples of this trade in the appendix.

The miniaturists depict many people in service: a maidservant in 43, 4; midwives in 108, 3 (pl. 19); male nurses in 67, 1 (pl. 58).

People who are connected with agriculture and husbandry are well represented: a wagoner in Villa Sirga in 31, 5 (pl. 15) drives a cart, drawn by oxen, with huge spiked wheels to give it traction. Beekeeping, and therefore the production of honey and wax, so necessary for the finest candles, is represented in 128 (pl. 27), whose setting is Flanders. The bees are enlarged so that the viewer can see them clearly and can see how well they are anatomically portrayed. Reapers of wheat near Segovia appear in F 12 (314), with their sickles. Since sheep raising was so important in medieval European cultures, several pages of miniatures contain shepherds, viz. 102, 5 and 147, 2. In 147 (pl. 17) we also see sheepshearers.

Silk culture in Segovia is well illustrated in 18, 3 and 4 (pl. 3). See our earlier discussion of this unusual and prized material.

Viniculture, which was all-important, is depicted in 132, 1; 161, 4; and F 13 (226), in which appear grapevines in full leaf and without leaves, with monks pruning them. This is in England. A large fig tree forms part of the setting of 107, 3 (pl. 67) in Segovia and a mulberry tree in Chartres is seen in 148, 6.

Minorities: Jews, Muslims, and Heretics

Hundreds of thousands of Jews and Muslims lived in thirteenth-century Spain, and it is quite natural that the former, believed to be enemies of Christianity, and the latter, enemies both of the Christian faith and of Christian kingdoms, should appear in so many miniatures. We suspect that heretics were few in number in the thirteenth century, but some heretics appear in miracles that occurred in the ancient world.

Jews, almost always seen as religious opponents of Christianity, are portrayed as murderers, blasphemers, and otherwise as vile and dangerous persons. One macabre example is 34, 1 (pl. 18) in Constantinople, where a Jew throws the portrait of Saint Mary into a privy because the devil tells him to. (Illustrations of privies are rare.) When a Christian buys the Jew's house, he finds the icon, removes it, and gives it a place of honor in his home. Once washed, it exudes a fragrant aroma and a flow of fine oil, and pilgrims visit it. A very interesting example of Jewish life can be studied in 108 (pl. 19), set in Scotland. In this

page of miniatures, we see the inside of a Jewish household and also the birth of a Jewish child, whose father is a pharmacist. In this page, Merlin rears the Jewish child, whom his own father wishes to kill because he has been born with his head on backward. Also we see Jews converted by Merlin, when he reveals the miracle of the Jewish lad's deformity. Jews are usually, but not always, portrayed in a negative light, as will be seen subsequently.

The conquest of most of Spain in the eighth century by Muslims was a part of Spanish history known to all, and of course in Alfonso's time Muslims still held Granada and other areas. Moors, as Muslims were called regardless of their appearance or origin, are characters in many miracles. Unlike Jews, they are respected as warriors and rulers, although they are usually depicted as cruel and dangerous enemies. Muslim armies are shown in many miniatures. Semitic Muslims are as white as Christians, but common soldiers and slaves and Muslims of the lower class are seen black with African features. In 185, 5 a blackamoor is a slave in a Christian household. The mother of the slave's owner hates her son's wife, so, in order to disgrace her, she orders the blackamoor to lie down in the wife's bed while she is asleep. When the mother shows her son this sight, he orders both his wife and the Muslim burned. The Muslim, innocent as he is, dies in flames, but the wife is unscathed (pl. 65).

Some of the scenes of Muslim battles and sieges are remarkably graphic and wonderful in their details. In 28 (pl. 20) we see the siege of Constantinople with catapults, and in 46, which deals with a Muslim raid on Christian lands, we see the Muslims taking booty; in 99 Muslim soldiers attack a Christian city. In both 99 and 46, much of the impedimenta and accoutrements of warfare can be seen—cavalry and infantry, armor, and so forth.

Few heretics are portrayed, and of these some lived abroad or in earlier centuries. Heretics in fourth-century Constantinople cause the eyes of Saint John Chrysostom to be gouged out in 138, reflecting times when the early Church in the East had problems with unbelievers. Other heretics in Cluny (156) cut out the tongue of a priest who writes songs for Saint Mary. Perhaps the best-known medieval heretic appears in 175A, 2, some of whose events take place in Toulouse. The heretic innkeeper places one of his goblets in the luggage of a young German pilgrim on the way to the shrine of Saint James. According to Filgueira Valverde (1985, 262), the heretics in 156 are Albigensians.

2
Clothing
Civil, Ecclesiastical, Military, Naval, and Constabulary

s mentioned in the introduction, we owe a great deal to the expert observations of Kathleen Kulp-Hill concerning the clothing depicted in the miniatures. Referring to the work of António H. de Oliveira Marques on daily life in Portugal and to Guerrero-Lovillo's treatment of attire in the *Cantigas* (1949), she invokes her own very special knowledge, gleaned from years of studying the miniatures, giving suggestions and insights best conceived by a woman.

We realized that pictorial representation of the garments of any culture reveals a great deal about social life. Kulp-Hill, in a paper read at the Kentucky Foreign Language Conference in Lexington (1985), offers ideas we had overlooked: "[C]lothing can convey inner states as well as the outward signs of joy, grief, penitence, modesty and dignity." Those scholars who study the *Cantigas* miniatures have been amazed at the remarkably detailed depiction of the attire of all levels of medieval Spanish society, from emperors, kings, and queens to peasants and common day laborers—Christian, Muslim, and Jewish. When we take into further consideration what was written about clothing in fictional and nonfictional books of the period, many of which were also illuminated, and look also at sumptuary laws, we can be certain of authenticity as regards medieval clothing in Alfonsine Spain.

Certain occupations and activities demanded clothing best suited to the work involved—for example, what butchers or hunters or farmers wore; but even such workers as these usually wore what we refer to as the basic masculine garb. Subsequently we point to the brother of an emperor wearing this basic attire for men and then reveal that masons and painters and other members of workaday society also favored it. This should hardly be strange to us, since twentieth-century men also generally follow the same basic style when they are formally dressed, for example in church, at the office, at business meetings, and often for travel—trousers, jacket, frequently a vest, a shirt, a necktie, and shoes. For informal attire men today wear jeans, shirts, and sandals or other informal footwear. Of course those in medieval Spain who dressed in basic attire also had garments worn on special occasions, just as do modern males. The same is true concerning the clergy then and now. We see bishops wearing miters and clerical robes, and they appear also wearing secular hats and garments.

Very good examples of male attire can be seen in T.I.1 42, 2, whose caption reads, "How young men were playing ball in a meadow." We see no undergarments here, of course, but in *Cantiga* 75, 4 we see *bragas* with knots clearly visible, which could be untied to lengthen them.

When the young men arose from their beds, they took off night clothing, if indeed they slept in any, and donned their *bragas*. These could be short, covering the body from waist halfway to the knee, as seen in panel 4 of *Cantiga* 22 (pl. 24), or as long as from waist to heels in cold weather. *Bragas* could be loosened for more freedom or tightened for support. We found no illustrations of longer *bragas*, since they would have been covered by the long stockings known as *calzas,* which, made of knit cloth, were tight enough to be shaped to the leg and to conceal the longer *bragas* if these were worn beneath them. *Calzas* were secured at the waist with laces. Over his *bragas* and *calzas* a man wore a *camisa* or shift, as seen in 148, 3 and 6, which was flowing and had long sleeves and an open neck with plackets (pl. 23) or binding.

Returning to the ball players, note the colors of the hose. The batter, the pitcher, and one of the youths ready to catch the ball wear black hose. We cannot see the hose of the third "catcher." The one wearing red hose has tucked up his tunic, as men often did when engaged in physical activities. In passing, it is interesting to speculate about the profession of the possessor of the red hose. We know that only the nobility could legally wear scarlet hose, with one exception: a *jograr* could wear red hose, if a noble had given them to him. The artist of 42 gave the youth scarlet hose, surely aware of this prohibition and of the exception. Was the youth in red hose a nobleman or a *jograr?* Or at times, did youths protesting the prohibition defy the rules? Inevitably, such conjectures may lead to unexpected information concerning aspects of daily life.

The basic outer garment worn by men was the *saya* or *cota* or a *capa* or tunic, which reached to the knees. It was belted so that it could be worn open or closed, and the sleeves were loose enough to permit active movement. It had an opening just wide enough to allow the head to pass through. This outfit was attractive in appearance and colorful. It resembled the riding coat worn by fox hunters today and derivatives of the redingote worn by women (pl. 50).

The ball players' white shoes are decorated by openwork, allowing the color of the hose to show through. The shoes have heels only slightly higher than the soles.

To complete the basic masculine attire, men generally wore a *cofia*, which appears to be a head kerchief designed to contain the almost-shoulder-length hair, reminding us of the "baseball" cap worn by so many males today.

To reinforce our statement that all classes wore the basic outfit seen in T.I.1, in 15A, 2 we see the brother of the emperor of Rome kneeling before the empress. His basic attire is slightly different in that he wears a ruffled collar and a long *manto* or mantle over his tunic. The material used in the basic attire of royalty would have been of higher quality than that of the average man. Such mantles would have been worn by men such as the ball players as protection against cold weather and the elements.

Men also wore *capas,* shorter than *mantos* and circular in cut and open on one side, but sleeveless on the other, as seen in 78. A heavier and warmer outer garment was the *garnacha* (*balandrán* and *gabán*), a cloak with full three-quarter bell sleeves, hood, and slits in the sides. Garin, the money changer, wears this garment in 41.

In 74 (pl. 14) the painter wears a *tabardo* over his smock. The sleeves are sewn only in the back so that the arms can protrude, letting the sleeves hang free. Slits in the *tabardo's* front and sides would also facilitate movement. The color of this *tabardo* is mauve and its sleeves are gray-blue.

The *manto,* the *pieza noble,* though any man might

wear it, was favored by royalty and nobility to represent dignity and ceremony. It was fastened with ties or *fiadores* or *fíbulas* (brooches). See the illustration in the frontispiece of this volume, where Alfonso on a covered bench wears the royal *manto.* The king in the songs of praise nearly always wears the royal *manto.* In 80, 6 he wears a long robe, over which is worn the *manto,* pinkish in color with a golden fringe. There is a design mostly composed of the three-towered castle of Castile. His gilded shoes are pointed. In 30, 1, he seems to be wearing a similar *manto;* however, he faces the viewer and his arms are outstretched, so we see only the lining of the *manto,* which is slate with a blue pattern. In 50, 1, he wears a gorgeously colored robe in which can be seen several patterns, but primary is the "clover leaf" or rosette seen in the border of many pages of miniatures. His *manto* is deep azure.

For a more detailed description of masculine attire, we have referred not only to the remarks by Kulp-Hill, but also to the descriptions provided by Guerrero-Lovillo (1949). We continue with the insights of Kulp-Hill because Guerrero-Lovillo does not link articles of clothing with specific illustrations in the miniatures. In 44 (pl. 44) the knight out hunting has gathered his tunic in his left hand to facilitate movement. He has a dagger in his belt, and his wide-brimmed sombrero, for sun and rain, hangs at his back. He wears a *birrete.* He has just launched his goshawk, and the glove in that hand is visible. His footwear may be *huesas (osas),* a type of boot. The same knight, who has lost his hawk, is in church begging for a miracle, as seen in panel 4. He wears a *capa* or *manto* trimmed with fur. He is clad in a jumper-like garment called a *pellote* or surcoat, which is also fur-trimmed. His tunic shows under his deeply-cut armholes.

The garments of professional people seem to have differed according to their occupation. In 88 appears a physician with a *manto* over his shoulder and a sleeveless *capa* underneath. He wears a *boneta* or *tutupía* as headgear. This hat is often the badge of physicians or sages. In F 95, 3 (209) (pl. 33) a physician treating Alfonso wears such a *boneta,* and in 157, 3 (pl. 10) and in 5, physicians treating the woman with the kitchen knife through her jaw wear *bonetas.*

In 8 (pl. 11) the *jograr* fiddling to honor Saint Mary wears a *tabardo* over his blue tunic. In 4, 1 (pl. 13) the clerical teacher wears a *tabardo* with a hood or *capuchin* attached, we believe, although it may be a separate hood called an *almuza.* Such gear in a chapel connected with a "schoolroom" may well indicate a cold temperature, offering an element of daily life associated with climate.

Pilgrims in 49, on their way to Soissons, wear the typical pilgrim cloak, the *esclavina,* similar to the *garnacha.*

The sleeves are sewn outside the armholes, forming a kind of cape. In 175A, 4 (pl. 45), the youth falsely accused wears a *esclavina,* as does his father, and both wear the pilgrim's hat. The pilgrim in 189, 1 (pl. 30) also travels to Salas wearing the *esclavina.* His sombrero hangs over his shoulder, fitting against his back. The blacksmith in 19 wears a conical hat and a heavy (leather?) apron over his tunic.

Jews and Muslims usually wear garments Alfonso's viewers would have recognized as eastern. The sultan in 28, 3 (pl. 20) is typical. He wears a flowing mantle or *alquicel* over a robe or *almexia.* Moorish undergarments were known as *aljuba.* Muslim knights in 63, 3 (pl. 60) in the midst of battle, appearing to be as fair as Christians, wear turban-like helmets, and blackamoors are bareheaded.

Jews were required by law to wear a sign, usually the Star of David, on their attire (*Siete Partidas 7,* title 24, law 11). They wore conical hats as in 34, 1 (pl. 18) and in 108, 1, 2, 4, and 5 (pl. 19). They wore mantles over full-sleeved tunics and pointed shoes.

The attire of women is not as well depicted as is men's. In 107 (pl. 67) we see the Jewess Marisaltos standing barefoot and in her shift *(camisa),* since she has been stripped prior to execution. The head covering is typically Jewish, that is, a scarf tied at one side and covering her throat.

The basic dress of women is the *brial,* as seen in 136, 2 (pl. 70). This rough and simple *brial* is worn by a woman gambler. Refinements of the *brial* were frequent. The go-between in 64, 4 (pl. 1), who from her attire seems to be well-off, wears over her tunic a heavy robe that trails on the ground. She wears a *touca* or headdress, which covers her hair and extends, shawl-like, around her neck.

Santa Maria wears over her *brial,* which is frequently blue, a lavish mantle. In 175B, 2, her mantle is white with a golden fringe, and the design on it features the "clover-leaf" cross in gold. In 47, 2 (pl. 8) she wears a deep blue *brial* and a pink mantle. On her head she wears the typical white wimple.

In 137, in which the lustful knight is seen embracing two courtesans, or well-off prostitutes, those women wear *tocas altas* (high-fashion sugarloaf hats) and *briales* with close-fitting bodices. One has lacings up the side to let the *camisa* or the skin show. The other wears a peplum at the waist. Another example of the sugarloaf hat can be seen in 64, 4 (pl. 1), in which the wife of the knight summoned to war appears wearing the beehive *toca,* supported by a chin strap. The *toca* is elaborately decorated. Her

brial is covered by a flowing mantle. The go-between's pink *brial* can only barely be seen, so long and flowing is her deep blue mantle. Her *toca* is round, and part of it serves as a chin strap to hold it in place.

In 23 the noble *dama de Bretanna,* as she serves her guest, who is a king, wears a lovely pink *brial* with a fringe on its *cinta* (band) almost covered by her floor-length deep blue mantle. Her *touca* (cap) has a *redecilla* (a type of snood to cover the hair).

Children, who are characters in many *cantigas* (See chap. 27, "Women and Children"), are clothed more or less as adults. In 122 the princess Berenguela, daughter of King Ferdinand III and Queen Beatriz, appears first wrapped in blankets and later, after dying and being miraculously resuscitated by the Virgin, appears wearing the miniature wimple of the order of nuns in Las Huelgas. Queen Beatriz is seen in panel 5 (pl. 61) as she stares through the open curtains of her litter.

In 44, 2 (pl. 44), in which the knight loses his goshawk, appears a little scout with a laced tunic looking for the lost hawk. In 79 appears Musa, the vain little maiden whose clothing represents her frivolity. She wears a *pellote,* lavishly trimmed with a long sash or ribbon in her hand. Her *toca* looks like a crown. We see her dancing and carefree in her garden.

In 135A, 1 (pl. 35) each of the two very young adolescents wears a *pellote,* hers pink, his blue, and she wears a cap resembling a crown. In 64 (pl. 1) the *cavaleiro* who receives a message from his liege lord to go to war wears a *birrete* and a *pellote* under his mantle. His shoes have a lattice design. In 178, 1 (pl. 69) a farmer and his family stand in front of their substantial-appearing house. The farmer is giving his son a pet mule. He wears a tunic with a dagger in its belt. His shoes are a frequently seen pull-on type. The little boy wears a simple tunic; the wife has a *crespina* (hair net) and a *garnacha* (robe) over her *brial.*

Armor, soldiers' uniforms, and accessories are treated at length by Guerrero-Lovillo (1949, 112-35). He offers line drawings of all such items. This very valuable book, in which he treats many kinds of clothing, has line-drawing illustrations of the clothing in sections titled "Atavío caballeresco" (112-35), "El traje civil masculino" (47-97); "Atavío femenino" (98-111); "Vestiduras religiosas" (163-82); "Traje de moros y judíos" (183-88); and "Tocado y calzado" (189-226). Unfortunately, the author did not indicate which miniatures he copied in his line drawings.

3
Death

he miniatures in the *Cantigas* depict death in many forms, and this is not strange, since people encountered it constantly. Diseases, some hardly known today, flourished—leprosy, small pox, erysipelas, and plague, to name only a few; feuds, murders and very violent acts were commonplace; executions for many more crimes than are so punished today were public—hanging, stoning, burning, and defenestration carried off thousands; starvation was always a factor; wild animals killed people; and war, nearly always in progress somewhere, brought death to the eyes of thousands; even art in many forms portrayed the grisly deaths of saints and martyrs, and everywhere were life-size crucifixes in which Jesus was portrayed with grim realism. And always the Church preached that death could not be escaped. Moreover, associated with actual physical death, the Church preached the damnation of the souls of the unrepentant, the wicked, and the unbaptized; and even the good had to face purgatory. So death and everything associated with it was dreaded.

We think Alfonso harbored the belief that the Virgin would pardon certain sins that the Church would not without the most dreadful penances and most convincing confessions. As the most loyal devotee of the Virgin, Alfonso apparently believed that with regularity she had saved him from death and from disease. He seems to have thought that his belief in her protection and the living proof of it in his recovery, in addition to the salvation she offered members of all social classes, could lead his subjects to depend upon him more than upon the Church itself. We are in debt to Maricel Presilla, who, in her doctoral dissertation, convincingly suggests that the *Cantigas* offered a kind of palinode to or rejection of the Church's more severe teaching. In the miracles, the Virgin sometimes forgives unpardonable sins even before confession and contrition and on occasions saves her devotees from death or even restores life to them when they have died. Obviously people realized that she would not save everybody; but when they read or heard the miracles recited and sung, or perhaps saw some presented in dramatic form, as some miracles were, for example, in France, they could hope that they might be the fortunate ones. Some she rescues from the trauma of facing death; others, who die, are resuscitated, even in some cases after the passage of considerable time; a few, due to be executed, through her aid do not die until they confess to a priest. Some die and are immediately taken straight to heaven, thus avoiding purgatory, for example the teenage girl Musa in *Cantiga* 79.

In 21 we see the violent death of a child, whom Saint Mary restores to life when the mother carries her to the Virgin's shrine; in 139 a child dies and instead of being resuscitated, goes to heaven; in 6, after Jews murder a lad because he sings *Gaude Virgo Maria,* she brings him back to life and allows Christians to slay the Jews; in 11 a monk commits the sin of fornication and drowns in a river unconfessed. Berceo told a version of the same story in his *Miracle* 17. In 122 (pl. 61) Alfonso's infant sister, Berenguela, dies but is resuscitated; in 5 Saint Mercurio slays the wicked Emperor Julian with a lance; in 124 (pl. 21) we see three methods of execution—stoning, piercing with a spear, and throat slashing with a knife; in 184, 4 (pl. 66) enemies kill a man and his wife with their swords. Hanging was cheap and popular, for example in *Cantigas* 13 and 175.

These are but a few incidents of death, but a great many more are listed in the index of categories under "Death" (see appendix).

4
Disasters and Accidents

isaster implies a great or sudden misfortune resulting in loss of life and property or one that is ruinous to an undertaking. Accident implies a happening that is unforeseen or un-suspected, or unintended. Since people of all classes and levels of society encountered natural and other disasters, some caused at work, Alfonso and his collaborators included miracles in which the Virgin saved people from the results of both disasters and accidents. Quite probably, such miracles came from hearsay, folk legends, and even from history.

Disasters

In F 79 (307) (pl. 12) when Mount Etna in Sicily erupted, killing many people and damaging the land and villages around it, the Virgin asked a young poet to write a song of praise in her honor. His work pleased her so much that she caused the eruption to subside. The miniaturists' conception of a volcanic eruption is naive yet convincing. Shipwrecks and storms at sea are well represented: in F16 (313) a ship is in a storm and has broken apart; we see in 33 a ship bound for Acre that sinks with many drowned; in F 53 (267) a storm strikes a ship en route to Flanders; F 65^1 (236) relates the sinking of a galley; in 39 the Church of San Miguel is struck by lightning and set on fire; in 113, 5 (pl. 22), when a huge stone is dislodged from a mountain and rolls toward the monastery of Monserrat, Saint Mary deflects it. The miniaturist depicts her angels lowering the stone away from the building; F 66^1 (266) depicts a church in which a beam falls on the congregation; in F 63 (252) she saves workmen upon whom sand collapses, burying them; when a mine being inspected by the emperor of Constantinople caves in, burying him and his companions, she saves them, permitting them to survive for a year underground (131).

Acccidents

In 35B, 1, the mast of a ship falls on an admiral and kills him; F 80 (276) depicts a man in church when a bell falls on his head; in F 53, 3 (267), a merchant falls overboard; in F 25 (322) a greedy man chokes on a rabbit bone. Falls are well represented: in F 52, 3 (241), a young man falls from a high window in his mother's house and his skull is crushed. When his mother begs Saint Mary to restore him to life, she does so. The resemblance to a similar event when Saint Paul resuscitated a young man named Eutychus is remarkably close (Acts 20:9-12). The accidental swallowing of a poisonous spider occurs in F 67 (225) and F 93 (222). See the appendix under "Disasters and Accidents" for a more complete listing.

5
Education

ducation was the obligation of the Church, although royalty, nobility, and the Church's own members, and occasionally the sons (rarely the daughters) of rich burghers had private instruction. *Cantiga* 4, 1 (pl. 13) depicts a cleric instructing a class of boys who sit on the floor. A Jewish lad learns with the Christians and is popular with them. This small facet of daily life reveals an unexpected custom, that race and religious faith could be overlooked by and with children. Please see the full discussion of this *cantiga* in chapter 1, the section titled "Commoners and Occupations," where we treat teachers. In 53 the Holy Spirit teaches an illiterate boy to read and speak Latin well, and we see him in panels 5 and 6 explaining Scripture to the people and also teaching them how to repair their church.

John of Damascus instructs a Persian burgher's son, especially in penmanship, in F 22 (265). In 111, 1, a man "instructs" women in the art of making love, reminding us that in Alfonso's *Cantigas de mal dizer* (MS Vaticana 76), the dean of Cález studied books that enabled him to seduce all sorts of women and to use them as he pleased, completely confusing them. In the *cantiga,* the above-mentioned cleric is seated on a four-poster bed with a woman and ardently kissing her. She seems to be grasping his arm as though to to resist him, but the caption, "How a priest was very fond of instructing women," indicates that he is successful in his instruction.

All of the *cantigas de loor* may be regarded as educational, since Alfonso dissertates on virtues and sins and Saint Mary's role in heaven's contact with mortals. The king is depicted in all but two of the *loores* in T.I.1—60 and 180; in F only three *loores* are illustrated (30, 40, and 96), and he is absent from F 40.

6
Fauna and Flora

In illuminating the *Cantigas de Santa Maria,* the artists naturally included domestic and wild animals in the settings of some *cantigas,* even though many times merely as a gratuitous addition, since they are not mentioned in either the captions or the text of the *cantiga* proper (Mâle 1972, 51). It is clear that the miniaturists often decorated their illustrations with animals and plants designed to provide attractive, realistic settings.

Domestic Animals

In *Cantiga* 148, 5 (pl. 23), "How a knight escaped from the hands of his enemies because of a shift of Holy Mary's he was wearing," we see a village scene with various domestic animals. There is a domestic sow that resembles wild swine with striped piglets also resembling wild piglets. We see a dovecote with the gray rock pigeons that had long been domesticated; we see a rooster scratching for food to tempt a hen. We see a flock of white geese, as well. Not one of these animals is mentioned in the text, which refers only to a village. All are the artists' additions to set the scene of the miracle.

Among domestic animals, many horses are depicted, both palfreys and war horses, some of which are perfect anatomical examples. Many war horses dressed for battle appear in *Cantiga* 63, "How Holy Mary saved from disgrace a knight who was to be in the battle of San Esteban de Gormaz, but who could not appear there because he heard three masses" (pl. 60). In *Cantiga* 22, "How Holy Mary saved a farmer from dying of the wounds dealt him by a knight and his men" (pl. 24), a horse is clearly depicted.

In *Cantiga* 171, 2, "How a woman from Pedraza was going with her husband to Salas and they lost their little boy in the river," a lady rides a palfrey, as does a lady in 135B, 3, "How Holy Mary freed from dishonor a couple who had sworn to her when they were children to marry each other" (pl. 36).

Mules were often ridden while hunting. Alfonso rides one as he hunts herons in 142, 1, 3, and 5, "How Holy Mary saved from death one of the king's men who had entered a river to retrieve a heron" (pl. 4), and another appears in *Cantiga* 178, 5, "About a little boy of Alcarráz whose father had given him a little mule and it died" (pl. 69). And in 179, 2, "How a woman who was crippled in her whole body had herself carried to Holy Mary of Salas and was cured at once," a paralyzed lady is strapped to the back of a large mule. In F 88 (228), "How a good man had a mule, diseased in all its feet; and the good man ordered one of his sons to skin it, and while the son was getting ready, the mule got up cured and went to the church," there appears a diseased mule, first swollen and hideous (pl. 25) and later in its natural form.

Numerous depictions of bovines appear. In 1, 2 (pl. 16), in the Nativity scene, we see an ox peering into Jesus' manger. In 31, 5 (pl. 15), a farmer plows with a team of bullocks, whose visible genitalia prove they are not castrated oxen. A remarkably well-depicted bull appears in 144, 3 (pl. 49). This bull is a *"toro bravo"* and was placed in the plaza in lieu of a bullring. He is baited by various *"toreros"* from the safety of a rooftop. In 47, 2 (pl. 8), we see a devil in the form of a fierce bull and in panel 4 a lion held at bay by Saint Mary.

Asses used as beasts of burden appear occasionally. In *Cantiga* 167, "How a Mooress took her dead son to Saint Mary's of Salas and she resuscitated him," panel 3 (pl.

26), we see an ass carrying a child's coffin. In 102, 5, we see rams with curled horns and also a goat. In 147, 2, more sheep appear.

Silkworms in 18 (pl. 3) are depicted with anatomic correctness except for size. Bees are also anatomically correct except for size in 128, 3 (pl. 27). In F 94 (208) also, bees appear, and in F 97 (211) strange white bees restore a melted candle.

In *Cantiga* 69 there are a rooster and a frog; in this case both are mentioned, because in the text a deaf-mute is cured and can hear both creatures. The rooster is depicted in panel 4; the frog is hidden in a marsh and cannot be seen. And from the mute's ear was extracted a fleecy worm that is not seen.

Pets

Since thirteenth-century Spaniards, according to the miniatures, had pets, we include them here. In *Cantiga* 135B, 3 (pl. 36), we see the heroine riding sidesaddle and holding a lapdog. Nothing is said about this little pet, which seems to be a gratuitous detail inserted by the miniaturist who created it. Shepherds' dogs appear in Cantiga 1, 3. In *Cantiga* F 4 (286) (pl. 28) a huge dog, one as large as a great Pyrenees or a Saint Bernard, appears. Of course, we could consider it to be a watchdog, given its attack upon a devotee who lay down in the street. In *Cantiga* 142, 3 and 5 (pl. 4), appear greyhounds, and in panel 4 is a spaniel looking into the water, probably a water spaniel. Many gentlemen kept falcons of various kinds. Such raptors, of course, were used in hunting. Even so, people who kept hunting hawks of necessity had to know the birds well in order to be able to control them. Therefore, falconer and hawk enjoyed the relationship of master and pet as well as that of master and hunting hawk. Alfonso is depicted hawking for herons in *Cantiga* 142 (pl. 4). Several *cantigas* reveal this tie between hawk and man. We see a gentleman in 44 (pl. 44) hunting quail with a goshawk.

Alfonso himself had a more unusual pet, one that people then used for hunting, especially hares. So fond was he of his pet ferret that he carried it about with him. One day it fell from the horse he was riding as he carried it, and horses trampled the beloved animal. Of course, when he begged Saint Mary to heal it, she restored the pet to life. It is a pity that this *cantiga*, "How Holy Mary saved from death a little animal they call *donezeña* (ferret)" (354) is not illustrated. We break our rule of discussing only what can be seen in the miniatures, because a ferret is an unusual pet. Alfonso's ferret is obviously described as a pet, but quite probably he used it to hunt rabbits. Ferrets in Spain today are used to hunt hares and to kill rats; but they are perhaps even more common as true pets, as they

have become in the United States. They can be tamed and can rival cats and dogs in affectionate behavior. They would be more popular but for the rank scent they share with their relatives polecats and weasels. It is possible, though not probable, that Alfonso's pet was a weasel. For millenia people have kept ferrets for hunting: they did not, to our knowledge, train weasels. The *Encyclopedia Britannica* and the *Oxford Dictionary* state that ferrets and weasels are of the same species.

It is doubtful that the animals sent to Alfonso by King Alvandexaver of Egypt (Keller 1972b) for his zoo could have been considered by him as pets: in 29, 5 (pl. 29), a zebra, a giraffe, an elephant, a bear, boars, and various exotic birds appear. But zoos were part of daily life and many kings proudly displayed various animals. King Frederick of Sicily (1272-1337) had a large number of animals that he sent here and there for display. The Cid had a lion, and Charlemagne kept lions. Henry IV of Spain (1425-74) had a large collection of animals. In *Don Quixote*, part 2, chapter 17, we read of the pair of lions sent to the king of Spain by the governor of Oran.

Wild Animals

A lion in 47 (pl. 8) is the devil in one of his disguises. He is well depicted, mouth open and paw extended. In 9, 4 (pl. 5), a lion confronts a pilgrim. In 67, 4 (pl. 58), a bear stands on its hind legs to attack a hunter. In *Cantiga* 82, 1, boars, with wings as demons, attack.

Mountain goats in 52, 5 (pl. 6), both male and female, with long curved horns, are illustrated. Hares are numerous, appearing often. Good representations can be seen in 52, 1 and 2 (pl. 6) and in 155A, 6.

In 189, 2 (pl. 30), a *bescha*, depicted as a dragon, appears. The title of this *cantiga* reads, "How a man who was going to Saint Mary's of Salas met a dragon on the way and killed it, and he became a leper from its poison and then Saint Mary cured him."

Many varieties of birds are represented. Falcons are seen in *Cantiga* 44, 5 (pl. 44) and 142, 2 (pl. 4). In the latter the hawk brings down a heron. In 124, 6 (pl. 21), appear two species of vultures, four ravens, and two magpies. In *Cantiga* 2 a white dove sits on Archbishop Ildefonso's shoulder as he writes a book sustaining belief in Saint Mary's virginity. It represents the Holy Ghost. Partridges are seen in 44, 1 (pl. 44). In 93, 4, in a tree are a hoopoe and an owl. A goldfinch in 93, 3 sings from a tree top, and owls appear in 135A, 6 (pl. 35) and 103, 3 (pl. 7).

Trees and Plants

Less identifiable are plants, especially trees and shrubs,

for example in 142, 2, 4, and 6 (pl. 4), in scenic backdrops. We clearly see pines in 42, 6 (pl. 50), and the Jewess Marisaltos stands at the foot of a tall fig tree in 107, 4 (pl. 67). Date palms are seen in 60, 2; 45, 6; and 100, 6. Most trees are stylized as in 155, 1. Ivy, covering a hermitage, appears in all the panels of 65B.

Roses, one of the Virgin's flowers, are seen in stylized design in 10, 1, where the Virgin sits among roses, and in 10, 2 among lilies and other flowers. In 56, 5 (pl. 31), five roses grow from the mouth of a dead monk. The lilies in 10, 2 and 140, 3 are more realistic. Most flowers are very small and are unidentifiable to us. A botanist might be more successful than we were at this task.

Wheat ready for harvest is depicted in F 12, 1 (314), and in 186, 2 (pl. 46), can be seen harvested grains of wheat. Grapevines appear well illustrated in 161, 4 and 5.

Although we have not discussed every example of every type of fauna and flora, we have treated these topics rather completely with illustrations.

7

Food and Drink

he two codices, T.I.1 and F, visualize food and drink, primarily bread and wine. Bread, of course, then as now, was served at all meals, usually in the form of small round rolls divided into six sections. They appear at every place setting at the wedding banquet in *Cantiga* 42, 4 (pl. 50). In 84, 3, we see the same rolls, and in 52, 3 (pl. 6), the table is in a monastery with the ever present rolls, knives, and bowls. In 67, 5 and 6 (pl. 58), a more formal meal appears at a table set for important people, including a bishop. In 23, 3, a king and a bishop are dining. It is interesting to note in passing that the same round, six-sectioned rolls were discovered in the ashes of Pompeii, reminding us of the sempiternal heritage of Spain's Roman past.

The miniatures, since they illustrate farm animals as well as wild creatures that formed part of medieval Spanish diet, reveal other comestibles: *Cantiga* 148, 5 (pl. 23), reveals farm animals that were eaten: chickens, pigeons, geese, and swine. In *Cantiga* 142 (pl. 4) Alfonso is seen hawking for herons, which were regarded as a delicacy in his time. Keller and Kinkade (1984, 27-28) describe the artistic techniques utilized to depict the action of this *cantiga.*

Cantiga 52, 5 (pl. 6), depicts monks milking mountain goats, and in panel 3 the same monks are at table, with the usual rolls, bowls for milk, in this case, and knives. Panel 5 shows a novice monk stealing a kid from the herd of goats, obviously planning to eat it surreptitiously. Fish, of course, was a great favorite and even a requirement on certain days and during Lent. *Cantiga* 386, which is not illustrated, tells of fish provided by the Virgin for a banquet given by Alfonso after the fish he had supplied were

consumed. Number 88 shows a physician-turned-monk who complains of the monastery's coarse food (wild greens without salt) because he had been used to "meat and fish, good wine and fine bread." The miniatures reveal him in panel 2 seated at a table weighted down with fine dishes and being fanned by a young man. In panel 4 we see him in monastic garb, chin in hand, gloomily gazing at the bowls of food on the table before him and at the brethren. The miniatures of 159 reveal in panel 1 butchers cutting up red meat into chops; panel 2 shows pilgrims seated and waiting for the meat to be cooked in a large cauldron. In the miracle, a maid stole a chop and it miraculously struck the sides of a chest in which the girl had hidden it. In panels 4 and 5 we see the stolen meat in the chest when the pilgrims open it. F 25, 2 (322) depicts a greedy man in Evora dining on rich food, including rabbit. He chokes on a bone, which, in answer to his prayer, the Virgin causes him to cough up. In 157, 1 and 2 (pl. 10), the artists depict fritters being fried in a large skillet over a fire on a tripod. Barley bread is seen in 65, and in 88, 5 and 6, electuaries are in evidence. Not always can food on a table be identified by sight; however, by reading the text or captions, or both, identity can usually be discovered.

Wine appears frequently in the miniatures, often in large pitchers placed on the floor near the table. Number 45A, 4 depicts a group of jovial young men at table, drinking wine while being fanned. Servants stand ready with pitchers. An especially well-set table with wine goblets appears in 132, 5 and in F 25, 2 (322). A large pitcher of wine placed on the floor is seen in 42, 4 (pl. 50).

Drunkenness naturally occurred in some miracles. One of the most interesting cases of inebriation can be seen in 47 (pl. 8). Panel 1 reveals the monk seated near a large hogshead in the monastery cellar with a pitcher at his side and a goblet held to his mouth. Panels 2, 3, and 4 show him staggering about as demonic visions assail him, all to be banished by the Virgin. Of course, wine is present at communion, depicted in many *cantigas.* In 73, 2 and 3, we see a white chasuble stained with red wine that a good monk had accidentally spilled on it.

8
Furniture and Furnishings

large proportion of the miniatures in T.I.1 and some in F contain illustrations of furniture in churches and private homes. Guerrero-Lovillo (1949, 286-315) illustrates and describes most of the objects we regard as furniture, both ecclesiastical and lay. Poets, scholars, and clergy often are seen seated in large chairs, with attached arms that are used as writing desks, as in T.I.1 2, 1, where Saint Ildefonso writes his book about the virginity of Saint Mary. Other examples appear in F 33, 1 (202). Armoires, usually seen open and filled with books haphazardly stacked, can be seen in many miniatures, for example in 2, 1; F 22B, 2 (265); and F 33, 1 (202).

Chairs of various kinds are depicted: in 153, a *cantiga* that we must consider humorous, a sick woman refuses to go on pilgrimage to the Virgin's shrine at Rocamadour. She states that she will not go unless her comfortable chair carries her there. In the miniature, panels 2, 3 and 4, we see her seated in her chair flying through the air toward the shrine. Panel 4 shows her standing in the shrine with the chair stuck to her buttocks, and even in panel 5 (pl. 32), when she lies down before the altar, it clings to her. When she sincerely repents, the chair releases her. This chair is large enough to have been quite comfortable. In F 98, 5 (269), appears a child's chair and table, with the child seated at it.

The artists depict many and various kinds of beds, since so many sick people appear in them (as well as people in bed for reasons amatory) and so many corpses lie in the beds in which they die. A beautiful four-poster nuptial bed, topped by a canopy, contains the young ballplayer and his bride depicted in 42, 5 (pl. 50); in 135B, 6 (pl. 36), a young married couple make love in a large bed; in

24, 4, a priest who was a gambler and a thief dies and is not buried in hallowed ground. Saint Mary appears to another priest, while he is in bed, and orders him to disinter the priest and bury him in hallowed ground; in 25B, 2, a Jew hides money under his bed; in 56, 4, a monk who composed psalms for Saint Mary dies in bed, and because of his devotion roses sprout from his mouth (pl. 31); in 75A, 1, appears a fine four-poster bed with a canopy in a dying rich man's house; several other miracles described in chapter 12 offer excellent depictions of beds. In 173, 1, 2, 3, and 4, we see a man suffering from a kidney stone. In *Cantiga* F 95 (209) (pl. 33) the miniaturists depict a lavish royal bed, Alfonso's own, during his ailment in Vitoria. It has four posts, a highly decorated canopy, a counterpane bordered by the royal symbols of the castle and the lion, and a colorful pillow. In contrast, in 166 we see a man on a mattress on the floor; and we see a cot in 75A, 2 (pl. 9).

Medieval Spaniards used many chests, but not chests of drawers, in which they kept relics, money, and other possessions. In 25A, 4, 5, and 6, we see a large chest into which the Christian who had borrowed money from a Jew, with Saint Mary as his guarantor to repay it, cannot return the money to the lender on the appointed day. Therefore, he places the money in a large chest and throws it into the sea. The chest miraculously floats to the Jew's house and is taken by him.

Numerous dining tables are visible. In 42, 4 (pl. 50), we see a wedding banquet with people seated, but the chairs are hidden by the table; in 115B, 3, appears another table; in 119, 1, we see the dinner table of a high judge and the judge eating; and in 88 we see a rich man at table and monks dining at a table in the monastery refectory. In 67, 5 and 6 (pl. 58), we see people dining at a fine table. Saint Ildefonso in 2, 1 rests his feet on a footstool; in 165B, 1 and 2, a sultan sits on a Moorish divan. Thrones are not frequently depicted, since monarchs are usually seen seated in chairs, but a true throne appears in 97, 3, 4, and 5.

Furnishings of various other kinds appear: curtains show in 108, 3 (pl. 19) and 174, 4; candles and lamps are usually seen in churches, as in *Cantigas* 8 (pl. 11). These are listed in chapter 18, "Religion," as are sconces, seen in 135B, 6, and lecterns, as in 94, 1, 3, and 5 (pl. 38).

9
Geographic Place Names

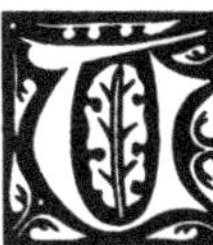he *Cantigas* contain a great many geographical place names from Spain and from abroad. Many are places of such importance as to be familiar to all classes of people; others might have been known to educated people in Alfonso's realm. Some are illustrated with miniatures that identify them clearly, as, for example, 107, 2 (pl. 67), in which the aqueduct of Segovia is seen. The aqueduct is drawn with Moorish arches, which would indicate that the artists knew of its existence but had not seen it. Many illustrations include representations of castles, fortifications, monasteries, and convents, few of which authentically depict these places. Examples of cities appear in the appendix, but a few we list here to convey an idea of the variety included: Alexandria in 65 and 145; Guadalajara in 142 (pl. 4); Pisa in 132; Vitoria in 123. Those who could read the *Cantigas* were probably educated enough to recognize the geographic place names mentioned. And because of travel in relation to pilgrimages, business, warfare, hunting, fishing, and so forth, the general populace would have been familiar with many of the places mentioned. We believe that if the geographical locale is real, it lends credence to the miracles and makes them more easily acceptable as having happened. In the appendix we list more than 150 geographical place names found in T.I.1 and F. Many more can be found in E.

Medieval Galician Portuguese did not use accent marks; therefore we, like Mettmann, leave geographical place names unaccented.

10
Health and Cures and the Human Body

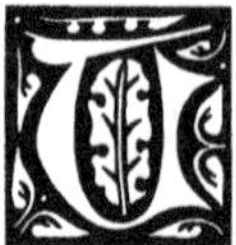he primary concern in human life across millennia has been health, its preservation and cures to keep it intact. Medieval Spain was no exception, and since the medieval world lacked the wonders of modern medicine and surgery, faith in curative measures from divine intervention was highly significant. Of course Scripture's miraculous cures were ever present in the medieval mind. Alfonso was mindful of this, as were his people of all classes, and everyone believed in divine intervention when health was in danger. Those who were exposed to his *Cantigas de Santa Maria,* through reading in public and possibly in dramatic presentations, believed that on several life-threatening occasions due to disease, Alfonso himself survived because of divine intervention. His patroness, the Blessed Virgin, they were certain, had saved his life. They believed that she was the primary source of curative power. We have stated earlier that the thirteenth century was the age of most intense Marian devotion. If we reflect, we know that Saint Mary has been, since at least as early as the fourth century, a protectress of her devotees and even of Jews, pagans, and Muslims who regarded her with respect. In more modern times her worship has flourished, as evidenced notably at Lourdes and Fatima; within weeks of our present writing, we witness multitudes, running into the thousands, going with frequency to sites such as Conyers in Georgia and places in Kentucky where she is said to offer advice. We know that hundreds of thousands still travel to Guadalupe in Mexico and to numerous others of her shrines in Europe. To the shrine of her mother, Saint Anne, additional thousands make pilgrimages to Beaupré in Canada. Still other myriads in the Middle Ages made their pilgrimages to the shrine of Saint James in Compostela in

Galicia, as they do today; and if not today, at least throughout the Middle Ages, other thousands traveled to the shrine of Thomas à Becket in Canterbury. Most pilgrims went for cures, as is attested by the vast number of ex-votos that decorate the walls of the shrines.

Scholars have wondered what disease afflicted Alfonso, since his several illnesses—at Vitoria, Valladolid, Requena, Montpellier, and in various other geographical regions—reveal a royal life constantly in danger from disease. His rebellious son Sancho, who dethroned him, leaving only Seville as his refuge, stated that his father was a leper, so terrible was his disfigurement. Maricel Presilla, the noted Alfonsine scholar, was given access to forensic tests on Alfonso's body; based on those and on reading about what the tests proved, she states that Alfonso suffered from a squamous cell carcinoma of the antrum (1989, 434-35). His eye, pushed out by the disease, indicated the seriousness of his ailment. This condition was terribly painful, so Alfonso prayed for the Virgin's help. Apparently the disease went into remission several times, and Alfonso believed the Virgin's mercy continually cured him until his final illness in Seville, where he died in 1284.

Several of the *cantigas* speak of Alfonso's illnesses. We offer here *Cantiga* F 95 (209) (pl. 33), which may be the most personal of all of Alfonso's miracles. This is truly an exceedingly beautiful page of miniatures. Even though Keller and Kinkade (1984, pl. 32) discuss it in detail, especially as to the artistic techniques employed by the artists, we shall also discuss its content here, so as to present important elements of daily life. Its title is "How King don Alfonso of Castile fell ill in Vitoria and had such a severe pain that he thought he would die of it." Panel 1 reveals the monarch lying supine on his royal bed, a four-poster. We see that his head rests on a striped pillow and that the counterpane bears the symbols of his house, the castle and the lion. A servitor comforts him by fanning him with a fan made of feathers from the tail of a peacock. Physicians, wearing the distinctive caps of their profession, proffer cloths soaked in hot water, but Alfonso turns his head away and with his hands commands that they forbear, since physicians, the king believes, will not relieve his pain. At the far right are seen mourners covering their faces in traditional gestures of grief. In panel 3 Alfonso has called for his codex of the *Cantigas,* and we see a priest handing it to him. The volume is covered in scarlet cloth and is framed in silver. Keller examined at the Escorial T.I.1, which he believes is the copy of the *Cantigas* seen in F 95. He saw the silver, black with age, and the velvet cloth turned dark brown. Alfonso is still supine in his bed. We know of no similar incident, for here we see in a miniature, in one manuscript of the *Cantigas,* a representation of another volume of this work. Panel 4 shows the king still reclining, but with the open volume on his body. His retainers kneel and pray. During all this, the youth with the fan never ceases to fan Alfonso. Panel 5 depicts the king sitting up in bed and kissing the volume. Its caption reads "How the King and all the others who were there highly praised Holy Mary." In panel 6 Alfonso with the open book on his lap prays with steepled hands. His retainers all kneel.

In F 71, which Mettmann does not list with 235, but which portrays the miracle herewith described, we read the title for 235 as offered by Mettmann in E and translated by Kulp-Hill: "How Holy Mary restored health to King don Alfonso when he was ill in Valladolid and given up for dead"; no captions are present. Alfonso is seen supine in bed, eyes closed. The Virgin stands at the head of his bed in panel 1, and in several arches we see mourners and physicians, one of whom holds a vial, probably containing the king's urine. In panel 2 we see many men, who according to the miracle's text are Alfonso's kinsmen, some of whom plot against him. Panel 3 contains three empty arches. Panel 4 shows a conspirator being burned. Can this be the friend (possibly the homosexual lover) of Fadrique, Alfonso's brother? That nobleman was Simon Ruiz de los Cameros (O'Callaghan 1993, 45). Panel 5 (pl. 34) shows the king still supine in bed under a large arch at the left. We see the Virgin standing at his bedside extending the Christ Child toward him. The Baby Jesus touches Alfonso's chest with both hands. At the right retainers cover their faces in token of their grief. Panel 6 depicts Alfonso kneeling and his retainers kneeling and giving thanks to the Virgin. Alfonso's physical body and face show none of the ravages of the illnesses he suffered.

The Virgin also cured him in E 279, which has no illustration and does not state the locale of his cure, and in E 367, which took place in El Puerto de Santa María.

The diseases cured cannot always be identified. Queen Beatriz suffered from a deadly fever in F 7, 4 (256), and her illness is illustrated only in line drawings. This same queen is depicted in color, of course, in 122, 5 (pl. 61). In 79 the frivolous maiden Musa seemingly dies of a fever sent by heaven, so that Saint Mary can take her to live with her. Some diseases are well known and were apparently widespread in medieval Spain as well as in the rest of Europe.

Among those is leprosy, an incurable disease in the Middle Ages, which figures among the miracles in which the Virgin cures the diseased. A strange case regarding the contraction of leprosy appears in 189 (pl. 30). A pilgrim on his way to Salas was attacked by a dragon whose blood, when he killed it with his sword, spurted on him and gave him leprosy; in panel 4 the red marks of leprosy are seen on his face.

The disease that afflicted more people than any other in the *Cantigas* was Saint Martial's fire, or erysipelas, an acute infectious disease of the skin and mucous membrane caused by streptococcus and characterized by local inflammation and fever. It seldom killed, but it caused extreme discomfort and even agony and persisted for long periods. In 37, 1, it caused so much pain in a man's leg that he had the leg amputated, and in 134, 1, the same drastic remedy was applied. The agony of a kidney stone in 173, 4, another affliction of medieval people, could not be cured by the physician, so the patient's promise to make a pilgrimage to Saint Mary's shrine at Salas caused her to make him pass the stone, which he found in his bed. Rabies is cured in F 81A (275); paralysis in 57, 4, and in 77 a woman crippled in all her limbs. Among several cases of blindness, a priest in 92 is cured at Saint Mary's altar; deafness is cured in 69 and 101 and drunkenness in 47 (pl. 8).

Wounds from battle and combat are prominent, especially in 126, 2, in which an arrow in a man's face is removed; a girl's heart is removed in an autopsy performed in 188, 5. In F 25 (322), a man chokes on a harebone; there is a miracle in which a child is delivered through a wound in the mother's side in 184, 5; there are many cases of childbirth, for example in 108 (pl. 19), and 89, 4 shows the practice of childbirth wherein the baby emerges while the mother is seated. A hospital appears in 67 (pl. 58) with male nurses; ambulance carts appear in 91, 2, as well as in other miniatures; a hospital litter is seen in 91, 2; pharmacies in 108, 1 and 2 (pl. 19) and in 173, 1.

The human body interested the miniaturists and no doubt Alfonso himself. Clothed bodies are depicted in realistic proportions. Obesity seems absent. We do not find dwarves, and we see only a few bodies that are freakish or abnormal. In 108 (pl. 19) a Jewish baby is born with his head facing backward because his father denied the Virgin birth of Jesus. In the *Partidas* (Partida 1, law 1 of title 6) monstrous births are mentioned: "Creatures born of women, and who are not formed as human as when they have two heads or limbs of beasts should not be considered children, . . . but where a creature is born with the form of a man, although he may have too many, or too few limbs, this does not prevent him from inheriting the property of his father or mother." Other abnormalities are aired in the *Cantigas:* in F 3 (224) a girl is born with her arm joined to her body down to her groin; many cases of twisted mouths are recorded, for example in 61 and in F 8 (283); feet and hands are paralyzed in 77; blindness was common, as in F 63 (233); many crippled people, both men and women, appear, as in 166 and 179; women are barren, as in 21; madness is represented in F 6 (254) and F 58 (319), and there is a lad who is a simpleton in 41.

The naked human body and the partially naked body are frequently depicted, without, it appears, any embarrassment. In chapter 12, "Love, Lust, and Marriage," nude bodies appear. The miniaturists depict such bodies in good proportion with attractive features. In 115A, 1 (pl. 37), can be seen a nude man whose entire body is visible except his genitals as he forces his sexual desires upon his naked wife, whose breasts are perfectly visible and well depicted, though her nether parts are under covers. In 135B, 6 (pl. 36), we see the young husband fondling his bride's breast. Both are nude to the waist. In 114, 4, a mother comforts her son, who sits naked in bed with cov-ers concealing him from the waist down. Marisaltos, the converted Jewess in 107, 6 (pl. 67), is seen nude as she sits in a baptismal font. In 105A, 4, we see a young man and woman, both nude in bed but covered from the waist down, and in panel 5 (pl. 42), we see the woman clothed, but with clothing pulled aside, as her husband mutilates her genitals; in 46, 6, a man kneels completely naked with his genitals exposed.

The partially nude appear more frequently: in 102, 3, a youth is stripped to his shift; in 22, 4 (pl. 24), we see a young farmer wearing his shift and *bragas*; 42, 5 (pl. 50) shows the ballplayer and his bride naked in bed but covered from the waist down. The bride's breasts are large and prominently displayed. In 102, 3, a youth is stripped to his shift; in 96, 6, we see a partially clothed man, wearing only *bragas;* in 93, 1, half-naked young men throw dice. In 7, 4, the pregnant abbess's illegitimate baby is removed from her swollen abdomen, and in panel 6, stripped to the waist, she is examined by the bishop and her abdomen found to be flat (pl. 40).

All of the people described above are slender and well formed, some of the men quite muscular. Muslims and Jews, both male and female, follow the same pattern. Even the diseased, those with twisted mouths and other physical deformities, such as gouged out eyes, are people with normal physiques.

There are many depictions of Jesus during his flagellation and crucifixion. In 59 (pl. 39) his life-size image on the cross strikes the would-be runaway nun. Jesus is depicted with a well-proportioned physique. Our listing of the items mentioned in this chapter and others associated with health can be found in the appendix under "Health."

11
Legal Matters

lfonso X caused various legal documents to be written. His *Fuero Real,* his *Espéculo de las leyes,* and the *Espéculo's* expansion, resulting in the *Siete Partidas,* treat an incredible number of laws. In the miniatures of the *Cantigas,* various facets of law appear. Representative of these are the following: in 62, 1, we see the drawing up of a contract. A woman in need of money pawns her son and cannot redeem him. We see the contract and the people lending her the money. When she cannot redeem him and appeals to the Virgin, the Virgin takes him right out of his irons and he is redeemed. In 64, 2 (pl. 1), a man receives a legal order from the king to join the army; in 75A, 1, a will is made; in 164, 2, a monk is accused of counterfeiting, and when he is arrested, he cries out to Saint Mary and she saves him, punishing his accuser; in F 47, 2 (291), a rapist is arrested, but Saint Mary saves him when he writes a long poem in her praise. Judges and magistrates carry out sentencing: in 175A, 5, a magistrate sentences an innocent boy who was framed (pl. 45, 4), and in 175B, 6, he sentences the guilty party and has him burned; in 119, 3, a high judge is himself a victim, in this case of devils, but Saint Mary saves him and later takes him to heaven. The judge wears clothes befitting his rank. In 48, 6, a gentleman gives some monks a deed to an estate, since he had refused them water from a spring and Saint Mary had moved the spring to the monastery. See the appendix under "Legal Matters" for other legal matters; see also the category "Punishments."

12
Love, Lust, and Marriage

We know that people from the beginning of literature until the present have been more interested in the sexual element of human life than in most other aspects. Out of sex, love developed on the higher plane and resulted in marriage; on the lower it became lust and led to casual affairs condemned by church and state, but all the same viewed with interest and even fascination. Lust enabled Gilgamesh to capture the virginal wild man as soon as he sampled the charms of the temple prostitute. We all are familiar with the lust of Samson for Delilah and David for Bathsheba, and those who study early writings of Egypt will recall the sexual elements in the *Story of the Two Brothers.* No period of human culture and literature has failed to use love, marriage, and lust as the bases for some of the greatest pieces of literary art. Sex attracts and holds attention, and it always has. It is among the primary motifs in the literature of our own times.

Alfonso el Sabio, his poets, and his miniaturists were interested in stories that caught and held attention, and therefore they included sexuality. Let us remember that the learned king fathered eleven legitimate and four attested illegitimate offspring. Quite probably there were others of the latter category from his youth spent in Galicia and in the army. When he was a young man, he wrote many profane *cantigas,* known as *cantigas de escarnio* and *cantigas de mal dizer.* Among those, many treated in satire the sexual deeds of various individuals, notably the camp follower La Balteyra. It is not strange, therefore, that he and his collaborators, in producing the *Cantigas de Santa Maria,* inserted a considerable number of stories based upon love, marriage, and lust. Such stories could catch and maintain attention, just as they have across millennia

and into our own times, in which they may have outstripped almost all other motivations for fiction. A high percentage of the miracles in the *Cantigas* capture audience attention because they tell tales of violence, cruelty, dangerous accidents, shipwrecks, falls from high places, drownings, kidnapping, battles, dreadful imprisonments, mutilations, murders, incest, infanticide, and execution by hanging, burning, stoning, and being dragged behind horses, to name but some of such attention-grabbing facets of daily life. See chapter 25, "Violent Acts."

We remind the reader that Maricel Presilla, in her very contributive, yet still unpublished, doctoral dissertation, suggests convincingly that Alfonso produced *cantigas* to convince his subjects that they should cleave closer to him and to the teachings of the *Cantigas,* rather than to the unrelenting severity of the Church. The Virgin could forgive the most atrocious sins and the most heinous crimes when repentance was clear, whereas the Church could not. The *Cantigas,* Alfonso's ex-voto, is a collection of miracles that taught forgiveness and even entry into paradise without purgatory, through Saint Mary's intervention in human life.

Since people were mightily interested in the sexual facets of other people's lives, the number of interest-catching and even titillating tales in the *Cantigas* is great. Moreover, whereas many sexually oriented miracles are told without the sexual act visualized, some may wonder why so many others are so specifically visualized. And when we consider that many, which are supported by miniatures, do not offer explicit scenes of lovers in bed and making love, we may question why so many other miracles are so illustrated in an ex-voto in honor of the Blessed Virgin. We believe that this matter needs deeper investigation, as does the entire narrative technique of the catching and holding of audience attention.

If Saint Mary, for the most part highly conservative as regards sexual matters, advocated sex primarily for procreation, as did the Church, how could Alfonso have thought that she would accept an ex-voto so colorfully filled with scenes of sexual activity? This also, which is an element of her character, should be studied more extensively. The Virgin is depicted as very human in her moods and actions. She demonstrates jealousy, wrath, revenge, and intolerance, along with all the more Christian virtues, which, as a woman and a mother, she should be expected to show.

In the *Códice Rico* she seems deeply concerned with sexual improprieties, and she undertakes to correct them, while, in an occasional miracle, she condones sexual pleasure in marriage. In most *cantigas,* men are the protagonists and aggressors. Such men appear in numbers 7, 11, 15, 16, 26, 55, 64, 68, 93, 104, 111, 115, 125, 132, 135, 137, 151, 152, F 45B (312), F 47 (291), F 90 (237), and F 92 (317). In these twenty-two miracles or *cantigas,* women play the secondary role, because male lovers or would-be lovers lead them astray. Some feminine protagonists are nuns, who either escape their convents to run off with their lovers or who are thwarted in the attempt—in 55, 58, 59, and 94.

As to MS F, a lustful man predominates in F 45B (312) and in F 47 (291), in F 92 (317) we read of a rapist, and in F 101 (336), which is not illustrated, we read about a lustful knight. As for lustful females, in F 28 (285) there is a runaway nun and in F 90 (237) a sexually wayward woman, a prostitute.

The illustrated as well as the unillustrated *cantigas* that concern sex add much to our perceptions of daily life. They reveal prevalent sexual immorality, the taste of the medieval audience, and much about bedrooms, blankets, beds, and so forth. We are tempted to accuse Alfonso and his miniaturists of an overly lively interest in sexual pleasure and resultant sin, since in the miracles' plots, and especially in their illustrations, so much sexual activity unfolds. We believe, therefore, that the king, his artists, and his audiences were titillated by matters sexual. Take for example 135A (pl. 35). Here various facets of daily life are seen. In panel 1 two adolescents make a secret vow to wed, and they consider this vow the equivalent of marriage; parental refusal appears in panel 2; in panel 3 an older suitor is rejected; panel 4 shows the maiden forced to marry a rich man; in panel 5 the rich husband, on learning of her love for her childhood sweetheart, does not force her; in panel 6 the rejected suitor captures her and her rich husband.

In 135B, 1 (pl. 36), the would-be ravisher is sent into a deep sleep when the maiden prays to Saint Mary; panel 2 shows her captor freeing her rich husband and releasing her; in panel 3 they all travel to Montpellier in search of her sweetheart; in panel 4 he is found and reunited with her; panel 5 depicts their formal marriage in church; all of the above is mild as compared with panel 6. The miniature shows the young groom actually fondling, in a carnal fashion, the breast of his bride. They lie in bed nude but covered from the waist down. The pertinent words of the captions read "and they did as a groom does with a bride in *solaz,*" a word that in this instance means "sexual pleasure."

Several attitudes, customs, and patterns of thought, all integral parts of daily life, reveal much about love, marriage, and lust among the middle class. F 45 (312), "How the gentleman could not do his will with his mistress in the house in which they had made an image of Saint Mary," possibly borders at least on the theme of the Virgin's acceptance of marital passion. A young noble falls madly in love with a beautiful maiden, and she with him, because he is handsome and well formed (panel 1); a go-between wins the girl's consent to go to his home and she goes (panel 2); the lover cannot function sexually and realizes this is because his large and comfortable bedroom is the very room in which he caused a sculptor to make a statue of the Virgin (panel 3). When they try to use a small and narrow room, their activity is unsatisfactory (panel 4). They try the large room again, with no luck, but when they decide to marry they are able to have intercourse (panel 5). They marry in panel 6, and the text suggests that their life was happy, since "afterwards he led a very good life and rid himself of evil conduct and bad judgment and all waywardness." Panel 3 leads the viewer now, and probably the viewer then, to smile at the sight of the frustrated lover, sitting in bed with his beloved, his chin resting on his hand as he very obviously cannot succeed in making love.

Cantiga 15, "This is how Saint Mary helped the Empress of Rome to endure the great trauma she suffered," reveals that the empress is threatened by lustful men on several occasions: the first lustful man is her husband's brother, who, when he tries to seduce her, is imprisoned by her (15A, 2); after the emperor returns from the crusades, she frees his brother, who quickly accuses her of trying to seduce him (15A, 3); the men ordered to execute her in a forest try to rape her, but a virtuous count saves her (15A, 4); she is put in charge of the countess's son (15A, 5); the count's brother attempts seduction, and when she refuses him, he kills the child and accuses her (15A, 6); the count sends sailors to take her to sea and drown her; when the Virgin keeps them from raping and drowning her, they maroon her on a rock to die (15B, 1); the Virgin saves her and gives her an herb that cures leprosy (15B, 2); her consequent trials do not concern lust.

This romance or Byzantine novel and Alfonso's *cantiga,* which borrowed from it, closely make use of the stock characters of lustful men from the highest level of society to commoners—here woodsmen and sailors.

In *Cantiga* 42 (pl. 50) (treated in chap. 17, "Recreation and Entertainment"), a young man forsakes Saint Mary, to whom he has promised fealty, in order to marry his sweetheart. We see bride and groom nude in bed but covered from the waist down (panel 5).

Cantiga 151, "How a priest who honored Saint Mary's churches and kept the Sabbath, but was lustful," is a tale of clerical fornication. In panel 3 the priest, whose tonsure identifies his calling, is seen in bed with his *barragana* (mistress). His lust cools when he sees through a window a statue of the Virgin.

Cantiga 115, "How Saint Mary took the child whose mother had given him to the devil out of anger toward her husband because she had conceived the child on Easter Eve," tells of a husband's lust. He and his wife had vowed chastity, but the devil drove him with lust so strong that he forced his wife and impregnated her. Panel 1 is divided into two incidents under separate arches. Under the first arch the husband, quite nude, is being urged by the devil to move into the second arch and into his wife's bed; under the arch we see him stark naked, sitting on the edge of her bed as she pushes him away. His hand is close to her breast (pl. 37).

The titles of the *cantigas* whose miniatures reveal no sexual activity in progress will make clear the element of lust as it afflicts male characters: 16 is titled "How Saint Mary converted a knight in love who was in despair because he couldn't have the lady he loved"; 125, "How Saint Mary separated the priest and the maiden who had married and made them both enter a religious order because the priest had arranged the matter through the devil" (pl. 55), reveals how the priest's lust for the maiden leads him to invoke devils to tempt her; F 54 (206), "How Pope Leo cut off his hand because he was tempted by love for a woman who had kissed it, and then Saint Mary healed him," stresses that the highest figure in the Christian faith sometimes burns with lust.

Lust, one of the seven deadly sins, was prevalent in both the civil and the religious sectors of society, to judge from the number of incidents in the *Cantigas.* Filgueira Valverde (1985, 233), as concerns *Cantiga* 137, "How Holy Mary made a knight who was formerly very lustful observe chastity," suggests that the "lustful gentleman" may

have been Alfonso himself, given what history tells us about Alfonso's carnal sinning. In panel 4 we can see a gentleman or a knight called "un cavaleiro" embracing two elegantly dressed *barraganas.* Possibly this miniature may have illustrated that the Virgin would gain grace for him at the Divine Tribunal as well as certain reception in heaven regardless of his sexual peccadillos. O'Callaghan in a genealogical chart in the front matter of *The Learned King* (1993) lists the four ascertained illegitimate offspring of Alfonso, as well as his legitimate heirs.

Fewer women than men were victims of lust in the *Cantigas de Santa Maria.* We are aware that more women were lustful in the *cantigas de escarnio* and *de maldezir.* Most notable in the *Códice Rico* are the four cases of illicit passion mentioned above, which recount the miracles concerned with love-struck nuns—55, 58, 59, 94, and F 28 (285). The miniatures in this series of lustful women depict no complete nudity but clearly reveal that the nuns are leaving the convents to be with their lovers. Panel 6 in 94, "How Saint Mary served in place of the nun who went from the convent" (pl. 38), shows the nun, her lover, and their three illegitimate offspring; in *Cantiga* 58, "How Saint Mary prevented the nun from going away with a gentleman with whom she had agreed to go," the first panel shows the nun making plans with her would-be lover. Panels 2, 3, 4, and 5 depict the Virgin's efforts to keep the nun chaste by showing her the horrors of hell. In panel 6 we see the gentleman as she rejects him, even though he had brought three companions and a horse with him. In *Cantiga* 59, "How the crucifix in honor of His Mother struck the nun in Fontebras who had agreed to leave with her lover" (pl. 39), we see her meeting him at the convent door (panel 1), asking the Virgin's pardon before she leaves (panel 2), being struck by the life-size crucifix (panel 3), lying unconscious at the foot of the crucifix (panel 4), explaining the miracle (the nail from the hand of the crucifix had wounded her cheek) (panel 5), and her repentance (panel 6). Unillustrated E 285, "How Saint Mary forced the nun, who would not for her sake, forgo running off with the gentleman, return to her order and she made the gentleman take up a religious life also," reveals much about daily life. The nun was noble, as was her lover. They married, had children, and lived in wealth and happiness, until the Virgin came to her in a dream, after which she and her husband-lover took religious orders.

In *Cantiga* 55, "How Holy Mary served in place of the nun who left the convent and reared the child the nun had while leading her sinful life," a nun leaves the convent with a tonsured priest. After living with him for some time in Lisbon, she becomes pregnant and he sends her away. She returns to the convent but has not been missed, as the Virgin has substituted for her. her sin is not discovered by the sisterhood, and as the time approaches for her to deliver the child, she begs the Virgin to help her not fall into disgrace. Holy Mary has the child delivered by an angel and whisked away to be reared by a hermit. When the son is older, he comes to the convent to sing, and mother and son recognize each other. The nun's confession to the sisterhood is proof of the Virgin's miracle.

Cantiga 7, "How Saint Mary freed the pregnant abbess, who had slept before her altar weeping" (pl. 40), indicates that even an abbess could harbor lust and sin with a man from Bologna. We see that nuns report such a sin by their abbess (panel 1); that the bishop rides to the convent to investigate (panel 2); that the abbess faces the bishop as her accusers watch (panel 3); that while the abbess prays and then sleeps before Saint Mary's altar, angels deliver her child (panel 4); that the angels take the baby to a monastery (panel 5); that the bishop in panel 6 makes the abbess strip to the waist (panel 40). We see her standing partially nude before the bishop, his retinue, and the nuns. Of course all signs of pregnancy and childbirth are absent. Her breasts are revealed and the flatness of her abdomen.

A mother's incest with her son in *Cantiga* 17, "How St. Mary saved from death the honorable Roman lady whom the devil accused to have her burned" (pl. 41), shows in panel 1 the mother and her son lying upon her in bed naked but covered by bed sheets from the waist down. The rest of the miracle is so horrendous that we interpret what its miniatures reveal: Panel 2, divided by three arches, depicts the lady squatting beside her bed giving birth to a child. In the right-hand arch we see a medieval privy, into which the lady is in the act of dropping her newborn infant. In panel 3 the devil in disguise accuses her to the emperor. She is ordered burned; she prays to the Virgin for aid (panel 4); the Virgin then leads the lady to the emperor (panel 5); the Virgin drives the devil away (panel 6).

In 68 a husband has sex with a harlot; in 93 a lustful burgher's son appears; in 104 a squire has a concubine; in 105A, 5 (pl. 42), a lustful bridegroom mutilates his wife because she denies him sex; in 111 a lustful priest "teaches" women about sex, and in 152 a knight is described as lustful. Two cases of rape or attempted rape are recorded in F 47 (291), and in F 90 (237) there is a rapist.

13
Personages

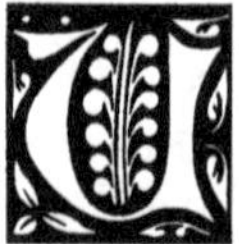nexpected and surprising numbers of individuals or personages are mentioned in T.I.1. and F. Many well-known people play roles (see the categories "Royalty" and "Nobility," under "Classes and Masses," in the appendix), among these Alfonso and his family, retinue, and friends. In the "Church Hierarchy" category appear members from the pope to the monks in monasteries.

Herewith we treat a few examples in order to provide the reader with an impression of the wide variety of people who appear. Many are personages well known to history, leading us to believe that the educated populace, and even the common people, knew more history than we had expected. Of course, such personages appeared in other literary works, in sermons, in folktales and legends, in books used by teachers in schools, and in the graphic arts—sculpture, frescoes, wood carvings, tapestries, and statues—all of which might have been explained or identified by preachers, teachers, and minstrels.

Among historical personages, we find depicted in *Cantiga* 5A, 1, the emperor Julian the Apostate, and we see his wicked deeds and persecution (pl. 43), as well as the violence of his death in panel 5. In 131 appears Alexios, emperor of Constantinople. Moving away from nobility, we encounter biblical characters, for example, Jesus in 30 and Mary Magdalene in 1, 5. Of the middle and lower classes, we see, for example, Tomé, a merchant, in F 89 (213); Elbo, a thief, in 13; Musa, a damsel given to frivolity, in 79; and in 41, Garín, a money changer.

Since nearly a hundred personages are named, we refer the reader to the listing in the appendix under the category "Personages" and to the listing by Agapito Rey (1927).

14
Pilgrimage

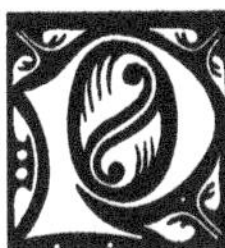

ilgrimage in medieval Spain, from very early times, was popular and continuous, certainly by the ninth century, when the sepulchre of Saint James was active in attracting pilgrims (Castro 1954, 130ff.). The saint's shrine in Compostela drew countless pilgrims from much of medieval Europe and even some from scattered groups in North Africa and the Middle East. Chaucer even sent the worldly Wife of Bath to Jacobsland, as Spain was known in England, and many royal and important people made the pilgrimage from Paris along the Camino de Santiago, as do many to this day. As the patron saint of Spain, James, known as Matamoros (Moor Slayer), did much in the popular mind to drive back the Muslims. Speaking of relatively modern pilgrims, we should never forget Georgiana G. King (1920, 14), who called attention to the syncretism of Saint James, in which she saw aspects of other Ibero-Roman divinities, namely the belief in Castor and Pollux. People in medieval Europe, and especially in Spain, believed that Saint James, or Santiago, was Jesus' own blood brother. This James was the "greater," another was the "less," and in the popular mind the two blended (Castro 1954, 138).

Alfonso respected pilgrims and took great pains to protect their persons and their rights in his *Fuero Real,* and especially in his *Espéculo de las leyes* (Martínez Díez 1985) and in the *Siete Partidas,* which was a greatly expanded version of the *Espéculo.* We are fortunate to have the knowledge of Joseph O'Callaghan, the distinguished historian of medieval Spain, to provide the historical and legal background in his book *The Learned King* (1993), which contributes to our study of the *Cantigas de Santa Maria.*

O'Callaghan, in a discussion with Keller, stated that it was not the shrine of Saint James in Compostela, nor any belittlement of the saint himself, that led Alfonso to include six miracles in which pilgrims to Compostela were not cured or otherwise aided by Saint James and who went to the Virgin's shrine in Villa-Sirga and were accommodated. Rather, it was the feud between the king and Bishop Gonzalo Games of Compostela, which led to the king's exiling the rebellious cleric. Alfonso, then, respected the miraculous powers of Santiago but nevertheless produced the seemingly anti-Santiago *cantigas.* We accept O'Callaghan's statement, but we qualify it with our own idea that the common people of Spain and from abroad would have had no knowledge of such political maneuvers. The six "anti-Compostela" miracles are numbers 26, 175, 218, 253, 268, and 278. Evelyn Proctor (1951, 28ff.), a distinguished scholar in medieval Spanish history from Oxford, first pointed out the rivalry between the shrine of Saint James and the shrine of the Virgin in Villa-Sirga, today called Villalcázar de Sirga. Keller (1959b, 1979a) elucidated 26, 175, 218, 253, and 278, the last three of which are not illustrated, and O'Callaghan added 268.

One other miracle in which Saint James plays a secondary role to Saint Mary is number 26 (pl. 56). Saint James's pilgrim, tempted by the devil disguised as James, castrates himself and cuts his own throat. Saint James struggles for his soul with devils and eventually appeals to the Virgin, who settles the case in favor of James's devotee. O'Callaghan (1993, 163-92) also believes that Alfonso's desire to expand his realm into Morocco caused him to develop Puerto de Santa María and Cádiz as ports from which his ships could attack North African Muslims. Puerto de Santa María, on the bay of Cádiz, became the site of twenty-four miracles, whose numbers place them beyond the codices that contain illustrations. Of the twenty-four, eleven deal with pilgrimages to Puerto, while the other thirteen miracles were wrought by the Virgin in Puerto or in nearby cities, in which people petitioned Santa María del Puerto for assistance.

More miracles occur at Salas in Aragon than at any other site, and all but one, since they are in T.I.1, are illustrated. Some of these were performed for pilgrims. Proctor (1951, 29) lists seventeen, to which we add numbers 176, 177, 178, 179, 189, and F 14 (408). Some of the most interesting miracles, especially those that contain pilgrimages, occur at Salas. Number 44 (pl. 44) relates that a gentleman who loses his goshawk goes on pilgrimage to Santa María de Salas. Suddenly the bird alights on his arm. We have discussed elsewhere number 189 (pl. 30), in which a pilgrim on the way to Salas slays a dragon whose blood makes him a leper.

There are seventeen miracles involving Villa-Sirga (Procter 1951, 29), and of these the five mentioned above were wrought for pilgrims on the way to or from Compostela. Other shrines are also the sites of miracles in which pilgrims are the protagonists. Soissons has nine miracles, of which three deal with pilgrims. *Cantiga* 49 relates that pilgrims en route to Soissons lose their way at night until Saint Mary leads them to her shrine. Miracles pertaining to Terena, in Portugal, are found in F, but few are illustrated. In one of these, F 89 (213), a merchant is wrongly accused of killing his unfaithful wife. His pilgrimage to Saint Mary's shrine in Terena exonerates him. Several miracles occur in Rocamadour. Representative of these is 22 (pl. 24), in which a knight tries to kill the servant of a man he hates, but the victim calls so devotedly to Saint

Mary that no weapon can wound him. He is then sent on pilgrimage to Rocamadour, in panel 5.

A few miracles occur in other places. A woman goes on pilgrimage to Valverde (*Cantiga* 98). The doors of the shrine close, and she cannot enter until she confesses and sincerely grieves over her sins. In 146 a woman's son, en route to Albeza, has his eyes gouged out by his enemies, who also cut off his hands, but they are restored when his mother appeals to Saint Mary. In 127 a youth kicks his mother. She asks for justice from the Virgin, who tells the son to beg his mother for pardon and that they should go together to Puy on a pilgrimage. On arriving at the church, the mother enters, but the son cannot. He is advised by the clergy there to cut off the offending foot, and he does so in order to enter the church. His mother, seeing her son so afflicted, begs the Virgin to restore his limb. The mother falls asleep at the foot of the altar, and the Virgin tells her in a dream to put the foot in its place and the Virgin will cure her son, which she does. In 175A, 4 (pl. 45), a father and son are on their way to Santiago, and a heretic places a silver cup in the son's sack, accusing the son of stealing the cup. In panel 4 the magistrates arrest the son. The father continues on his way to Santiago, and on returning to Toulouse he finds his son alive and well on the gallows. The magistrates then punish the guilty man, and the father and son return home together. Well over eighty poems (Procter 1951, 29) relate to the Virgin's shrines in the Peninsula. In 9 (pl. 5) a cleric goes on a pilgrimage to Jerusalem. The importance of pilgrimage, then, is certainly confirmed since almost one-third of the *cantigas* make pilgrimage the background for as many miracles.

15
Places, Sites, and Locales

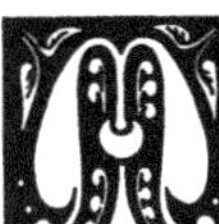iracles occur in a large number of places, all of which contribute in one way or another to depicting daily life. In 4, 4 (pl. 13), we see a glass furnace, a picture that clearly indicates how such a furnace appeared with its door opened and closed; 186, 2 (pl. 46), reveals an *hórreo,* a storage bin or granary mounted on four smooth columns to protect the contents from rodents. The Alfonsine representation closely resembles *hórreos* seen today in Asturias and Galicia.

An open-air shop is seen in 9, 3 (pl. 5), with a customer on horseback buying an icon; we see a kitchen in 157, 1 and 2 (pl. 10); countless church altars appear, for example in 11, 1; 16, 3; and 21, 4; stables serve as the background for many miracles, as seen in 31, 4 and 48, 5. There is an excellent illustration of a privy in 17, 2 (pl. 41) and another in 34, 2 (pl. 18); and even heaven (in 85B, 1) and hell (in 85A, 6) are depicted. This section of the index in the appendix is copious and runs to one hundred sites.

16
Punishments

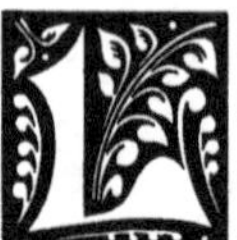

iterature, Scripture, and the visual arts represent many punishments, since punishments offer interesting narrative segments. Some of art's most vital and famous works dwell upon Jesus on the Cross, the martyrdom of saints, and punishments for crimes and sins in the secular world; there are also many incidents of punishments inflicted upon private citizens by their enemies or lovers. Mankind has always been fascinated by punishments. Legal punishments in medieval Spain were often overly severe, cruel, horrible, and even macabre, and they are depicted in the miniatures of the *Cantigas*. The miniatures sometimes portray punishments in foreign lands and in bygone days, for example, crucifixion. Aside from truly legal punishments, many illegal punishments are performed in the miniatures by the victims' enemies, lovers, and masters and by pirates, Moorish invaders, and Jews. We list some of these in the appendix under "Violent Acts." In F 22 (265) (pl. 64) John Damascene's hand is cut off because the emperor thinks he has written treasonous letters. Treason was more often punished by death. In the *Cantigas* a Jew might be seized by Christians and beaten because he was a Jew, as in 85. In 95 a Christian is seized by Moors and imprisoned and whipped because of his faith.

Legal punishments are amply represented in the *Cantigas*. Many people were punished according to the law's demands: in 13, 3, authorities hang a thief, but because of his devotion to Saint Mary, she sustains him on the tree gallows; in 107, 3 (pl. 67), a Jewish woman, who has sinned according to Jewish law, is cast down from a high cliff by her coreligionists, but she is saved when she calls to Saint Mary for aid; in F 47, 3 (291), a rapist is imprisoned but is saved by Saint Mary. A man is stoned, pierced with a lance, and has his throat cut for supposed treason in 124 (pl. 21). Other examples may be found in the appendix. Illegal punishments are less frequently represented: in 6, 6 and F 18, 6 (294), mobs burn people as punishment. For other instances, see the appendix.

Divine punishment occurs in a variety of instances. It is imposed upon wicked people and heretics, usually by the Virgin. Many punishments are more terrible than those the law allowed: in F 48, 5 (318) and F 85, 4 (316), people who have desecrated Saint Mary's images are blinded; lightning strikes merchants' wool because they have not fulfilled a vow made to her in 35B; Saint Martial's fire is a punishment in 105B, 1; in 157, 2 (pl. 10), a knife pierces a woman's jaw when she eats fritters made from stolen flour; penance is exacted for false witness in 164, 5. Many more examples are listed in the appendix.

17
Recreation and Entertainment

Not for nothing was Alfonso X known as El Sabio (the Learned). So conscious was he of the everyday needs of his subjects that in law 21 of his famous *Siete Partidas* (seven divisions of law) we read: "There are other joys besides those we spoke of in the laws prior to this one, which were found to give man comfort, when he had cares and woes, and these are hearing songs and the music of instruments, playing chess or backgammon or other games similar to these. We say the same regarding stories and romances and other books that speak of those things from which mankind receives joy and pleasure" (Scott 1931, 80).

We believe that by *hestorias* Alfonso meant "stories," not "histories," and in fact many *cantigas* are indeed short stories or, as some would prefer to say, "brief narratives." In many cases the *hestorias* of the *Cantigas* are well-known short stories found in collections of *exempla,* sometimes with the Virgin as a central character, sometimes with a central character in the form of a mortal or even a pagan goddess.

In F 37, 1 (293) (pl. 47), we see an entertainer who is a minstrel or *juglar,* whose specialty is mimicry. We read that he is so successful that his audiences give him all sorts of presents, an observation that reveals again a facet of daily life. He receives, according to the text of the miracle, clothing, saddles, reins, and other generous gifts. One day, he gazes at an image of Saint Mary holding the Christ Child on her lap, and in order to amuse people, he attempts to mimic her posture. This displeases Jesus, who causes his mouth and his arm to be twisted. Later, when he repents, the Virgin cures him.

Interesting also is *Cantiga* F 59, 1 (363), "How Saint Mary freed from prison a gentleman who wrote a song for her." This gentleman has been imprisoned by Count Symon for an insulting song he wrote about him. The songwriter—a *trobador*—apparently sang insulting songs, not only about the count, but about other people as well. Here, we are certain, is a singer of *cantigas de escarnio* or *de maldizer,* both satirical and scurrilous. It appears that important and powerful people, such as a count, could arrest and condemn such songsters to death. Of course, when the man writes a song for the Virgin, she frees him from prison.

F 85, 1 (316), "How Saint Mary took vengeance upon a cleric who ordered a hermitage burned and made him build a new one," depicts a troubadour cleric *(crerigo trobador),* whose poems concerned mockery rather than love *(d'escarnio mais ca d'amor).* The *cantiga* even names this man, a certain Martin Altivez, who was the prior of the church. Usually in such songs of mockery, the person pilloried was named, lest anyone fail to know who he or she was. Alfonso had cause to know much about such songs of mockery, since he wrote a great many himself; the most famous (or infamous) were about the camp follower La Balteyra (Braga 1878, 64). If he ever needed forgiveness for his having composed scurrilous songs, we do not find evidence of it in the *Cantigas de Santa Maria.* In panel 1 we see the *crerigo trobador* reading or singing a song from a large page of paper.

When the *Partidas* mentions *romances,* the meaning is "romance novella" or even "novel." The best example is *Cantiga* 15, "How Saint Mary helped the Empress of Rome to endure the very great troubles which she experienced." In the Byzantine romance upon which *Cantiga* 15 is based, the Virgin is absent.

Illustrating the recommendation in the *Partidas* for

listening to musical instruments is *Cantiga* 120, 1 (pl. 2), a *cantiga de loor* (song of praise). We see musicians seated with their instruments entertaining Alfonso or the Virgin. A fiddler stands and plays, and behind him and the seated musicians, we see the arms of dancers. *Cantiga* 62, 5, "How Holy Mary restored the son to a good lady who put him up as security and the interest increased so much that she could not retrieve him," reveals a similar dance; clarions are raised as they are played. Other examples of musical instruments are in 100, 6, where we see a rebec (a kind of mandolin) and two other instruments, which are plucked or strummed. In F 6, 2 (254), we see two runaway monks dancing in their shifts.

Games involving dice can be seen in *Cantiga* 6, 2, "How Holy Mary revived the little boy whom the Jew killed because he sang 'Gaude Virgo Maria,'" with both women and men throwing dice. It is a feast day, and Jews and Christians are playing. In *Cantiga* 38, 3, "How Saint Mary extended her arm to grasp that of her Son who was about to fall due to the stone which the rogue had thrown" (pl. 48), we see the gambling den, and in panel 2 gamblers are drinking and dicing. A woman draws wine from a large wineskin. At least one player is only half-dressed, while another wears only a chemise. Hideous devils violently punish the wicked people.

Cantiga 136, 2, "How in the land of Apulia, in a city called Foggia, a woman was playing at dice with some companions in front of a church" (pl. 70), shows more gamblers at dice, with a woman taking part in the game. *Cantiga* F 6 (254) shows monks dancing. In *Cantiga* 140, 6, we see gamblers and a scene of general debauchery, with a man kissing a well-dressed woman. *Cantiga* 76, 1, "How Holy Mary restored a good woman's dead son to her on condition that the woman return hers, whom she had taken from the arms of her statue," depicts a scuffle between two men in a tavern, where people are gambling at dice.

Entertainments not included in law 21 of the *Partidas* appear in some miniatures. One was bull-baiting, a precursor of present-day *corridas.* Panels 3 and 4 of *Cantiga* 144, "How Saint Mary saved a good man in Plasencia from death by a bull which came at him to kill him" (pl. 49), depict such a bull-baiting in progress in Plasencia. We see a plaza used as a bullring for entertainment at a wedding celebration. The audience, observing from the rooftop of a house, arouses the bull by throwing feathered darts with sharp points at him, while others hurl spearlike instruments attached to ropes so as to be pulled back and thrown again. In panel 3 we see a young man also on the roof, waving a cape to try to attract the bull. The crowd, successful in arousing the bull, causes him to threaten a devotee of the Virgin.

A ball game takes place in 42, 2, "How the postulant placed the ring on the finger of the statue of Holy Mary and the statue curved its finger around it" (pl. 50), which is a scene of dual action, with young men playing ball in a meadow. The batter has hit one ball with the bat, and his companions try to catch this fly. The pitcher is prepared to throw him a second ball. The game and the equipment resemble those used in baseball or softball. The bat tapers, the ball seems to be covered with cloth, and the pitcher throws underhanded. For more freedom of movement, one of the men in the outfield has tucked up his tunic. See Keller and Kinkade 1984, pl. 2, and their lengthy discussion of the miniatures (12-18).

Hunting and fishing, obviously recreations, are represented in detail. *Cantiga* 142 (pl. 4) shows Alfonso himself, accompanied by his followers (a hunting party), hawking for herons. For a description of this page of miniatures, see Keller and Kinkade 1984, pl. 30, pp. 27-28. *Cantiga* 67, 4 (pl. 58) depicts a gentleman seining for fish and the same man mounted on his horse, spearing a bear. In 44, 1 and 2 (pl. 44), a falconer launches his hawk at quail. In 95A, 4, we see a fisherman using a fishing pole.

We agree with Ana Domínguez Rodríguez that some miniatures portray Alfonso involved in rituals, protodramas, or proto-operas in some of the *cantigas de loor* (Keller 1990). The songs of praise, of course, present lessons of a pietistic nature. Alfonso, ever conscious of the value of entertainment as a means of capturing and holding the attention of his audience, utilized this pedagogical technique. We believe that, if staged, such lessons inserted in dramatic pieces were used by him. This suggests the presence of drama as a facet of daily life, which needs more attention than it has received. We believe that some of the miracles, and not only the songs of praise, may have been dramatized, as they were in France. *Cantiga* 90, 3 (pl. 51) and 4 in effect seem to visualize stage settings and staging devices. A people's, a century's, and a culture's recreations and entertainments are crucial to a complete understanding of how life was led. Consider our own.

18
Religion

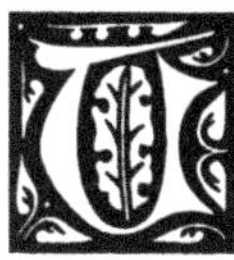

his somewhat all-inclusive section contains so many details that here we can relate only representative aspects of it, leaving the rest to the appendix. Obviously, since most of the *cantigas* concern religion, clerics, pilgrimages, and so forth, we have included some items and aspects of religious daily life in other sections; for example, when we list devils or angels in the appendix, we place them under "Supernatural Beings."

One of the Virgin's greatest boons to her devotees was their resuscitation or the resuscitation of their family members. No more impressive miracle could be performed. In *Cantiga* 11 a monk who has visited his harlot drowns in a river, and devils are carrying off his soul when Saint Mary saves it from them and resuscitates him. In panel 3 devils are depicted dragging the soul, which, as usual, appears as a childlike figure, as angels watch. Panel 4 reveals Saint Mary with a wand driving the devils away as one of her angels retrieves the soul. The scene of resuscitation (panel 5) is remarkable. Saint James in *Cantiga* 26, 4 (pl. 53), is also depicted as he saves a soul from a devil in a kind of tug-of-war. In 14 a monk of Saint Peter dies without confession and devils take his soul. It requires Saint Peter's request to Saint Mary to persuade Jesus to allow her to save the monk's soul. The naive yet beautiful depiction of Peter, other apostles, and Saint Mary and Jesus are noteworthy and reveal considerable artistic skill. Jesus tenderly embraces his Mother (panel 5) as her retinue of saintly virgins surround the altar on which she kneels at Jesus' feet. Visions are numerous. A representative one appears in the miniatures of 66, 2. Therein we see the bishop lying asleep at the foot of Saint Mary's altar. Vows are well represented, for example in 42, 3 (pl.

50), where we see the young ballplayer promising the Virgin to be faithful to her rather than to other women, even his sweetheart.

Mass is illustrated in at least fifteen *cantigas*. Representative is 32, 1, in which a priest can be seen preparing communion. Penances are frequent. *Cantiga* 16 is an unusual story: a gentleman seeks a lady's love and she refuses him. A saintly abbot, with a halo, tells him as a penance to recite two hundred Aves a day for a year; if he does so, he can win the lady. This he does before the Virgin's altar. She appears to him and he recites as many Aves to her as he has for the lady. Then Saint Mary takes him with her to heaven. In panel 2 the abbot gives him the penance, and in 6 we see his soul taken by her.

Prayer, of course, is very frequently depicted in the miniatures of both T.I.1 and F. We offer a few examples here: in 5A, 2, people pray to be saved from Julian, the Apostate; a monk prays at the altar in 11, 1; in 14, 2, Saint Peter prays for the soul of his devotee; in 18, 1 (pl. 3), a woman prays to Saint Mary to save her diseased silkworms; in 30, 1, Saint Mary prays to Jesus; in F 8, 1 (283), a priest prays at her altar; in F 9, 1 (298), a woman beset by devils prays to her; and in F 95 (209) (pl. 33), Alfonso himself prays to her to save him from disease. One *cantiga*, F 5 (205), begins by invoking prayer: "Oraçon con piadade oe a Virgen de grado."

In the appendix we list many items associated with religion; for example, in 55, 1, appears a book of hours; in 73, 2, a chasuble; a cowl in 54, 3; a fresco in 74, 1 and 2 (pl. 14); a censer in F 60, 6 (272); relics in F 44, 1 (257); and a waxen image in 167, 2. This section reveals probably more of daily life than any other.

19
Sins and Crimes

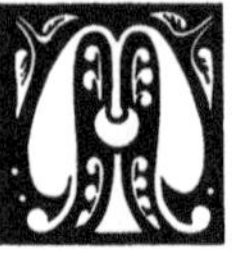edieval society regarded as sin a great many more actions than we do today, for example, the seven deadly sins, which are not even crimes in modern society. Alfonso and his legists did not promulgate laws and punishments even for some of the "thou-shalt-nots" of the Decalogue. Covetousness was not a crime, but it was regarded as sinful in the eyes of God. Separation of church and state was not a problem in the Middle Ages. Therefore, church law and civil law often overlapped. Some sins were also crimes and certain crimes were sins: adultery was one of these, as were blasphemy and homosexuality, which last was punishable by death; the *Siete Partidas* leaves no doubt that this "crime against nature" was a most serious offense. Boswell (1980, 289) and the second *Partida,* law 21, 1-2, offer considerable detail about it with, of course, reference to Sodom. Boswell (289) mentions that the *Partidas* did not go into effect until the fourteenth century; he even doubts that the law was regularly enforced, even though we know that Alfonso had his brother Fadrique and his brother's friend (lover?), Simón Ruiz de los Cameros, executed, Fadrique by strangulation; Simón was burned at the stake (O'Callaghan 1993, 241-42). The only reference to homosexuality in the *Cantigas* is in F 71, (235) where we read these words: "Just as the candle burns, so also burned the flesh of those who did not love womankind." In panel 4 of this miniature appears a man being burned. He could be Simón Ruiz.

Some of the most abominable sins appear in the *Cantigas* and even in the illustrations that visualize sin. In *Cantiga* 17, 1 (pl. 41), the miniaturists depict the incest practiced by a mother with her son. The Church would have punished such a sin by execution, and the law of the land would have done the same; however, the Virgin forgives the sinful mother and saves her. We repeat that we believe that her forgiveness strengthened the populace's concept that Alfonso, through his divine patroness, superseded the often harsh influence of the ecclesiastical hierarchy.

Blasphemy appears frequently in the two codices: in 34, 1 and 2 (pl. 18), we see a Jew throwing an icon of Saint Mary into his privy, for which deed devils kill him; in 72 a gambler insults Jesus and Mary and is gruesomely slain by devils; in 136, 2 (pl. 70), a woman who loses at dice throws a stone at the image of the Child Jesus in his Mother's arms. For this the king has her dragged through the streets behind horses until she is dead. In F 18 (294) the woman is burned to death. The king was Conrad and the site of the miracle was Foggia in Apulia. For other incidences of blasphemy and blasphemous acts, see the appendix.

Murder and blasphemy appear in 19, 1, where three knights kill another who has sought sanctuary in a church. Suicide, a capital sin, is treated in 84, 3 in a *cantiga* fraught with pathos. A gentleman leaves his bed and his wife each night to go to worship the Virgin; the wife asks him where he went and jokingly he tells her he went to see another woman. At this his wife stabs herself to death. The husband entreats Saint Mary to bring her back to life, and when he returns home, he finds her alive and well. Again the Virgin pardons a capital crime. Another suicide appears in *cantiga* F 2 (201), where a young girl tries to commit suicide, first by stabbing herself and then by swal-

"

lowing venomous spiders. The Virgin forgives and resuscitates her. Three runaway nuns and one who tries to desert her convent surely are committing blasphemy in *Cantigas* 55, 58, 59 (pl. 39), and 94 (pl. 38), and so is the abbess in 7 (pl. 40). We list such sins as greed, lust, pride, and other sinful deeds in the appendix. We treat thievery and gambling and the actions of highwaymen, counterfeiters, and others in chapter 22.

20
Structures

The illustrations depict many cities and villages in Spain, as well as in other lands and centuries. As Guerrero-Lovillo (1949, 227-65) so cogently puts it, the depiction of cities is not exact and indeed follows a style nearly always only suggestive of what these cities actually looked like—crenelated walls, towers, barbicans, and so forth. Since there are so many backdrops of cities behind their walls, we do not list every one depicted in the miniatures. We believe the depiction of the Arreixaca section in Murcia is a good example of a city in 169, 1, with many towers and tiled roofs and Saint Mary's church. Could viewers of the miniatures recognize it? We doubt it. However, in 107, 1 (pl. 67), there can be no doubt that the city concerned is Segovia, since the aqueduct in panel 2 identifies it, even if the walls and other structures do not. It is strange that the miniaturists have painted the aqueduct with Moorish, rather than with the actual Roman arches.

Plazas appear from time to time. An excellent, representative plaza converted into a bullring is the locale for a bull-baiting in 144, 3-6 (pl. 49). City streets are not carefully delineated but can be identified by the buildings and houses beside them and by the action taking place on them (Guerrero-Lovillo 1949, 230-32). In 12, 4, an *alguacil* and his policemen hurry along a street to interrupt a desecration by Jews; in 12, 3, an archbishop stands in a street to ask if the congregation heard a voice complaining about the Jews; in 25, 1, a man carries a chest on a street; in 64, 4 (pl. 1) and in 68, 5 and 6, a go-between confers with a customer. In 136 (pl. 70) a woman is dragged along a street.

Many facades of various buildings on city streets appear (Guerrero-Lovillo 1949, 232-38). An excellent example can be seen in 9, 3 (pl. 5), where there is a shop open to the street, from which a pilgrim purchases an icon; in 41, 1, the facade of a money changer's establishment is seen; in 59, 1 (pl. 39), the facade of a convent door; in 27, 1, the facade of a Jewish synagogue; in 108, 1 and 2 (pl. 19), an open-air pharmacy.

House interiors are too often not very detailed, but there are exceptions. Dining rooms provide the background in some miracles; in 42, 4 (pl. 50), a wedding party sits at table; in 45A, 4, we see another dining room; in 67, 5 and 6 (pl. 58), we see a dining table at which a bishop sits as he, in panel 6, exorcises the devil who had possessed a corpse; in 52, 3 (pl. 6), monks sit at table in the monastery refectory.

In 108, 3 (pl. 19), we see the bedroom in a Jewish house and a woman in labor. The bed is large and the curtains are visible. In 15A, 6, a royal bedroom in a palace appears. In 17, 2 (pl. 41) and 34, 2 and 4 (pl. 18), a privy is depicted. A kitchen, which shows fritters being cooked in a large skillet on a tripod, is clearly illustrated in 157, 1 and 2 (pl. 10), and in the same panels there is a cauldron that can be lowered over a fire.

In 143, 1 and 6, appears a detailed depiction of Jerez de la Frontera, in which Guerrero-Lovillo (1949, 228) sees elements of realism. Houses and other structures usually abutted on streets, leaving no space for sidewalks. City walls rise behind gamblers in 136, 1, 2, and 3 (pl. 70); besieged cities appear—28, 1, 3 (pl. 20), and 4; 51 in every panel reveals a city under siege. The wine cellar of a monastery with huge hogsheads of wine is seen in 47, 1 (pl. 8). Other structures, streets, and so forth, are listed in chapter 16, "Places, Sites and Locales," and in the appendix under "Structures and Streets."

21
The Supernatural
Angels, Devils, Spirits, and Souls

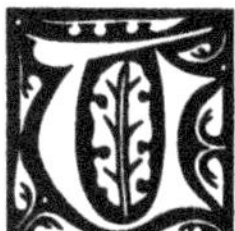hroughout the miniatures the hosts of heaven and of hell are constantly at war. The Virgin, of course, is the primary foe of all forms of evil and its advocates. The miniaturists depict both angels and devils, often in the same illustrations. Angels appear wearing albs, most are blond, and their wings are brightly colored. There are some truly exceptional wings, which often extend beyond the full body length of these spirits and are exquisitely represented. They shimmer, appear diaphanous, and seem truly celestial. So many of the heavenly host appear in the miniatures that to describe them all would consume most of our book. Therefore we treat some of the most representative and striking and refer to the others listed in the appendix. As might be expected, an angel appears to the shepherds in 1, 3; in 2, 5 (pl. 52), we see angels with haloes and colorful pinions standing at either side of Saint Mary as she offers to Saint Ildefonso the alb made in heaven; in 3, 3, a pair of angels flanking Saint Mary drives off horned devils; in 7, 4, two angels with white wings in white albs deliver the child conceived by the abbess, and the caption realistically reads, "How St. Mary removed the abbess' child through her side." We see the Virgin standing over the abbess, but in the miniature the angels are actually removing the baby. In panel 5 one of these angels hands the newborn infant to a bearded hermit to be reared; in 11, 3, white-winged angels in albs, whose sleeves and robes are bordered in gold, watch as a lustful monk drowns in a river and as dreadful winged devils seize his soul. In panel 4 the Virgin with a ray of golden light has caused the devils, as they fly upward, to drop the soul, which angels then recover; and in panel 5 the Virgin, flanked by groups

of monks, holds the resuscitated monk's hand while an angel supports him as he sits up. Very beautiful angels stand on either side of Saint Mary in *cantiga* 100, as Alfonso kneels at her feet.

Devils and demons are more plentiful than angels. Some of the most hideous appear in 109, 1, 2, and 3, as they try to take a man to perdition. One is completely naked; the others wear breachclouts of long hair. Most have beards. In panel 1 two have the talons of birds of prey and one has cloven hooves. In panel 2 a devil has webbed feet; in panel 3 (pl. 54), as monks take the devil-beset man to the shrine, we see a bat-winged devil standing behind him with its arms around the man's neck. In panel 5 tiny demons scamper up a column in Saint Mary's shrine at Salas, as they flee from her image. In 111, 4, devils are boiling souls in a huge cauldron. One uses a bellows to fan the flames as he dives into a hole, and angels flank Saint Mary as she saves a soul.

In 115A, 1 (pl. 37), devils urge a man on as he is seen in bed with his wife. In *cantiga* 125A, 4 (pl. 55) and 6, we see a host of devils called up by a young cleric to help him win a girl for whom he lusts. To protect himself from them, he sits within a circle lined with cabalistic symbols and a star; in 125B, 1, the devils are trying to seduce the girl, and in panel 2 they hold back the sword wielded by the girl's father as he tries to kill her.

Souls frequently appear, always in the form of naked childlike figures. In 149, 6, two angels carry upward the soul of a priest who had doubted the authenticity of the Host; in 138, 6, angels carry to heaven the soul of John Chrysostom; in 75B, 2, Saint Mary takes a poor old woman's soul with her, whereas in 75B, 5, black devils with two-pronged hooks hold a rich man's soul. *Cantiga* 26, 3, reveals devils carrying off the soul of a pilgrim, and in panel 4 Saint James has a tug-of-war with a devil over the same soul (pl. 56). Demonic boars with tusks and batlike wings appear in 82, 2.

Cantiga 72 is a fearful tale: we see gamblers in panels 1 and 2; in panel 3 one of the gamblers, who insulted Saint Mary and Jesus, is being ripped open by a devil; and in 4 (pl. 57) we see the man's ghost, a white shrouded figure, as it appears to the dead man's father to tell him that his son is dead. This, we believe, is a most characteristic depiction of a ghost.

One of the most fearful depictions of a devil, who possesses a dead body in order to use his destructive powers, can be seen in *Cantiga* 67 (pl. 58), whose page of miniatures is one of the most beautiful and artistically presented in T.I.1. See Keller and Kinkade (1984, 67-68) for a lengthy discussion of these miniatures. Nearly a hundred appearances of angels and devils are listed under "Supernatural Beings" in the appendix.

22
Thieves, Gamblers, Highwaymen, Counterfeiters, and Other Criminals

riminals who exist today appear in the *Cantigas*'s miniatures: in 9, 4 (pl. 5), we see highwaymen, who would have stolen from a monk but for Saint Mary; in 45 a knight is a highwayman and a robber of monasteries; in 106, 1 (pl. 59), thieves on horseback steal cattle; in 13 a thief who always commends himself to Saint Mary is arrested and condemned to hang; she holds him as he hangs from the gallows.

Gamblers figure frequently in the *Cantigas,* and their portrayal in taverns and on the street enables us to see features of daily life found in such places (see chap. 15). Representative *cantigas* about gamblers are *Cantiga* 24, 1, in which a novice for the priesthood dies without confession; 136 (pl. 70), where we see a woman gambler; and 140, 6, where a gambling house is depicted. See the listing in the appendix of numerous other criminal acts.

"

23
Tools, Implements, and Weapons

e believe that the illustrations of items used by medieval Spaniards, as seen in the miniatures of T.I.1. and F, provide exceptionally detailed depictions. Our index in the appendix is copious in this area, but even so, and in accord with our plan to describe how some of these items appear in the miniatures, we relate herewith some representative examples. Armor in a world in which warfare was almost constant is exceptionally well presented. *Cantiga* 63 (pl. 60), in all six of its colorful panels, reveals armor worn by cavalry. The story is well worth telling. Panel 1, at the left, depicts the knight, mounted and wearing distinctive black and white armor, under which is chain mail. In the same panel to the right, he is received by his liege lord, who needs his help in battle. In panel 2 the knight is hearing mass and is being admonished by his squire, who fears that his reputation will suffer because the liege lord has already gone to the battlefield. The squire points to his master's helmet on the ground. Panel 3 shows the cavalry moving into battle. We see mailed horses, knights in full armor of several sorts (Guerrero-Lovillo 1949, 112-35), lances couched as well as carried aloft, shields, several types of helmets, and a banner—in short, a well-armored army marching against an enemy. Panel 4 is remarkable in its presentation of action in battle. Christians rush at Muslims, also in full armor, and meet them in full career. The Muslims are Semitic as well as black. The knight, who was still hearing mass, seems to be in the thick of the fray on his horse. Some miraculous substitute for him spears a knight in Christian armor, who is evidently a mercenary for the Muslims or perhaps a renegade Christian. This knight is seen toppling from his horse, which, in its effort not to fall, stretches its forelegs to support itself. Moorish shields and spears are clearly depicted. All this is seen by the knight's liege lord, who is gratified to see how well his knight fights in battle. In panel 5 the liege lord, returning from battle, meets his strong supporter just then setting out for the encounter. He embraces him. All praise him for his prowess and for the number of Muslims he slew. He is mortified, for he has never entered the battle, but behold, his armor and helmet are dented. Panel 6 shows the Christian knight kneeling before Saint Mary's altar giving thanks. The knight who is the center of the miracle bows low. Interesting also is the helmet of one of the knights, in panel 6, upon which appears a lily of France.

In 28, 3 (pl. 20), we see a catapult constructed by a sultan to knock down the wall of a besieged city; in 99 we see a Muslim army in armor, carrying weapons and shields; in 165A, 3 (pl. 68), we see Moorish tents, some of which are being erected, and we see the stakes to hold them steady being driven into the ground by servants.

In the world of civilians, we see fishing nets in 183, 6; in 31, 5 (pl. 15), appears a cart drawn by bullocks; there is an ambulance cart to carry the sick in 91, 2 and 3; forges appear in F 31, 2 (253); a cauldron for cooking in 68, 1 and in 157 (pl. 10); bellows in 111, 4, and much more. In the world of the Church, a censer can be seen in F 60 (272); a silver bowl in 152, 4; and many, many garments and implements used by the clergy are depicted throughout the miniatures. For these see chapter 18, "Religion." In the category of medical instruments, forceps appear in 126, 2, and a crossbow is used in panel 3 to extract a dart when the forceps fail. Agricultural implements are frequently represented: in 48, 5, we see a plow; in F 12, 1 (314), sickles; in 52, 2 (pl. 6), a milk pail; in 136, 6 (pl 70), a painter mixes paint and paints a statue.

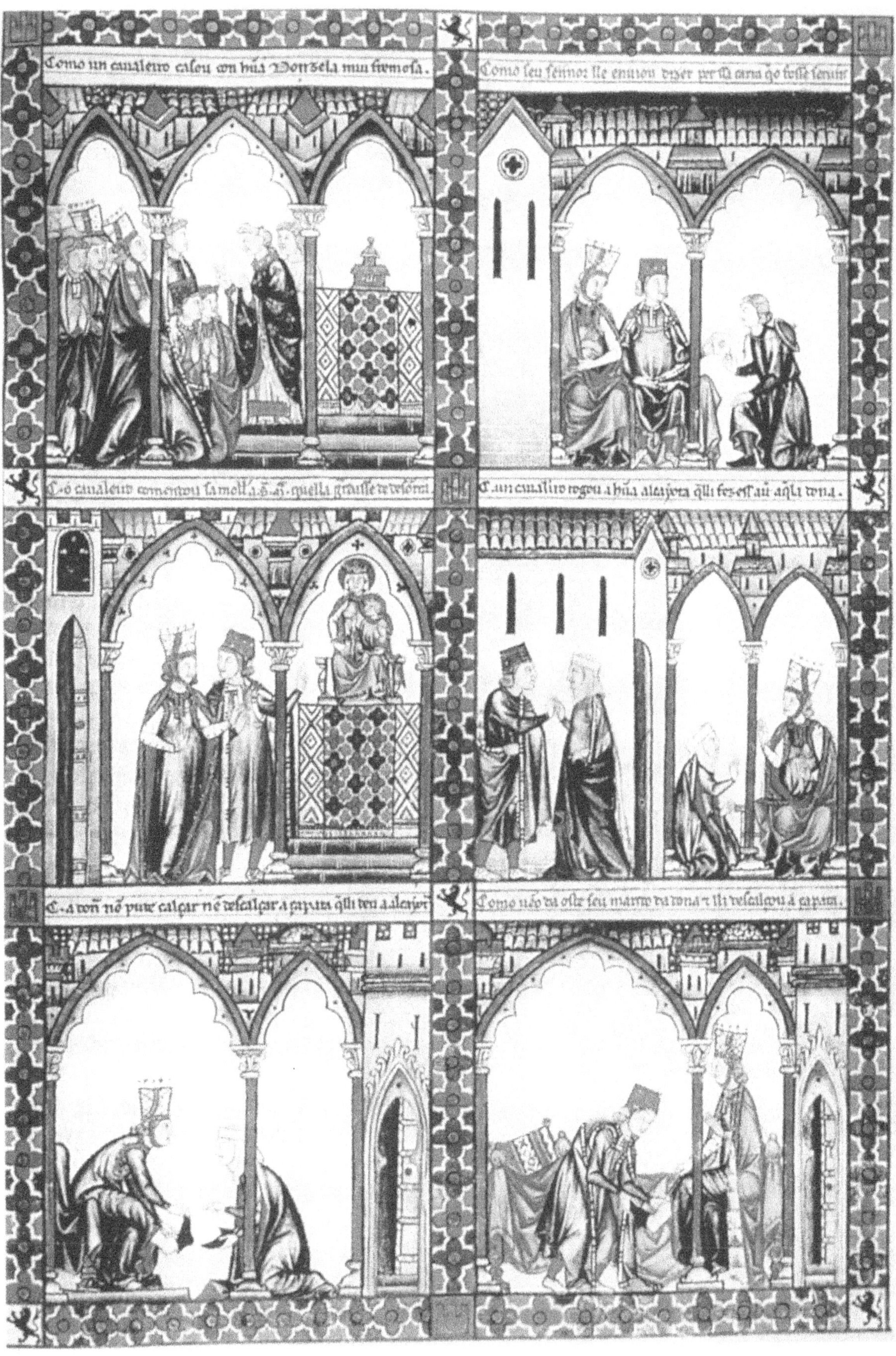

Plate 1: Cantiga 64. "This is how the wife whose husband had left her under Saint Mary's protection could not put on or take off the shoes her suitor had given her."

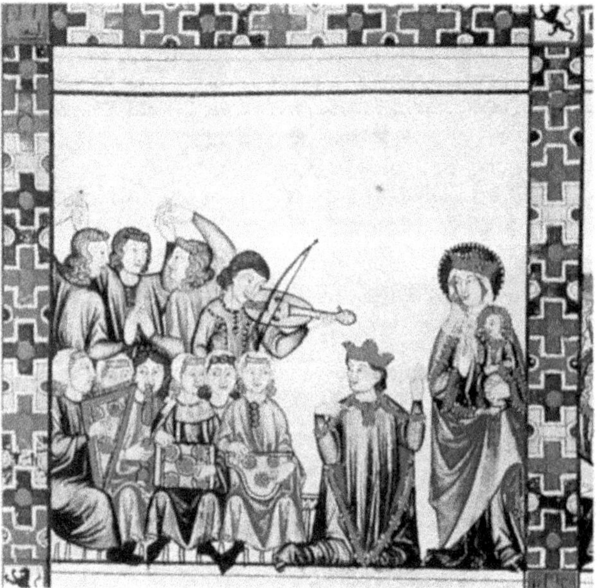

Plate 2: Cantiga 120, panel 1. This is a song of praise to Saint Mary. Panel 1 has no title, but it shows musicians, singers, and dancers.

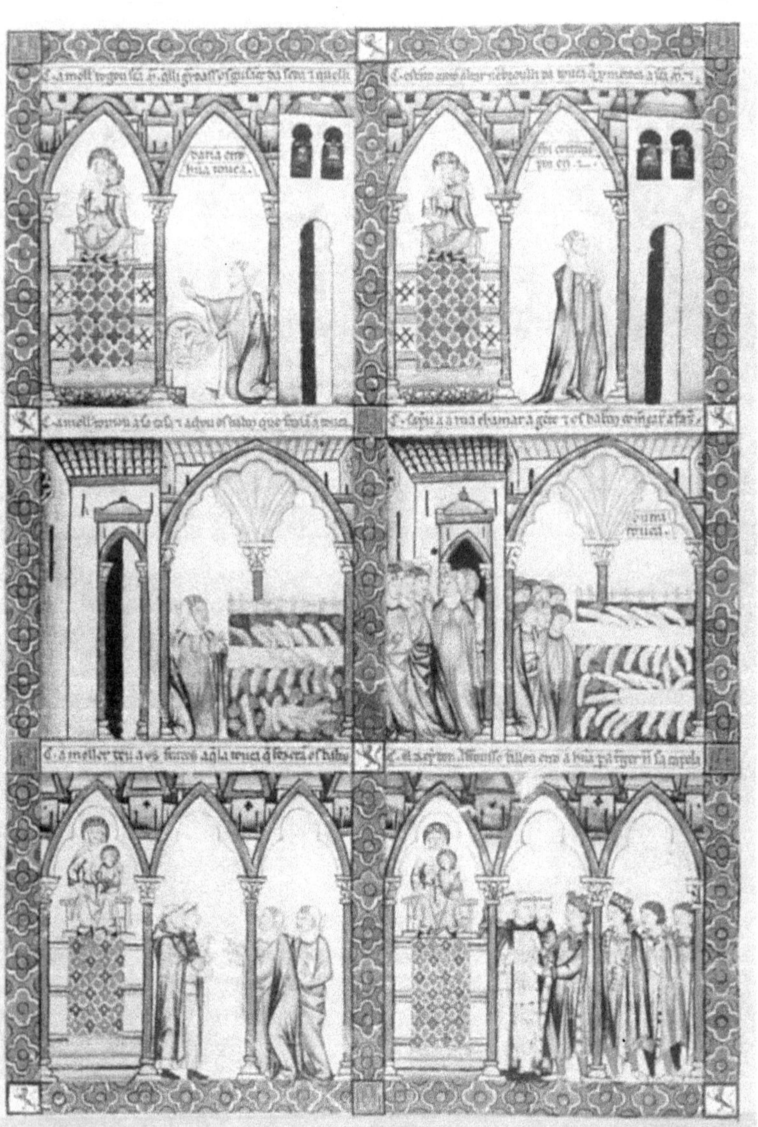

Plate 3: Cantiga 18. "This is how Saint Mary made the silkworms spin two veils . . ."

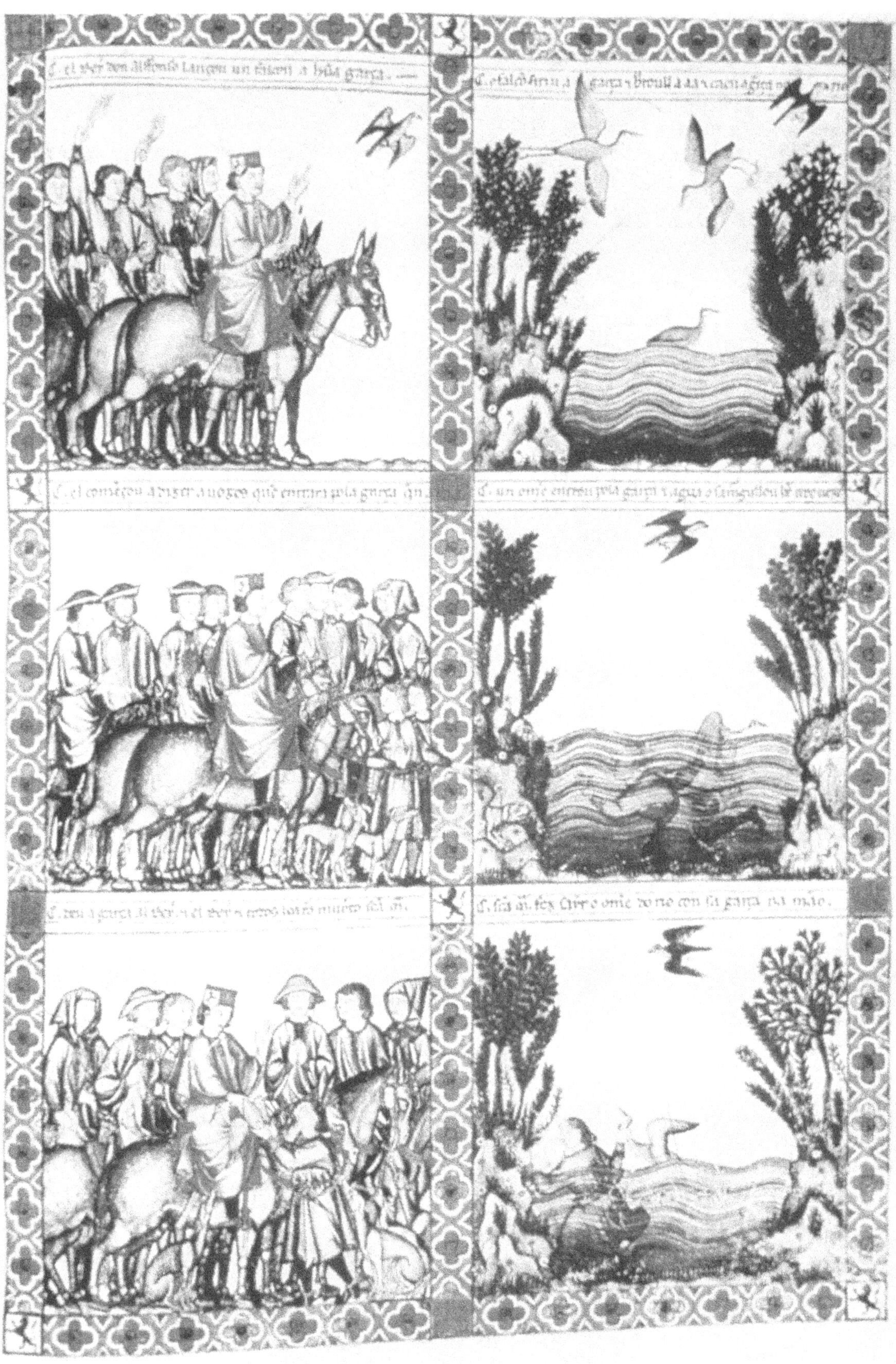

Plate 4: Cantiga 142. "This is how Saint Mary wished to save a king's man from death . . ."

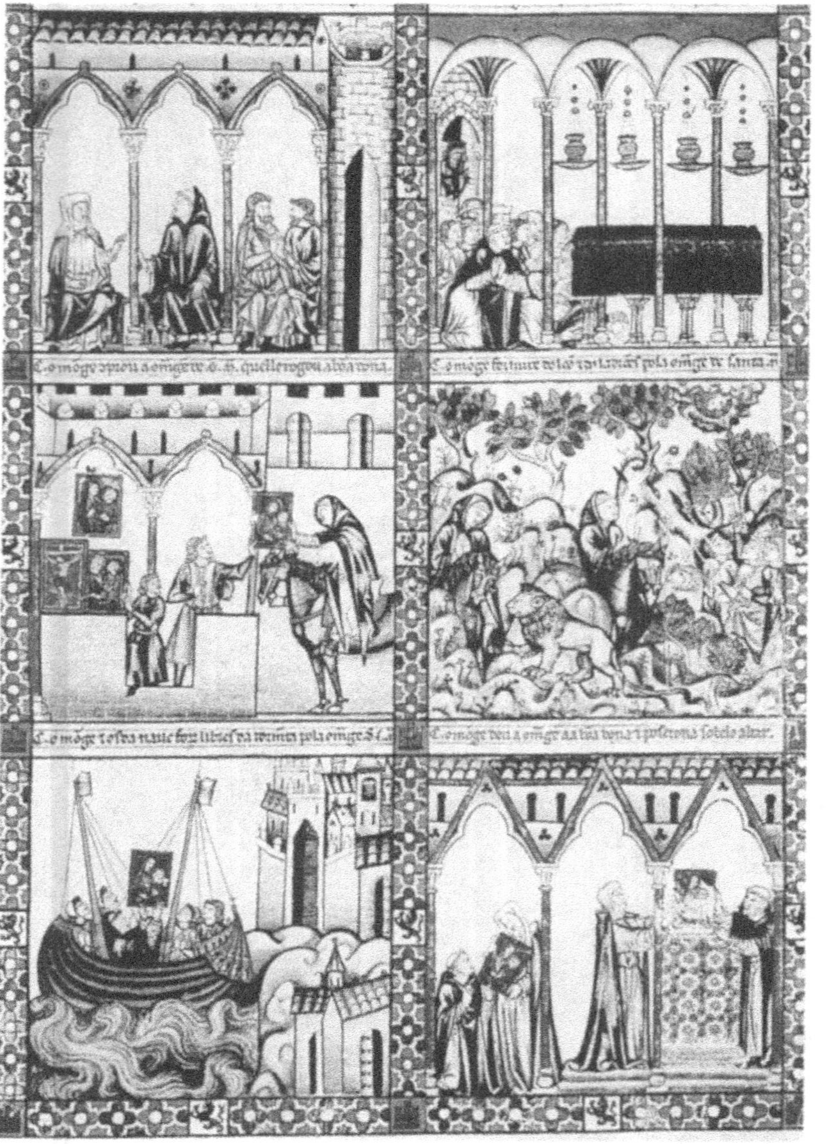

Plate 5: Cantiga 9. "This is how…St. Mary made her image painted on a wooden tablet exude oil."

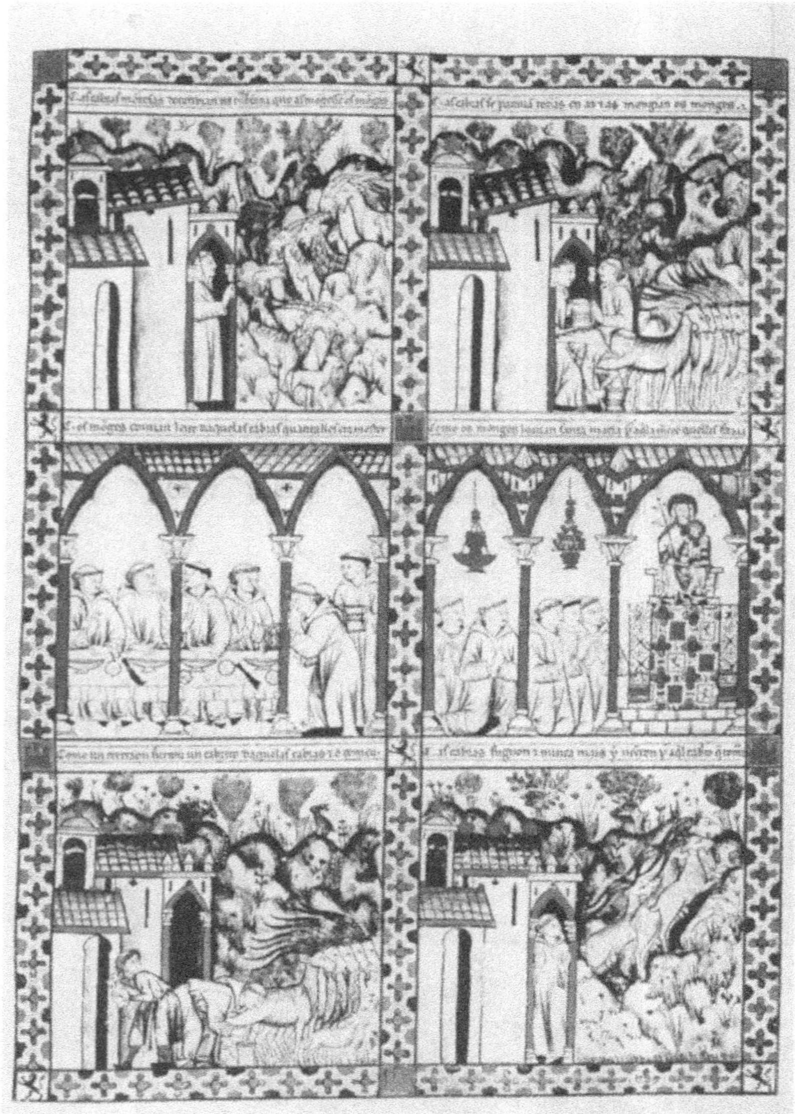

Plate 6: Cantiga 52. "This is how Saint Mary made the mountain goats come to Monsarraz . . ."

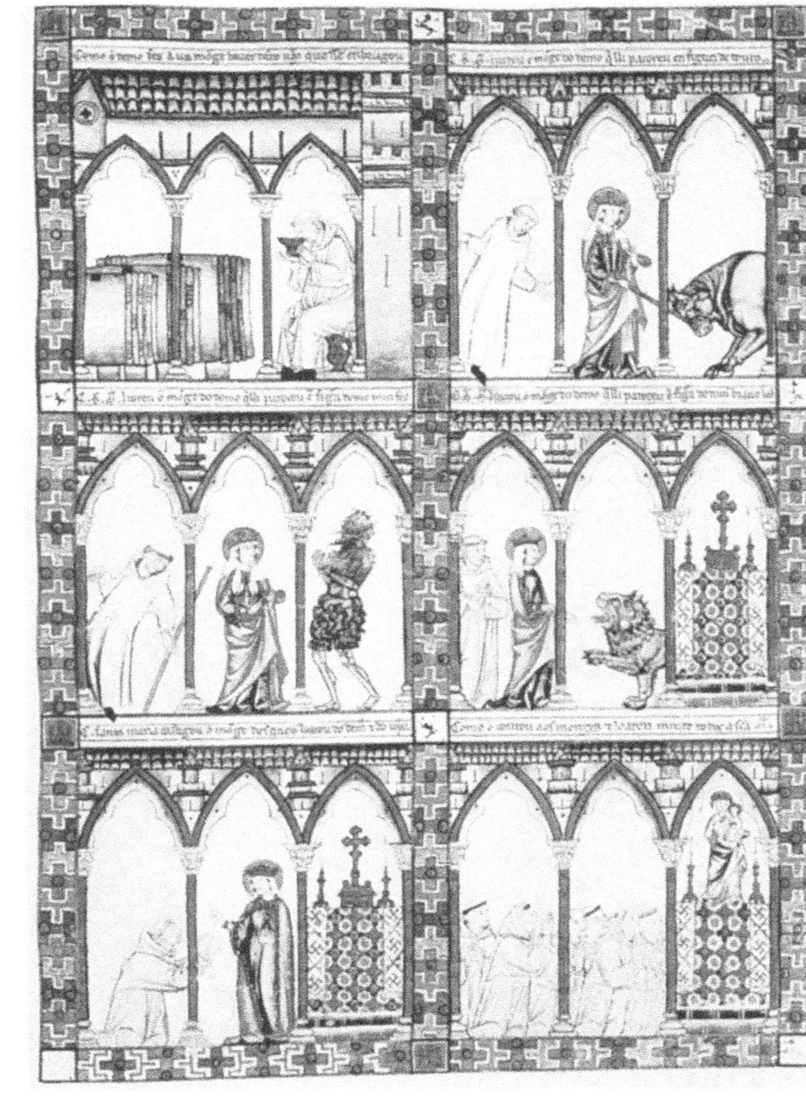

Plate 7: Cantiga 103. "This is how Saint Mary made a monk remain three hundred years [listening] to the song of a bird . . ."

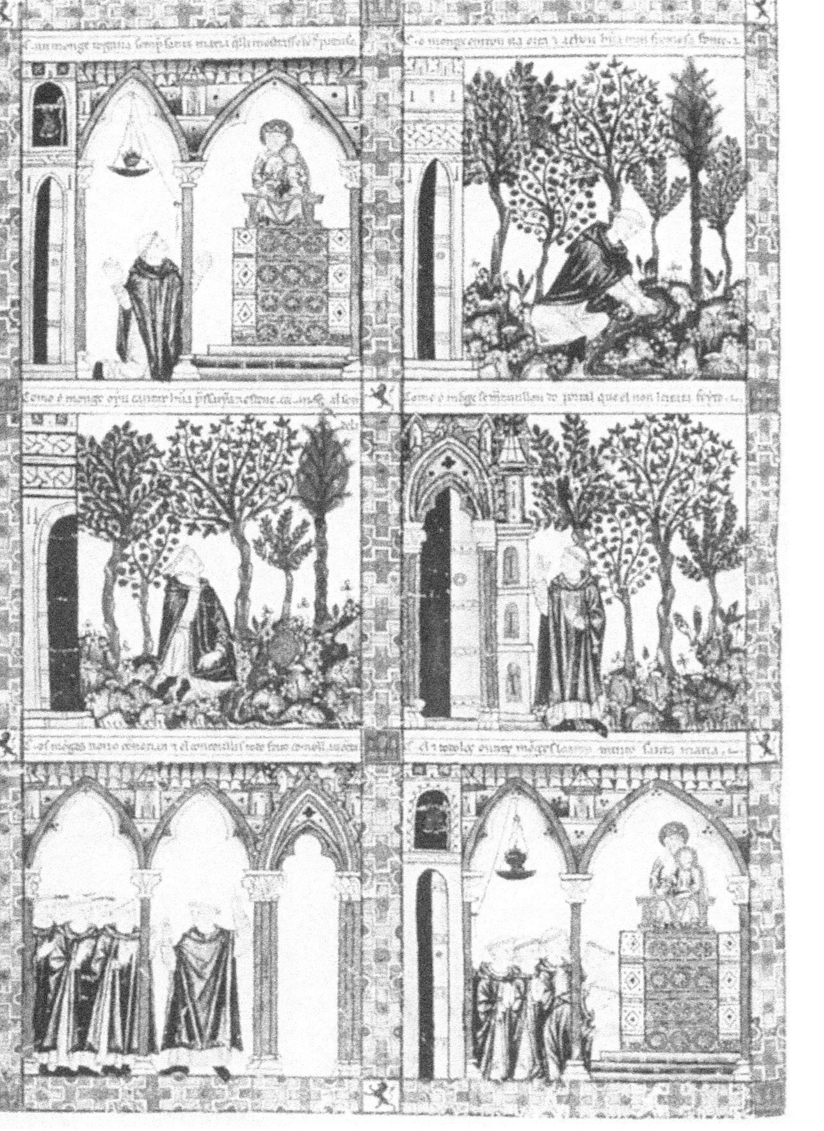

Plate 8: Cantiga 47. "This is how Saint Mary saved the monk whom the devil tried to frighten in order to destroy him."

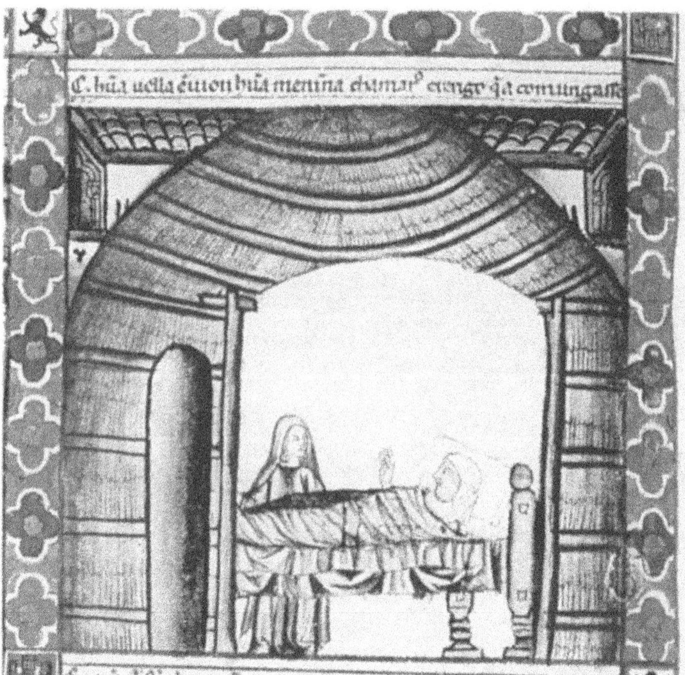

Plate 9: Cantiga 75A, panel 2. "How an old woman sent a girl to call the priest to give her communion."

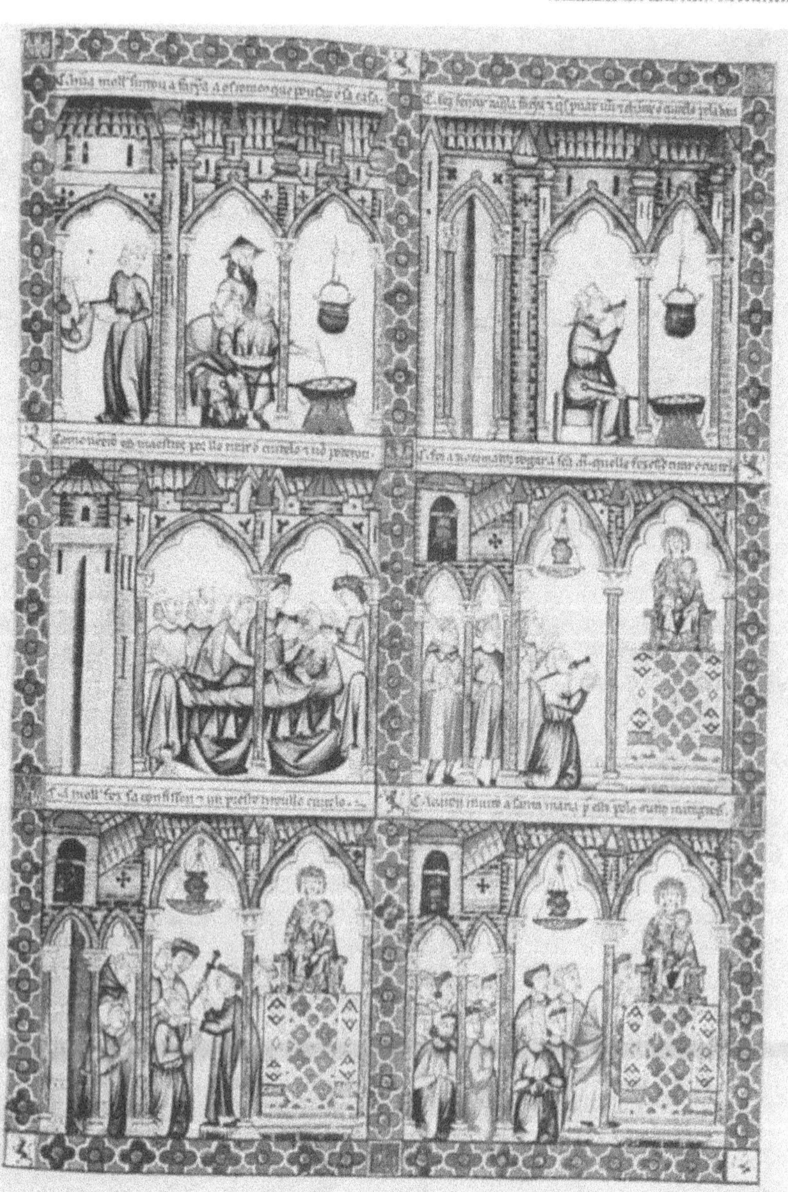

Plate 10: Cantiga 157. "This is about some pilgrims who were going to Rocamadour . . ."

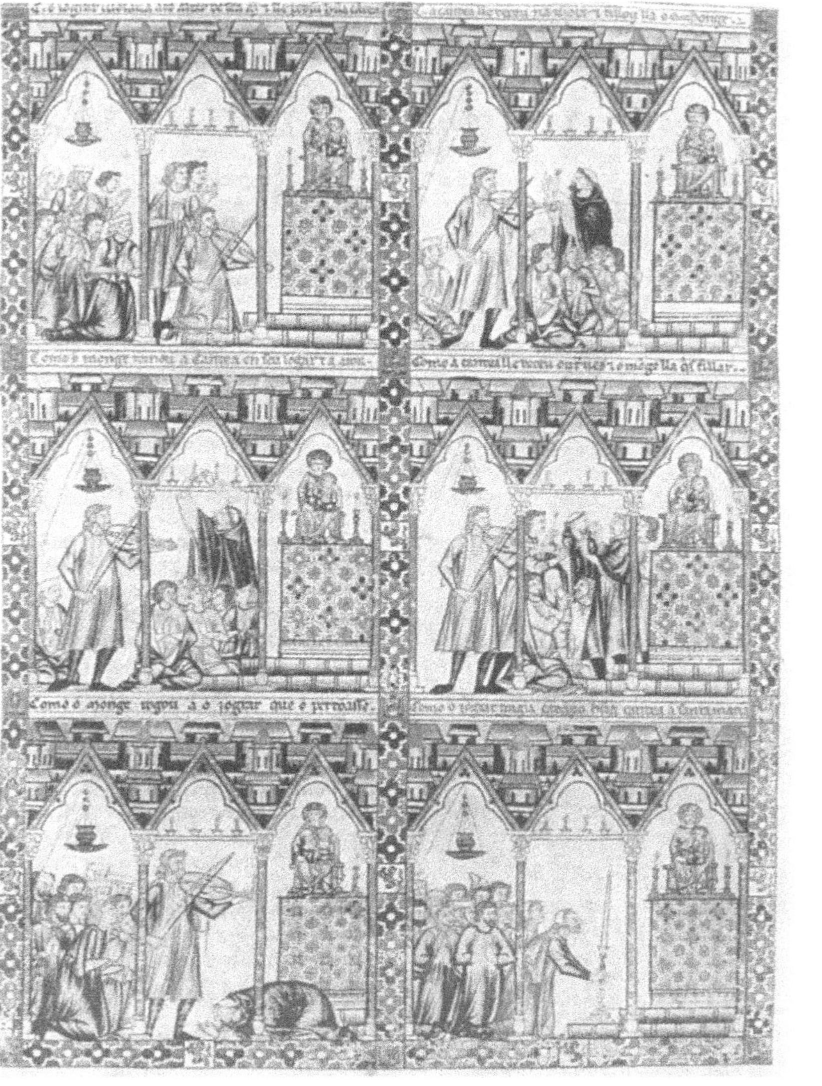

Plate 11: Cantiga 8. "This is how Saint Mary made a candle descend on the fiddle of a minstrel who sang before her."

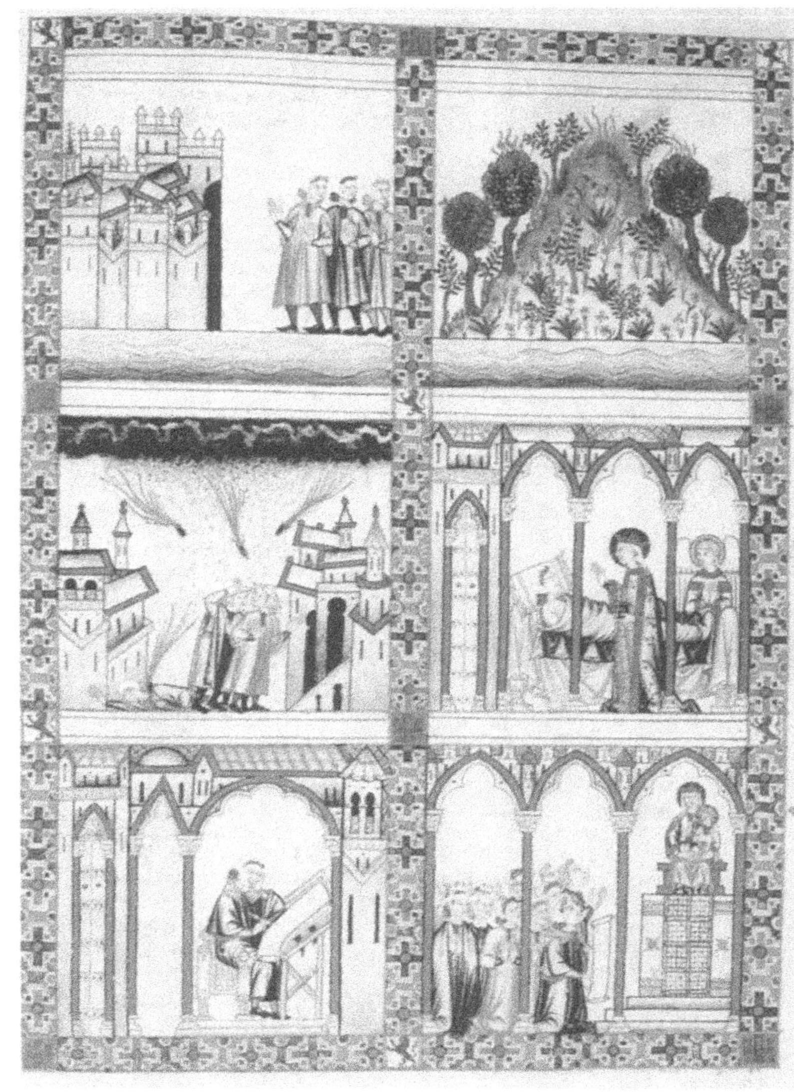

Plate 12: Cantiga F 79, panel 4. "This is how Saint Mary took away a great fire storm in the land of Sicily."

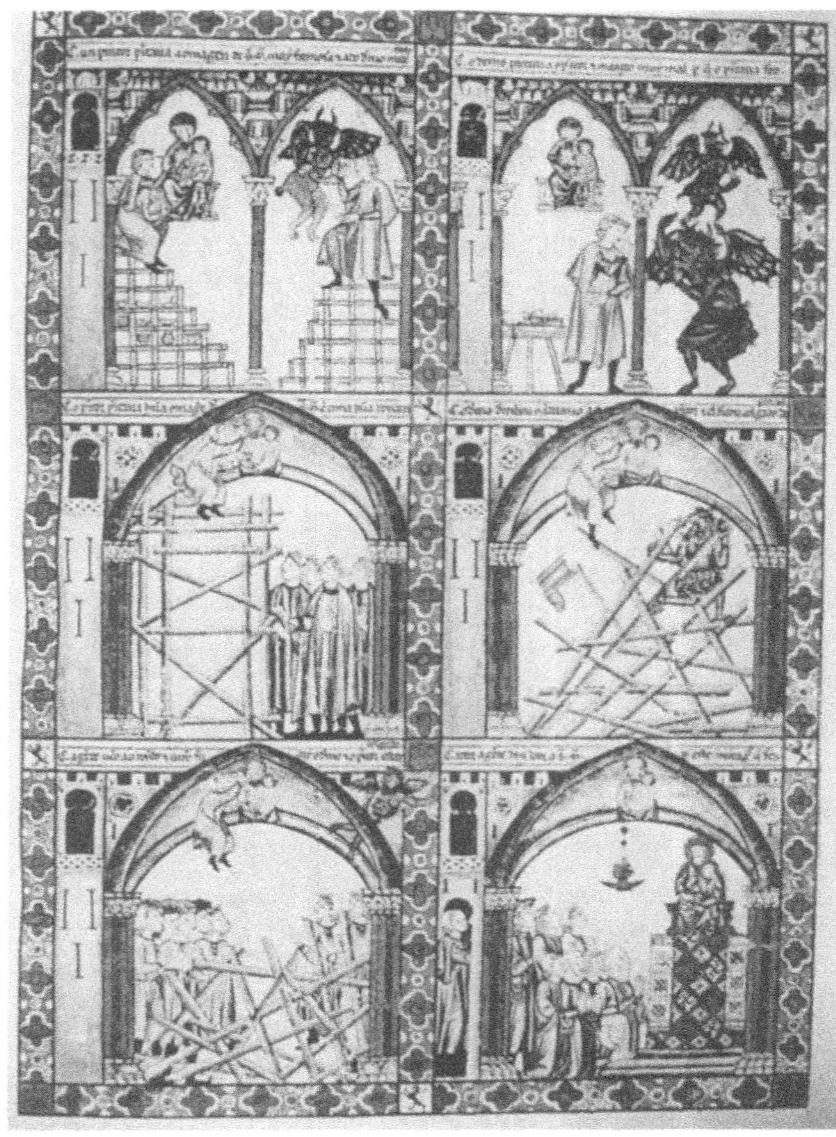

Plate 13: Cantiga 4. "This is how Saint Mary kept the Jew's son from burning . . ."

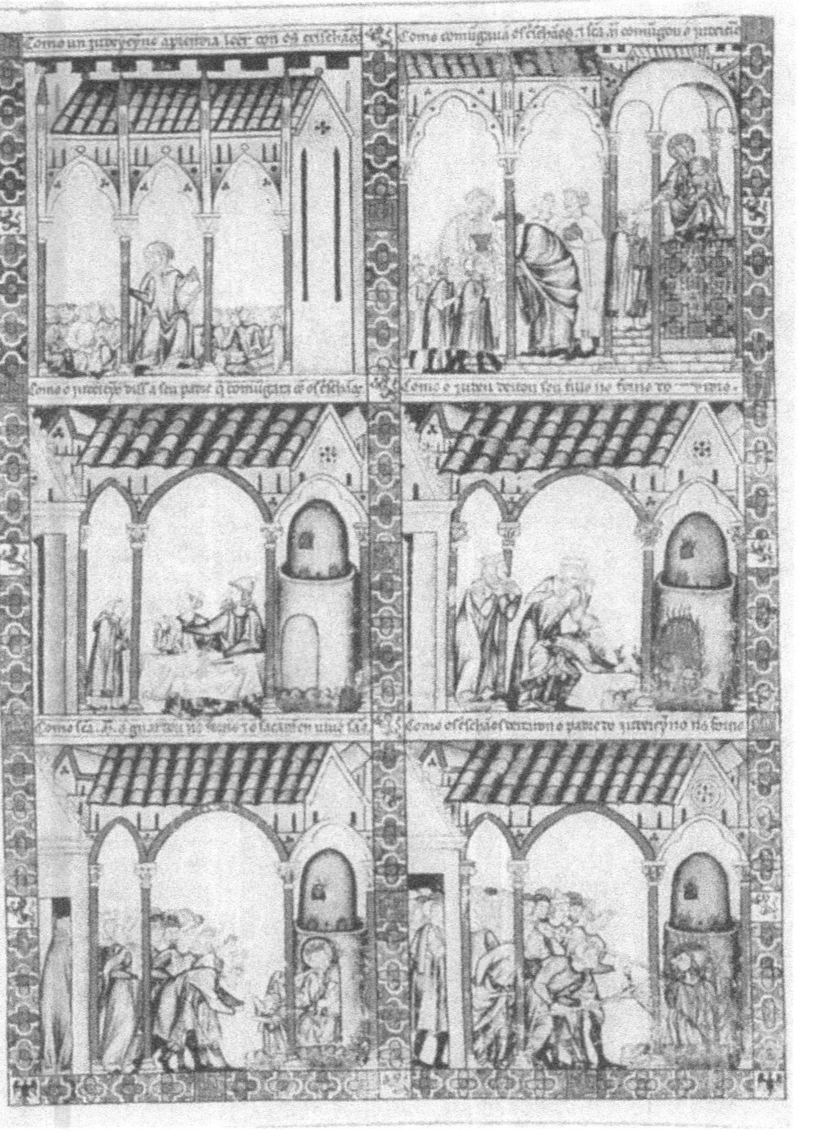

Plate 14: Cantiga 74. "This is how Saint Mary protected the painter whom the devil tried to kill because he was painting him ugly."

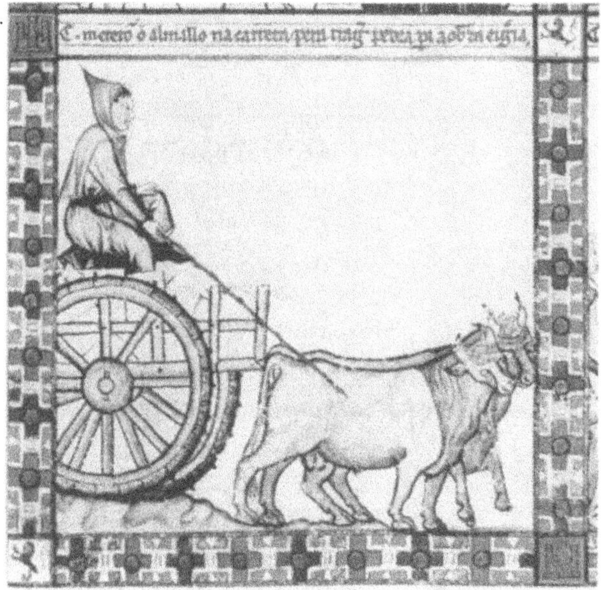

Plate 15: Cantiga 31, panel 5. "How they hitched the bullock to the cart to carry stone for the building of a church."

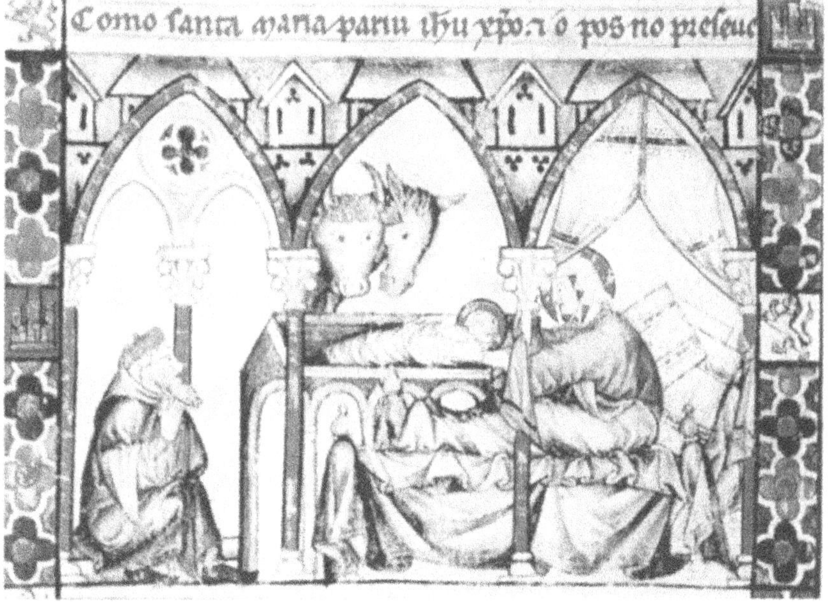

Plate 16: Cantiga 1, panel 2. "How Saint Mary gave birth to Jesus Christ and laid him in a manger."

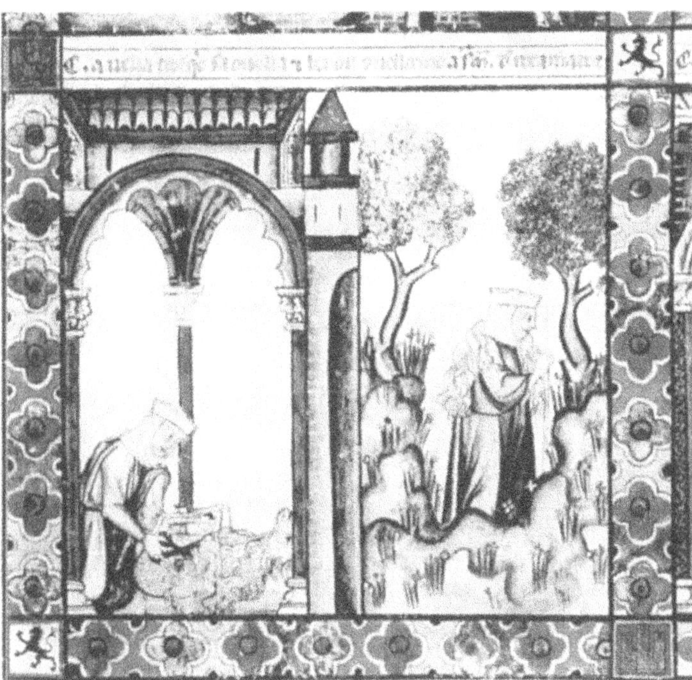

Plate 17: Cantiga 147, panel 5. "How the old woman sheared the sheep . . ."

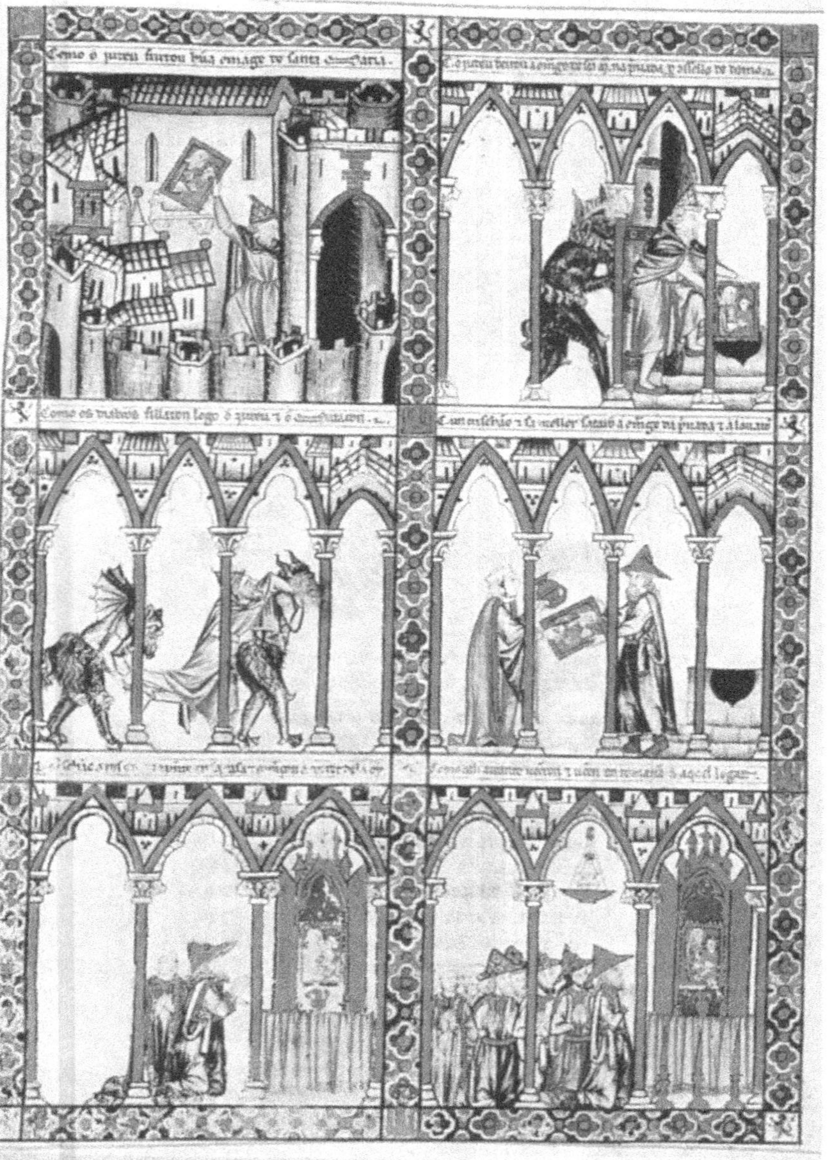

Plate 18: Cantiga 34. "How Saint Mary got the better of a Jew for the dishonor he had done her image."

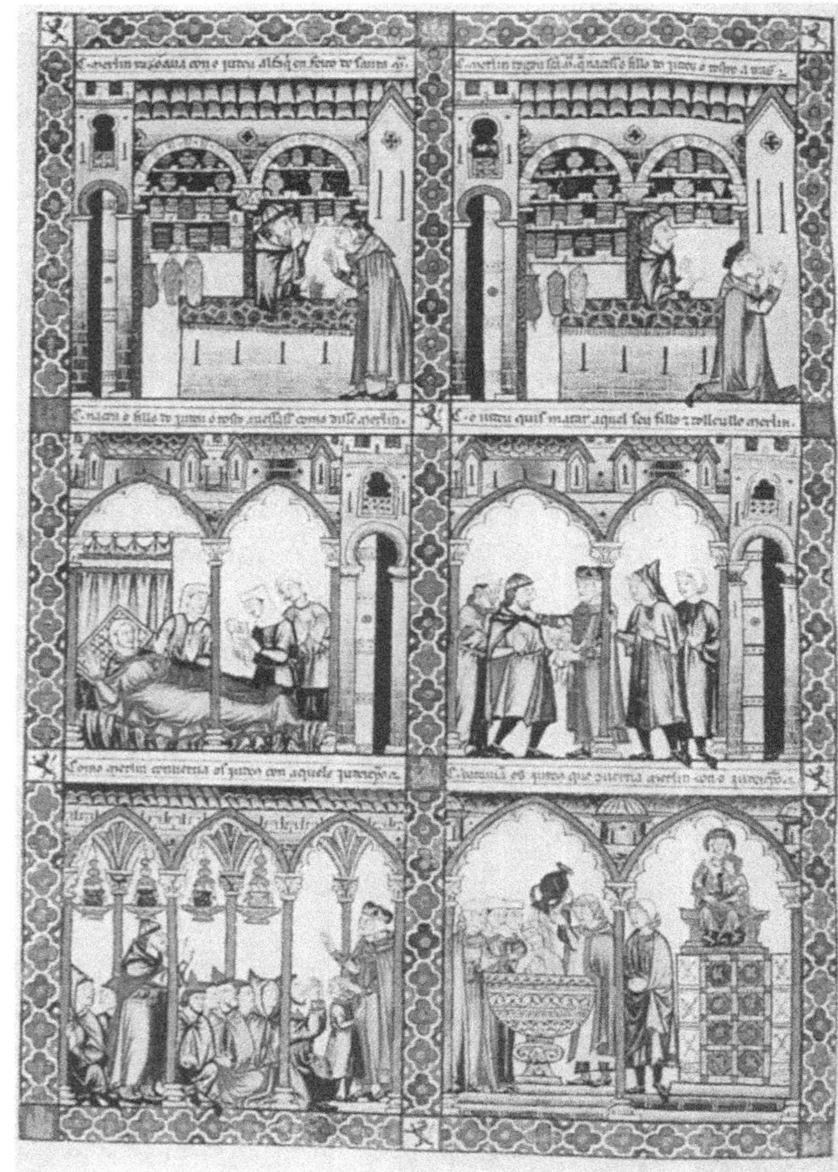

Plate 19: Cantiga 108. "This is how Saint Mary made the son of a Jew be born with his head on backwards . . ."

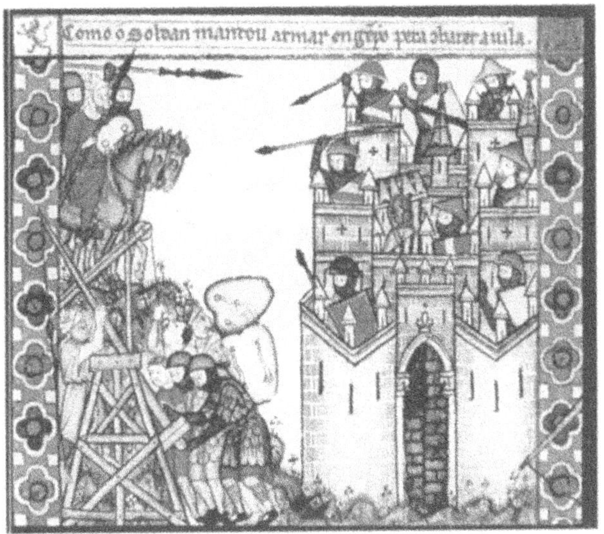

Plate 20: Cantiga 28, panel 3. "How the sultan ordered siege engines set up."

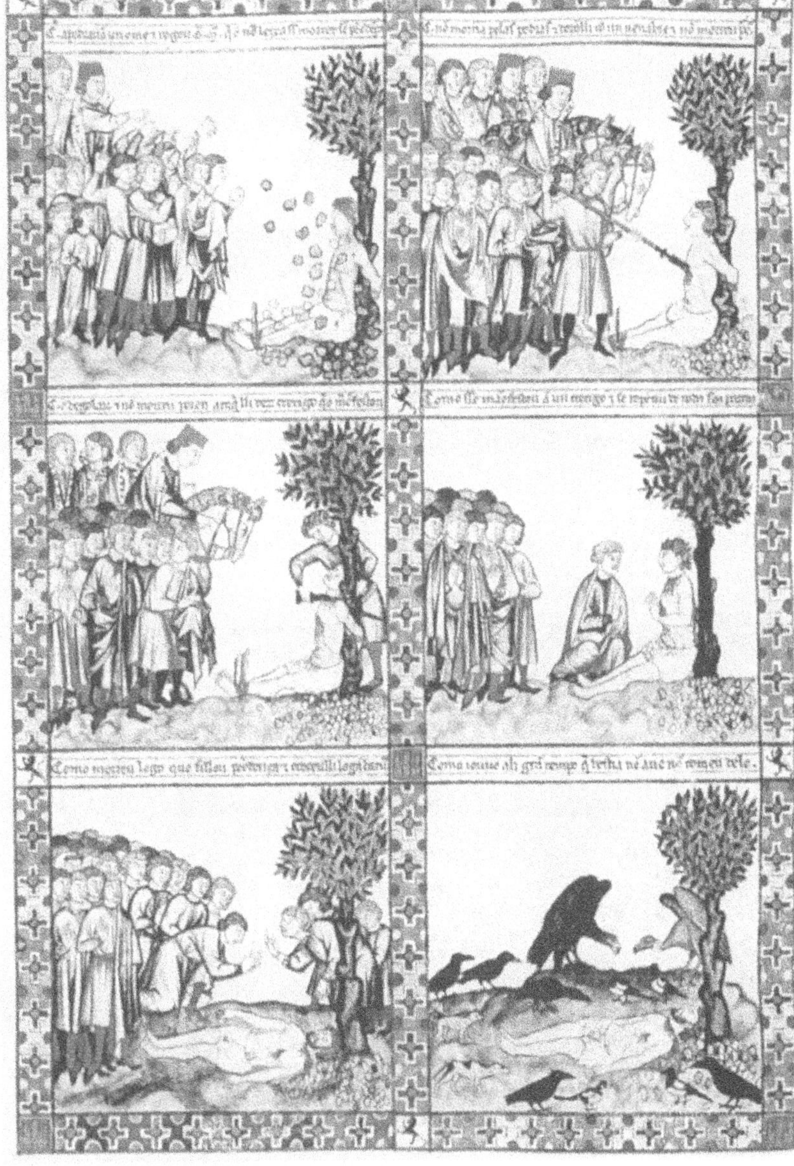

Plate 21: Cantiga 124. "This is how Saint Mary saved a man whom they stoned . . ."

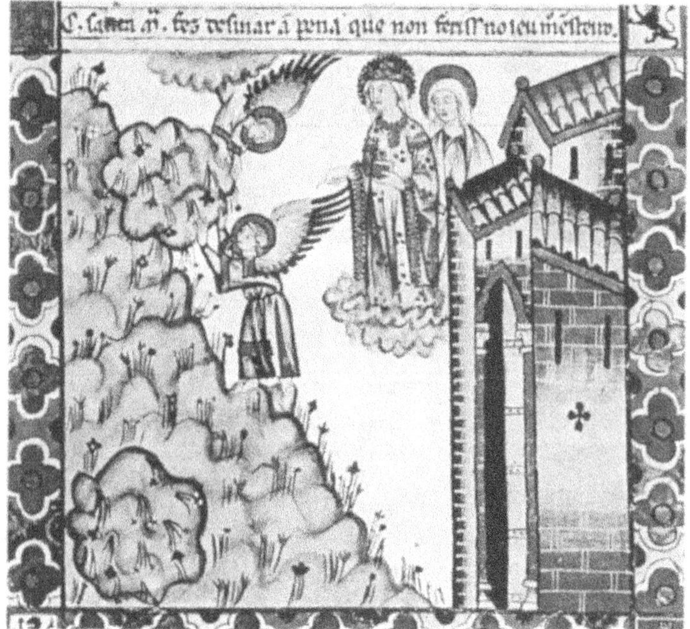

Plate 22: Cantiga 113, panel 5. "How Saint Mary made the rock change course so that it would not strike the monastery."

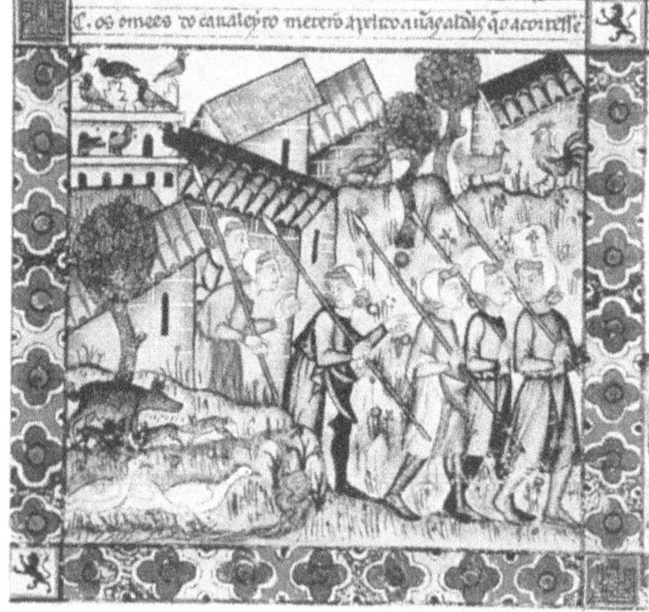

Plate 23: Cantiga 148, panel 5. "How the knight's men went to some villages to ask them to help him."

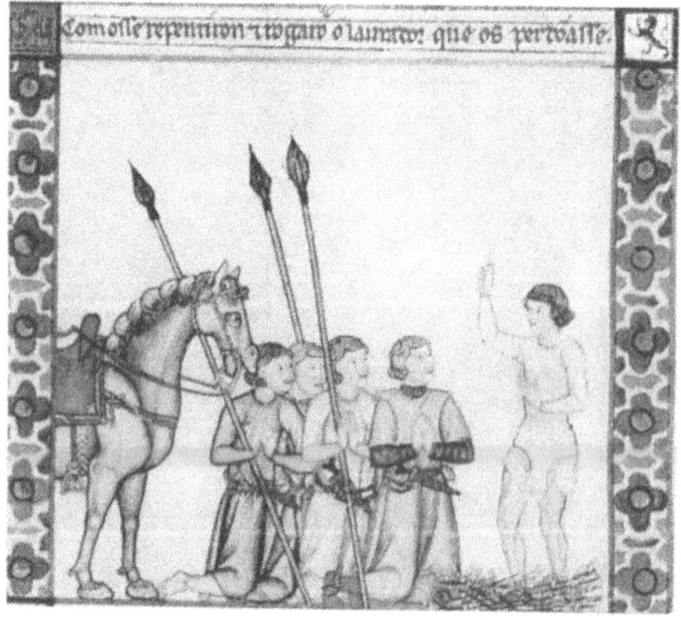

Plate 24: Cantiga 22, panel 4. "How Saint Mary protected the farmer so that he would not die from the wounds a knight and his men gave him."

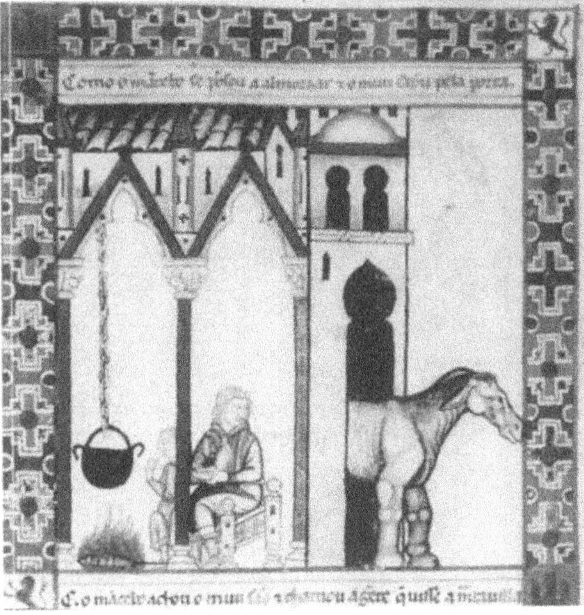

Plate 25: Cantiga F 88, panel 2. "How a good man had a mule which was swollen in all four legs."

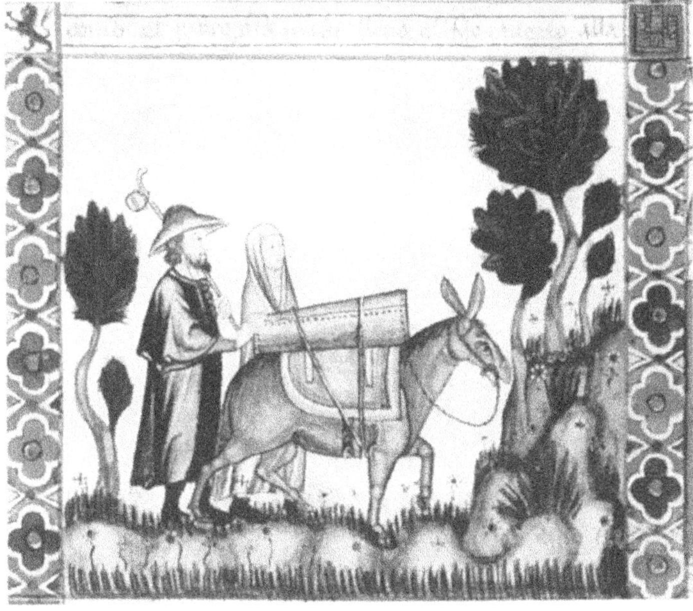

Plate 26: Cantiga 167, panel 3. How she was going with her son to the Lady of Salas.

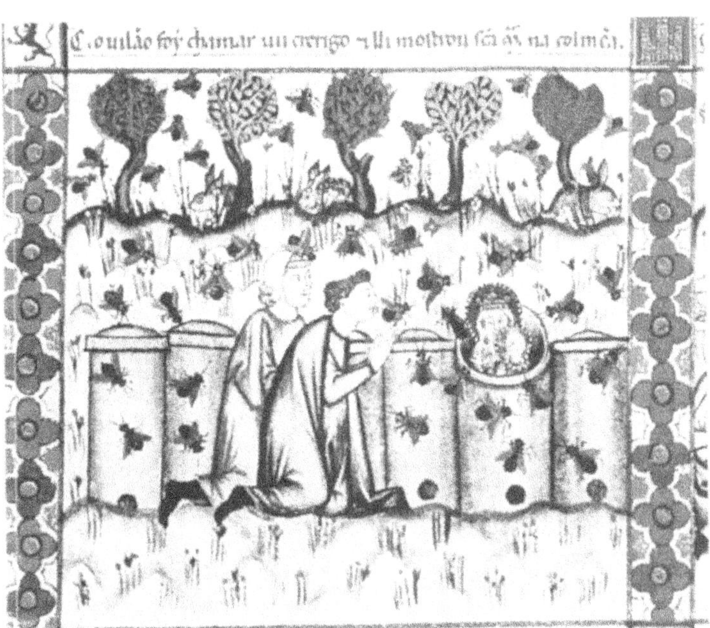

Plate 27: Cantiga 128, panel 3. "How the peasant went to call a priest and showed him Saint Mary in the beehive."

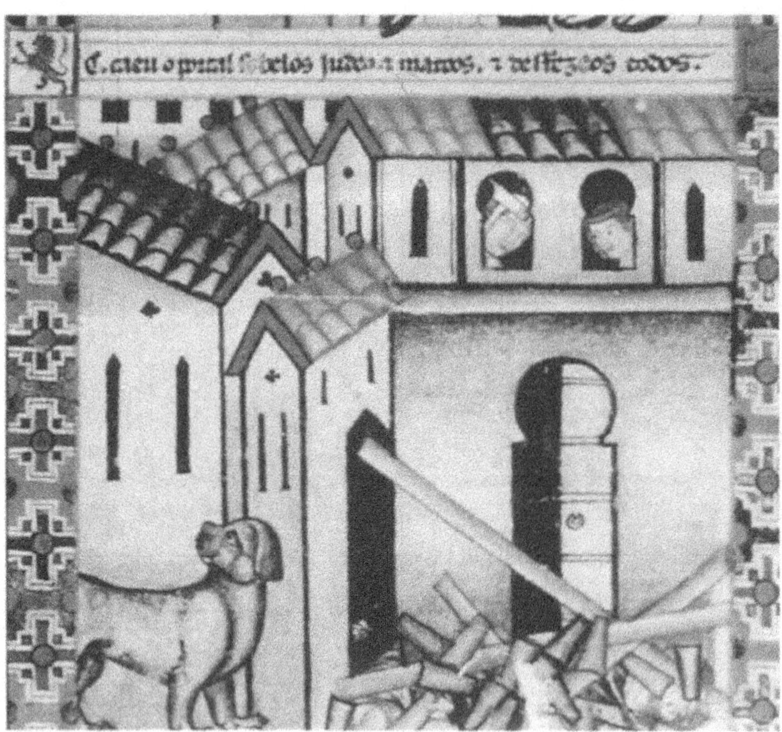

Plate 28: Cantiga F 4, panel 4. "How a huge dog passed by there . . . and attacked a good man."

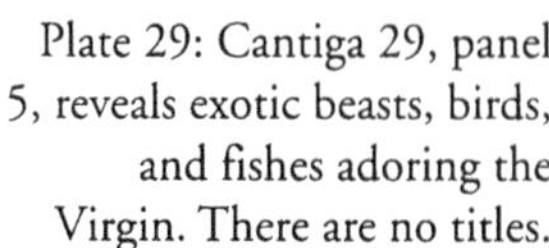

Plate 29: Cantiga 29, panel 5, reveals exotic beasts, birds, and fishes adoring the Virgin. There are no titles.

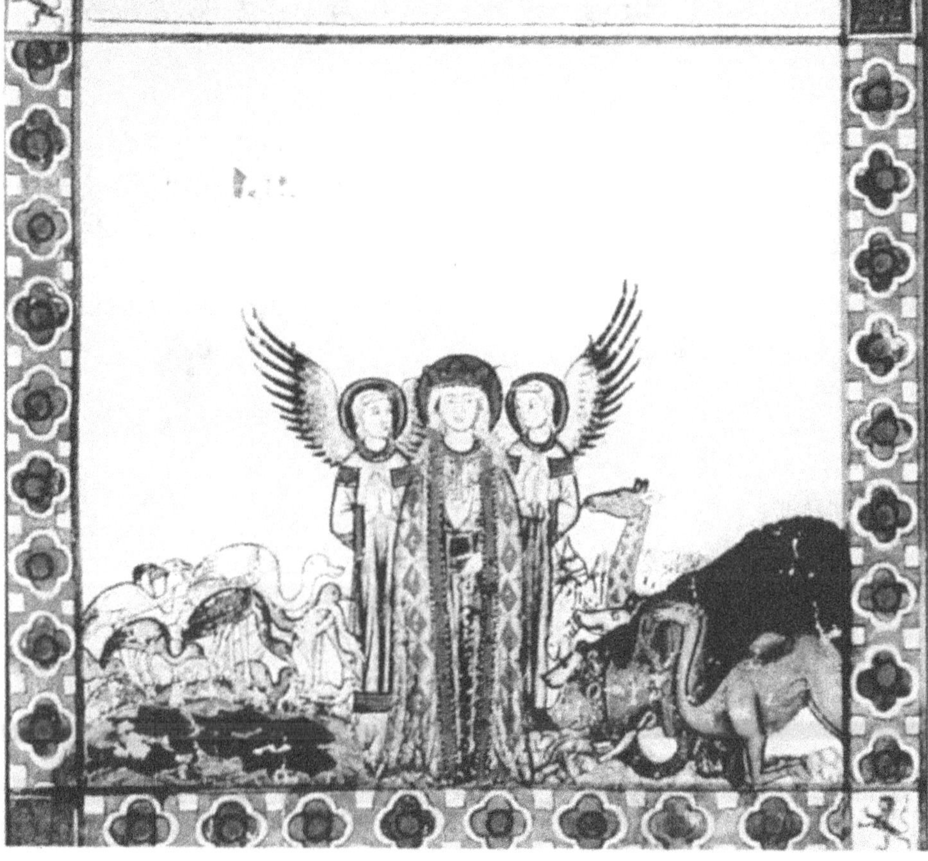

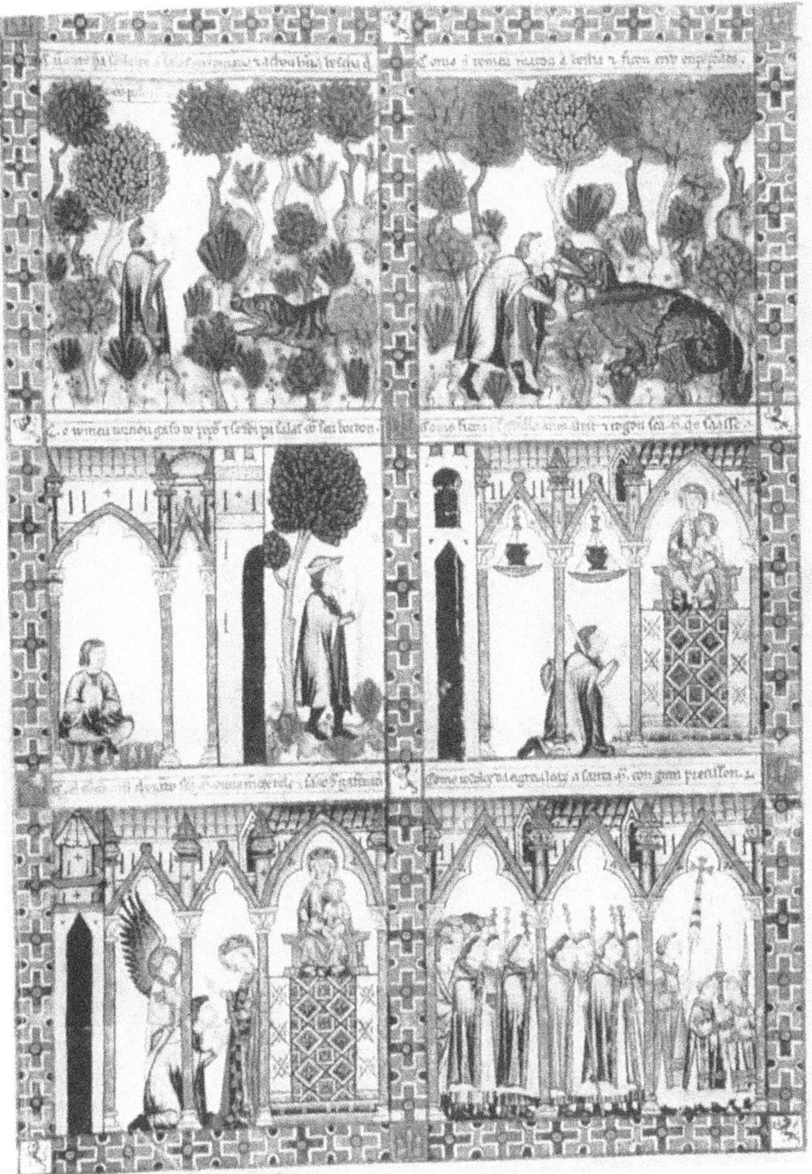

Plate 30: Cantiga 189. "How a man went out to Salas on a pilgrimage and met a dragon which came to kill him."

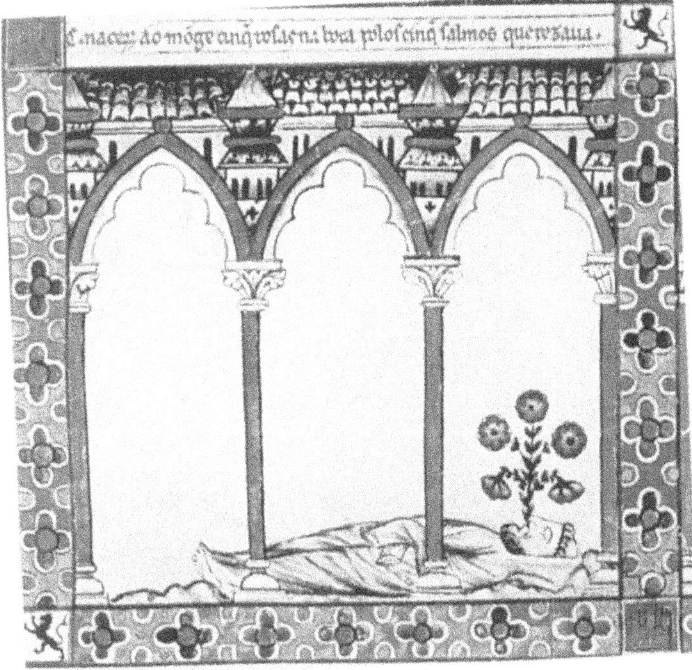

Plate 31: Cantiga 56, panel 5. "How five roses bloomed from the mouth of the monk because of five psalms he recited."

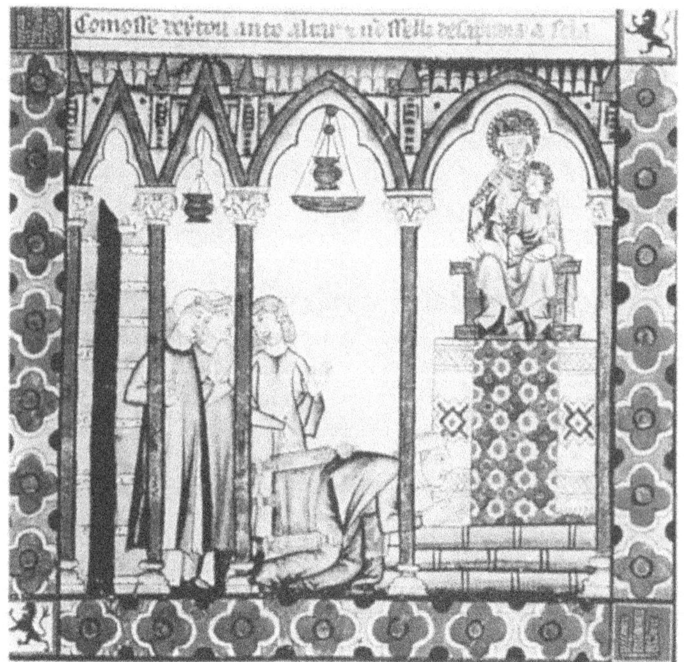

Plate 32: Cantiga 153, panel 5. "How the woman lay down before the altar and the chair did not let go of her."

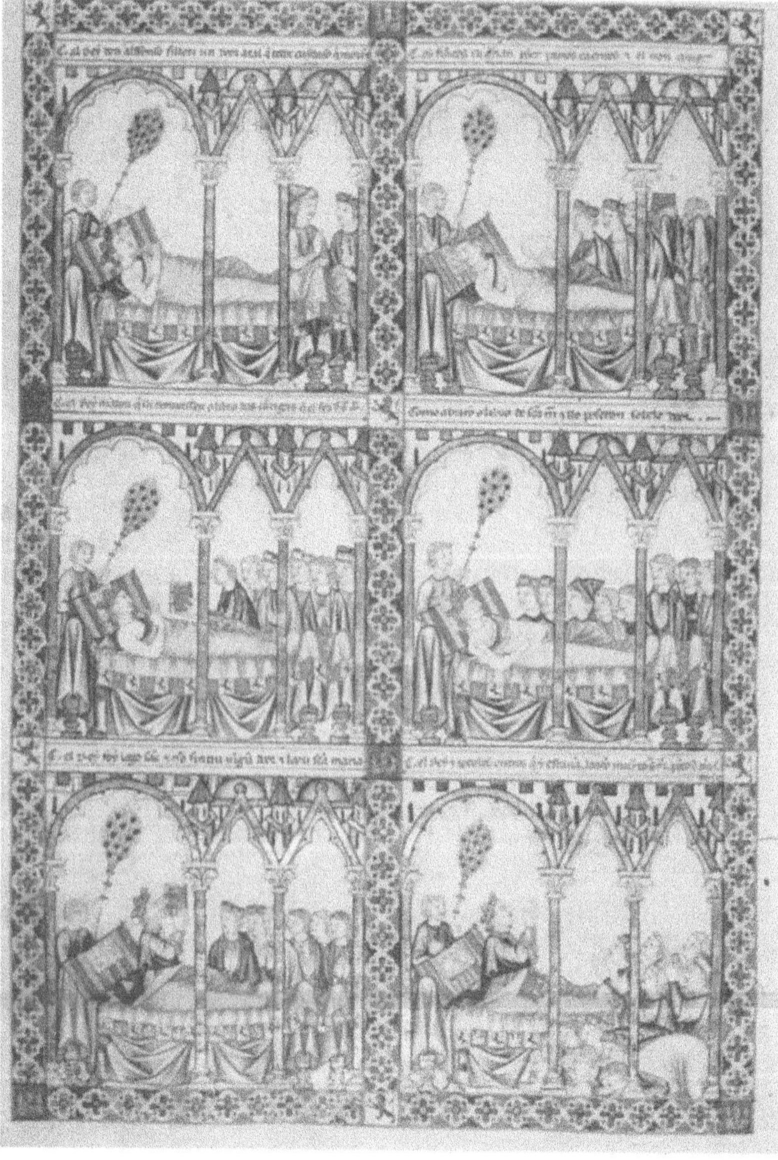

Plate 33: Cantiga F 95. "How King Alfonso fell ill in Vitoria . . ."

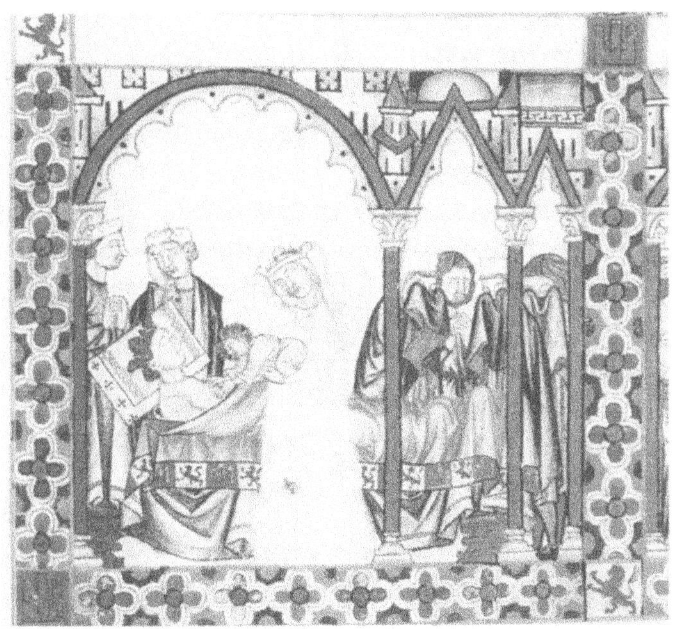

Plate 34: Cantiga F 71, panel 5. "How Saint Mary cured King Alfonso in Valladolid who was judged to be dying."

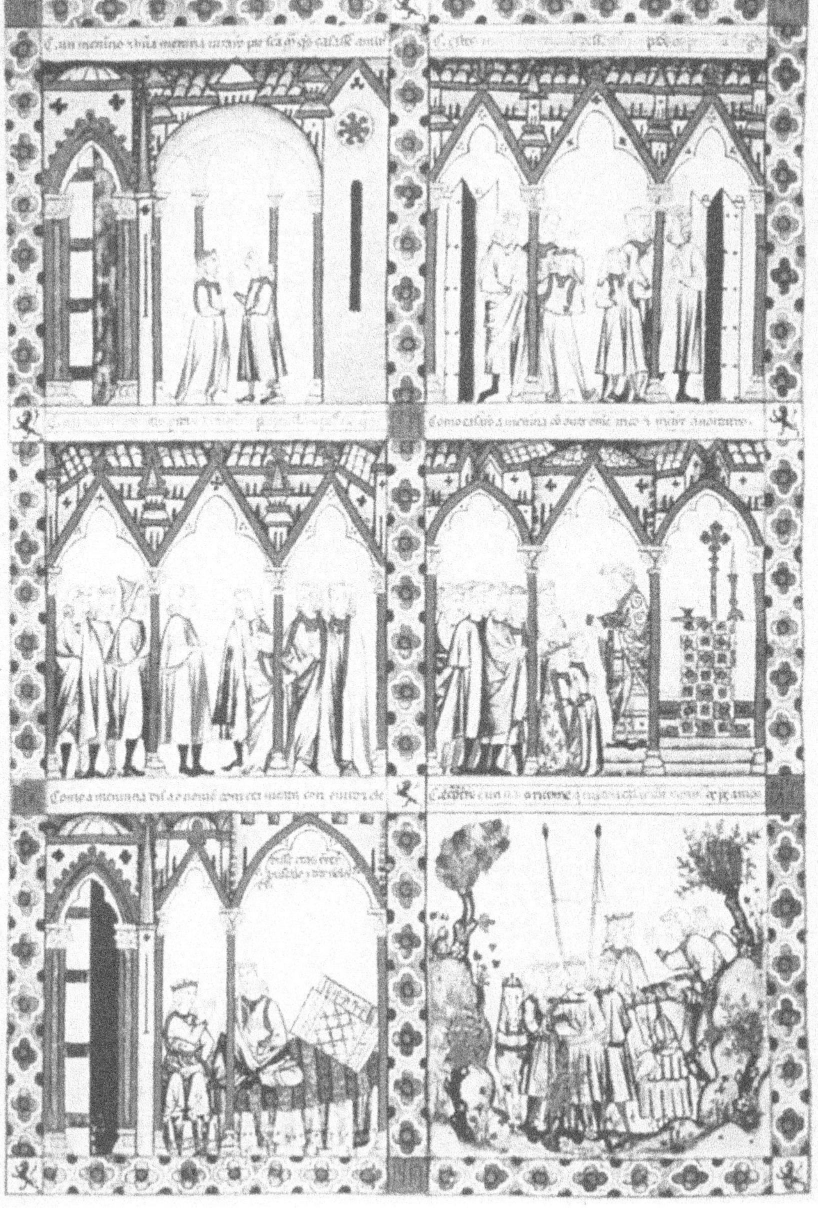

Plate 35: Cantiga 135A. "This is how Saint Mary confirmed the marriage of a boy and a girl.

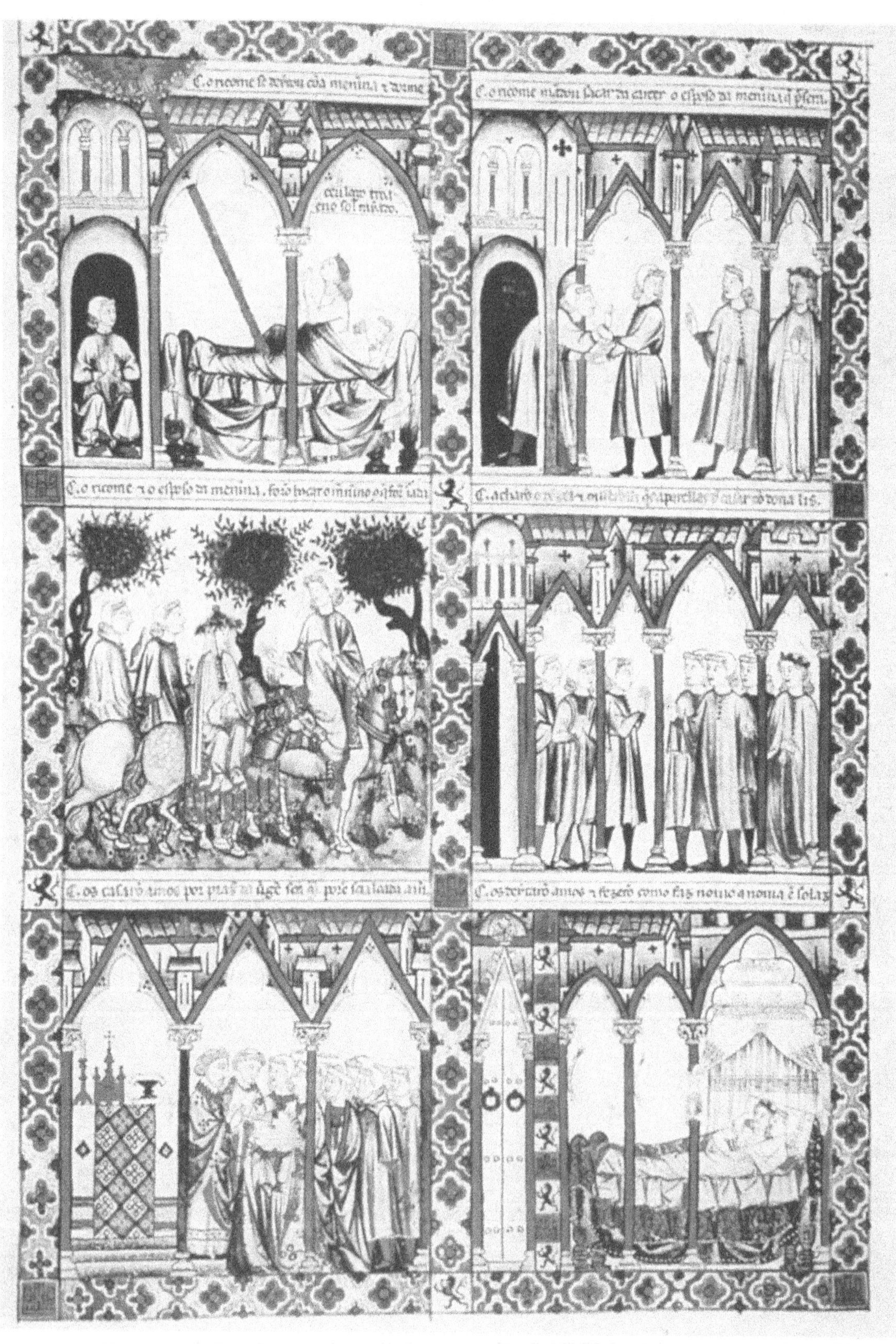

Plate 36: Cantiga 135B. There is no title for this page, which treats further adventures of the two young lovers.

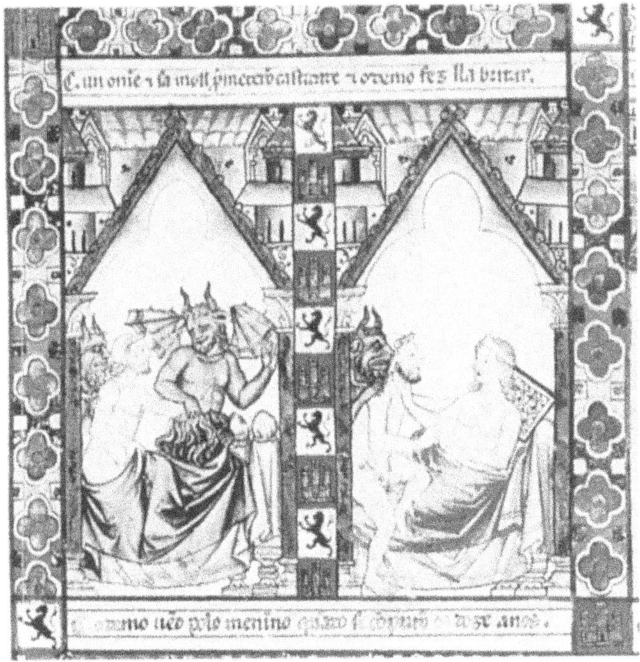

Plate 37: Cantiga 115A, panel 1. "How a man and his wife vowed chastity and how the devil made them break it."

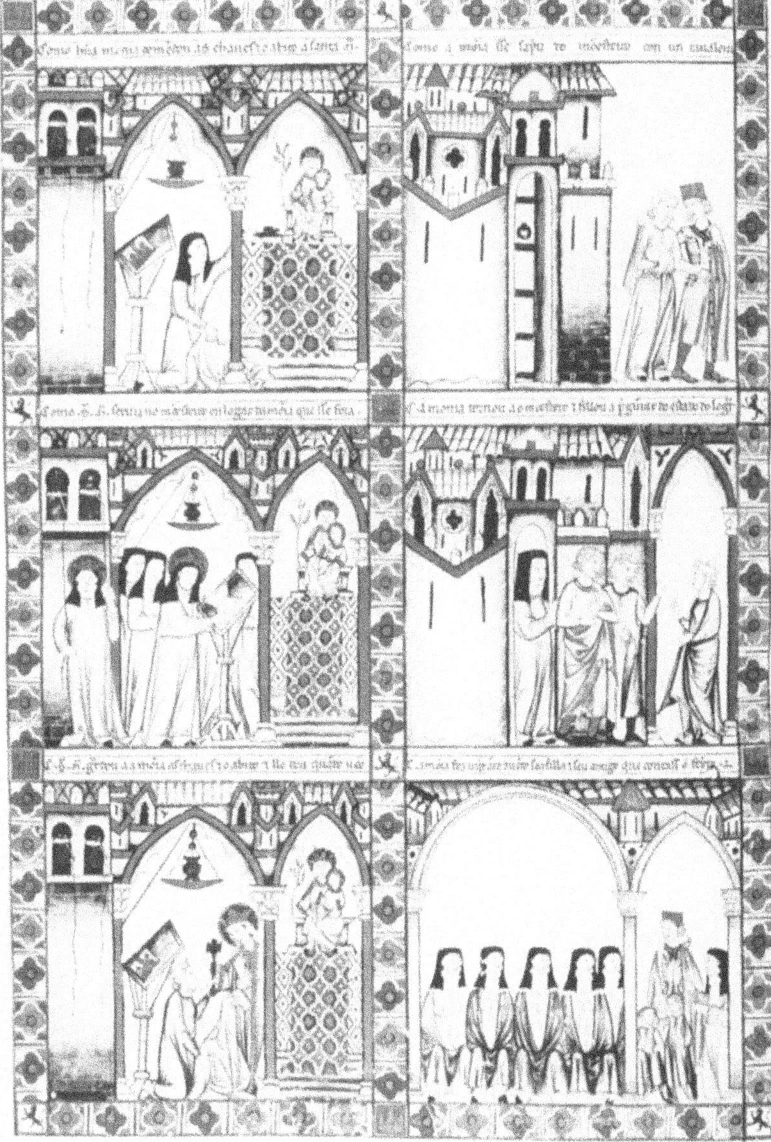

Plate 38: Cantiga 94. "How Saint Mary served in place of the nun who left the convent."

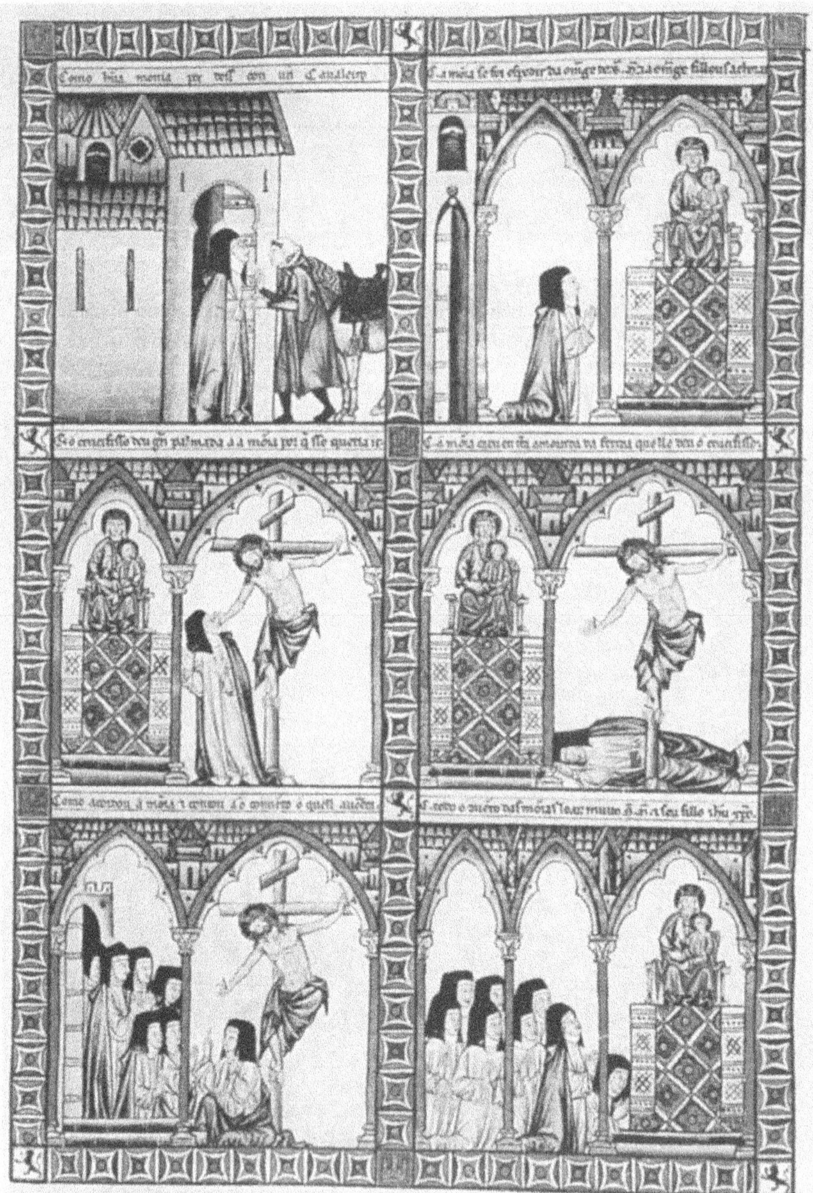

Plate 39: Cantiga 59. "This is how the crucifix for the honor of His Mother slapped the nun who had promised to go away with her lover."

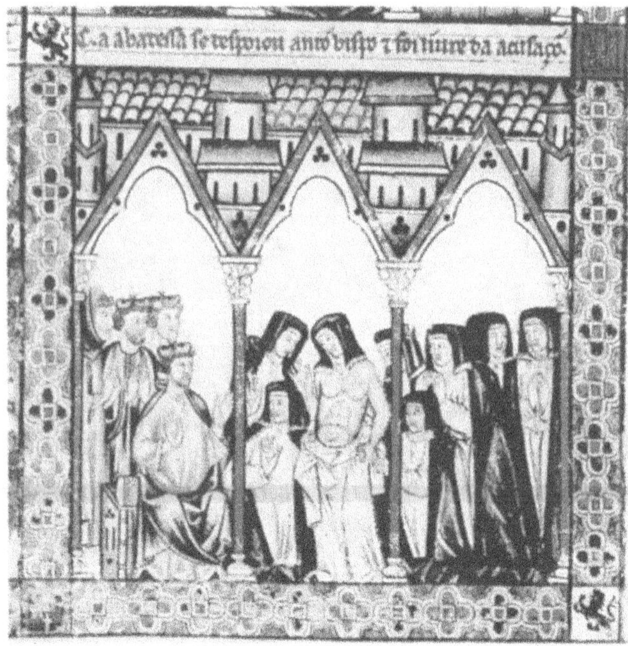

Plate 40: Cantiga 7, panel 6. "How the abbess disrobed before the bishop and was cleared of the accusation."

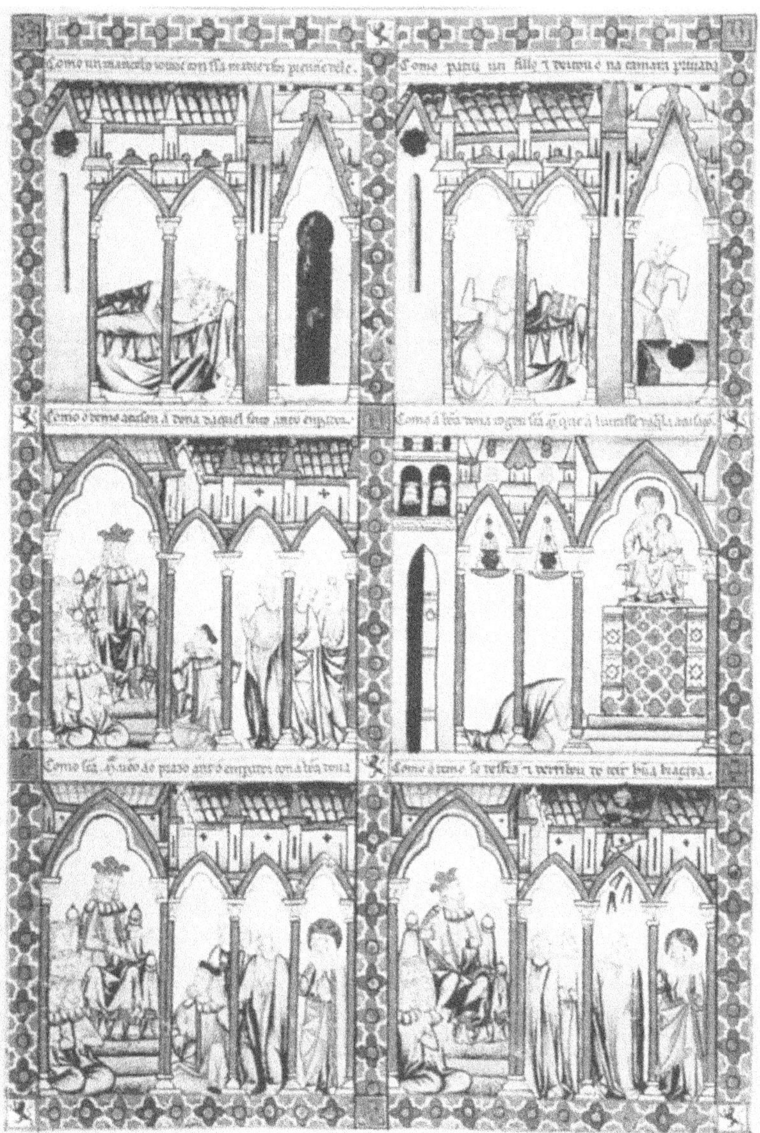

Plate 41: Cantiga 17, panel 1. "This is how Saint Mary saved from death the honorable lady of Rome whom the devil accused in order to have her burned."

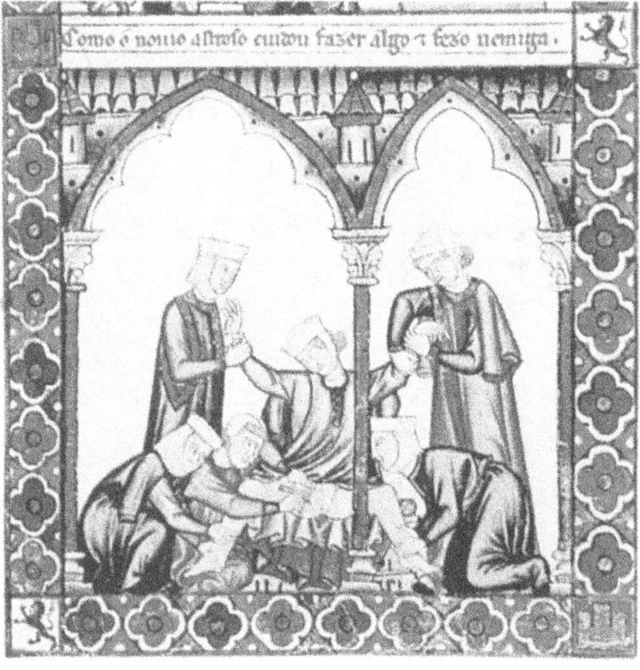

Plate 42: Cantiga 105A, panel 5. "How the wicked bridegroom planned to do something and committed a shameful deed."

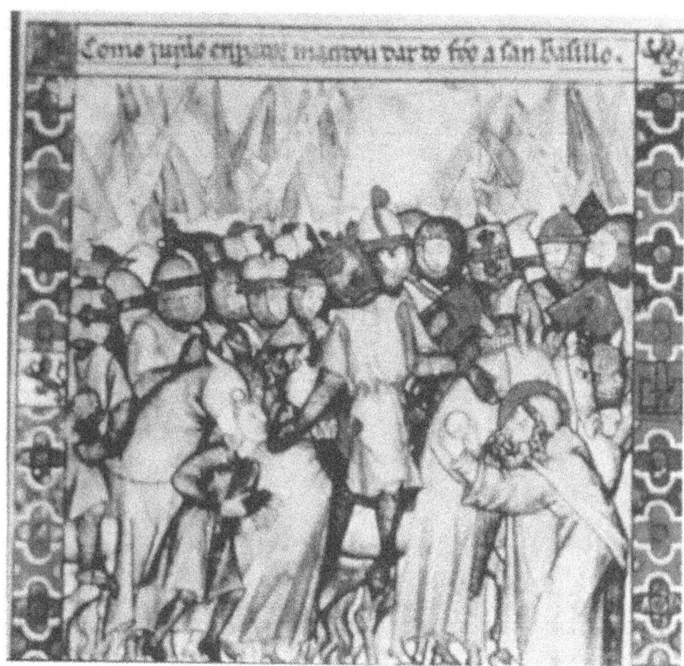

Plate 43: Cantiga 5A, panel 1. "How Emperor Julian ordered hay given to Saint Basil."

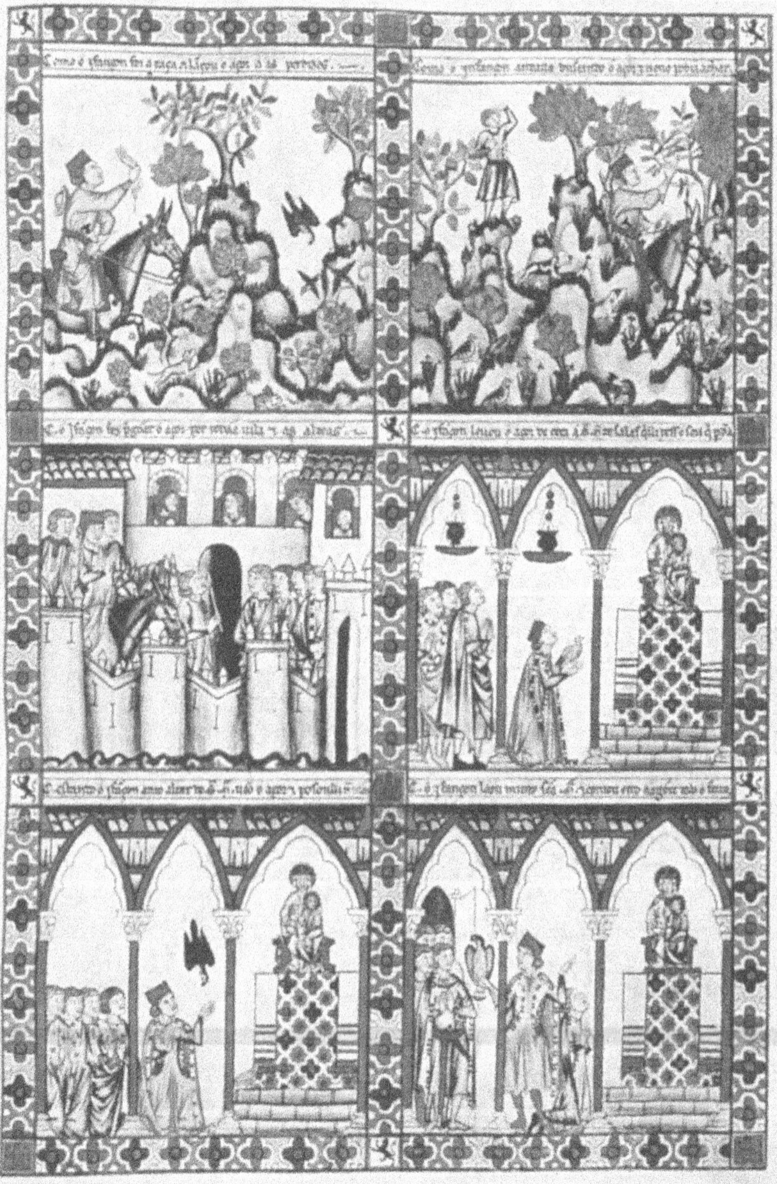

Plate 44: Cantiga 44. "This is how the gentleman lost his goshawk . . ."

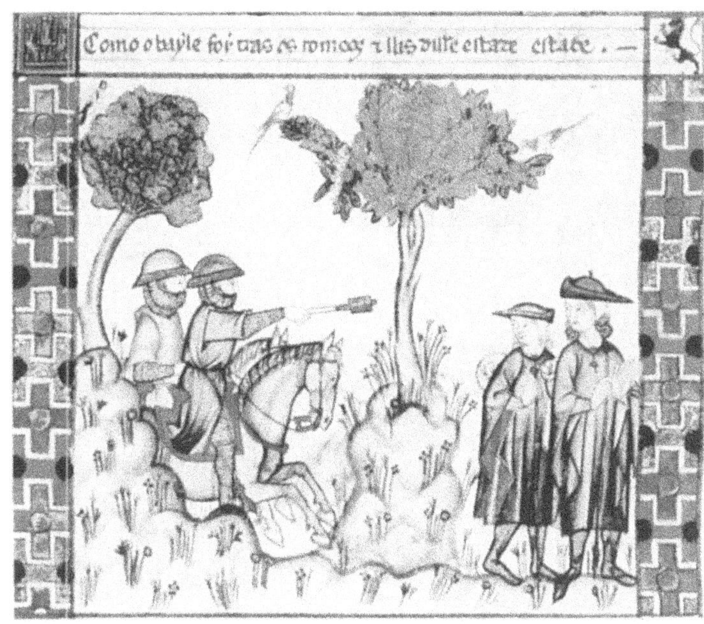

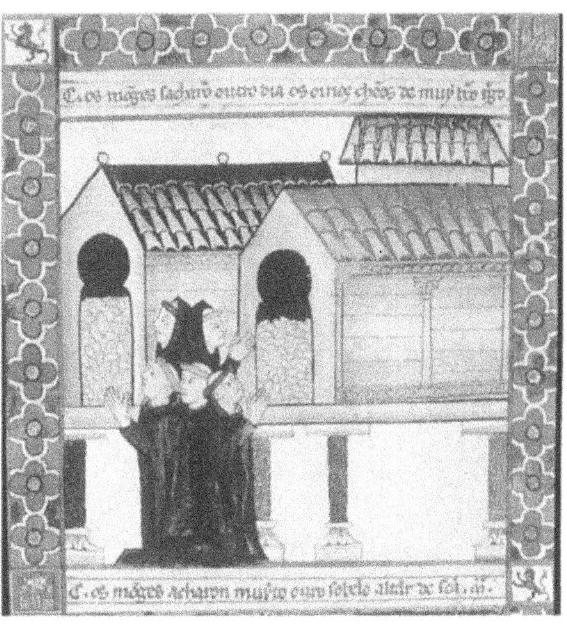

Plate 45: Cantiga 175A, panel 4. "How the magistrate went after the pilgrims and told them to halt."

Plate 46: Cantiga 186, panel 2. "How the next day the monks found the storage bins filled with very good wheat."

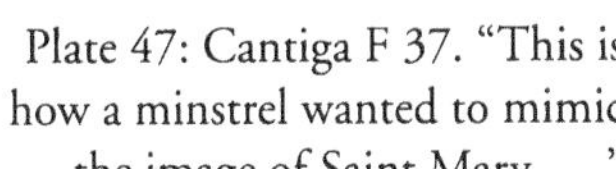

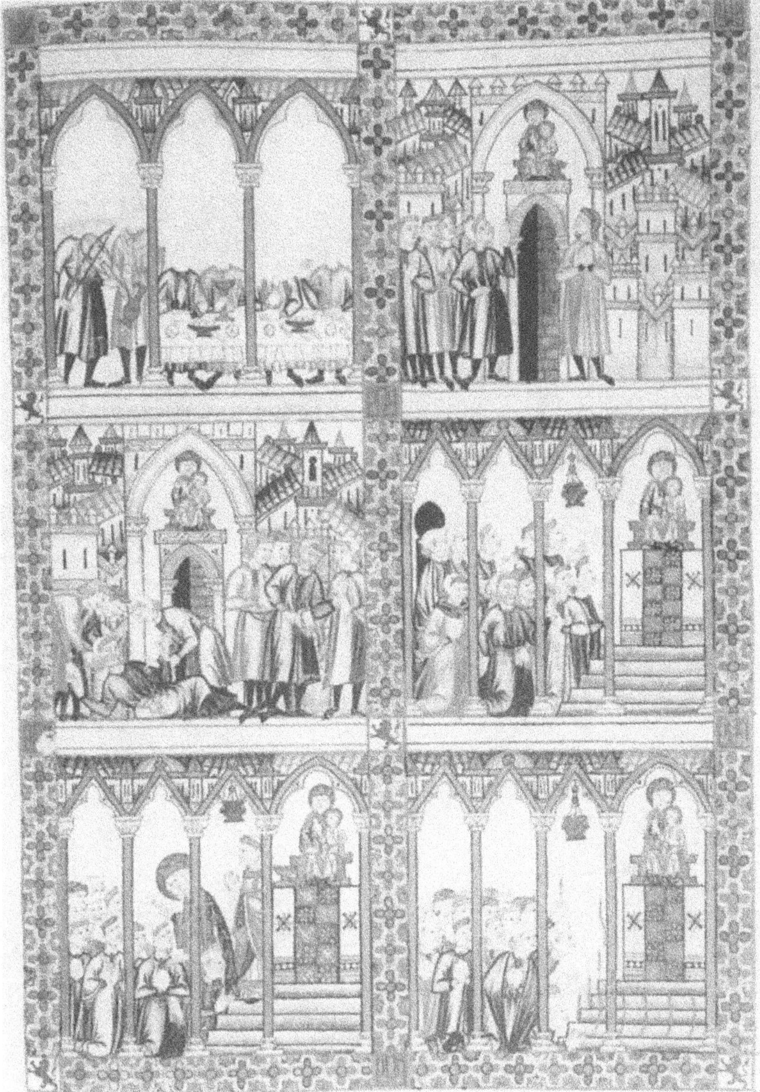

Plate 47: Cantiga F 37. "This is how a minstrel wanted to mimic the image of Saint Mary . . ."

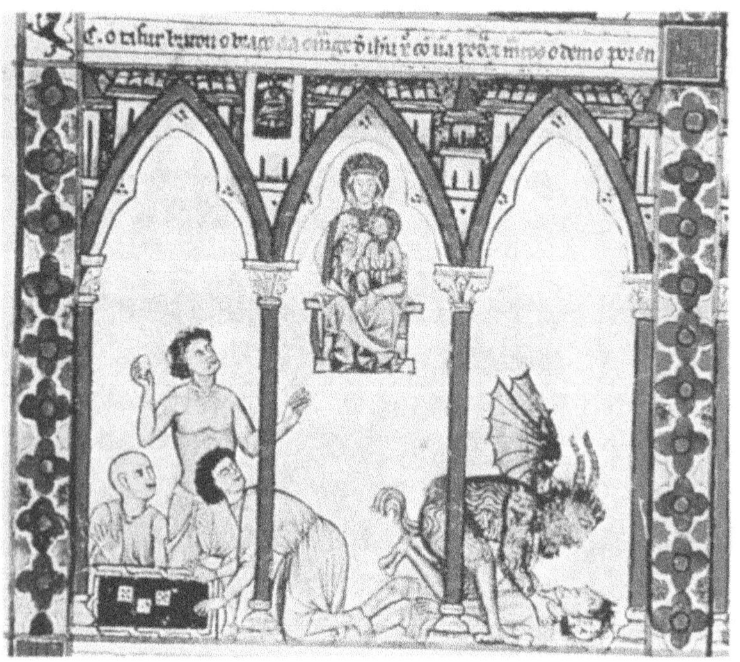

Plate 48: Cantiga 38, panel 3. "How the rogue struck the arm of the image of Jesus Christ with a stone and the devil killed him."

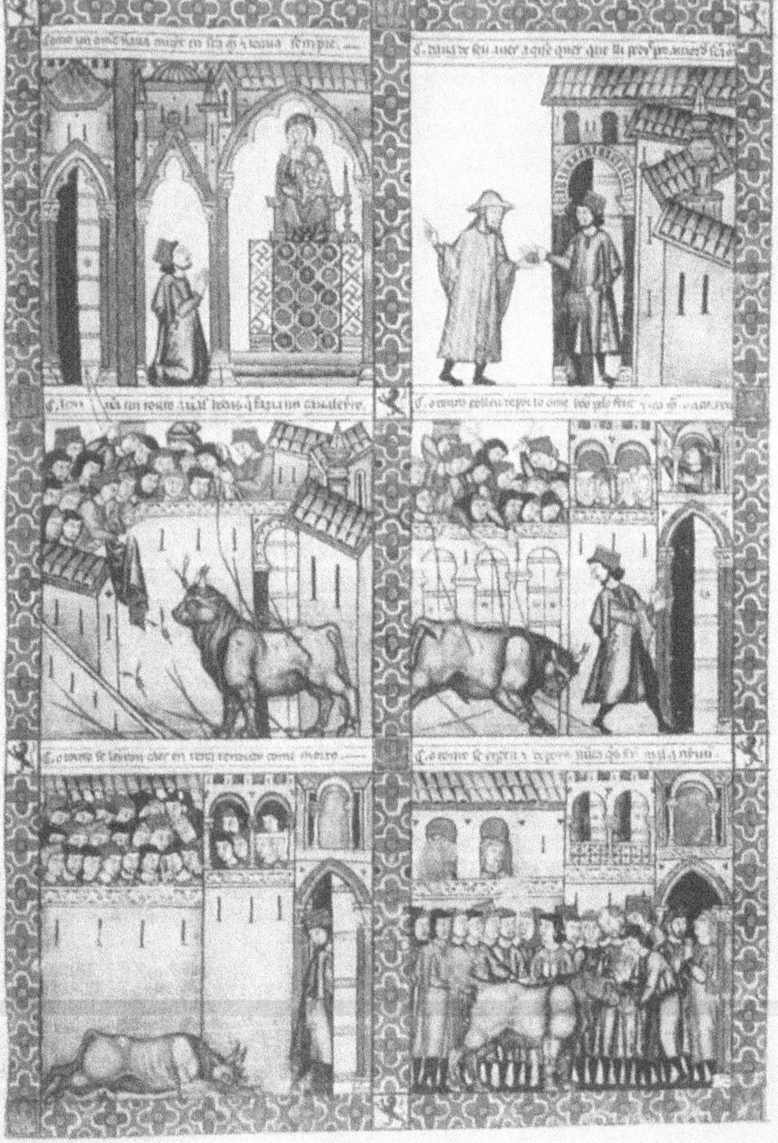

Plate 49: Cantiga 144. "This is how Saint Mary saved a good man in Plasencia from a bull which charged him to kill him."

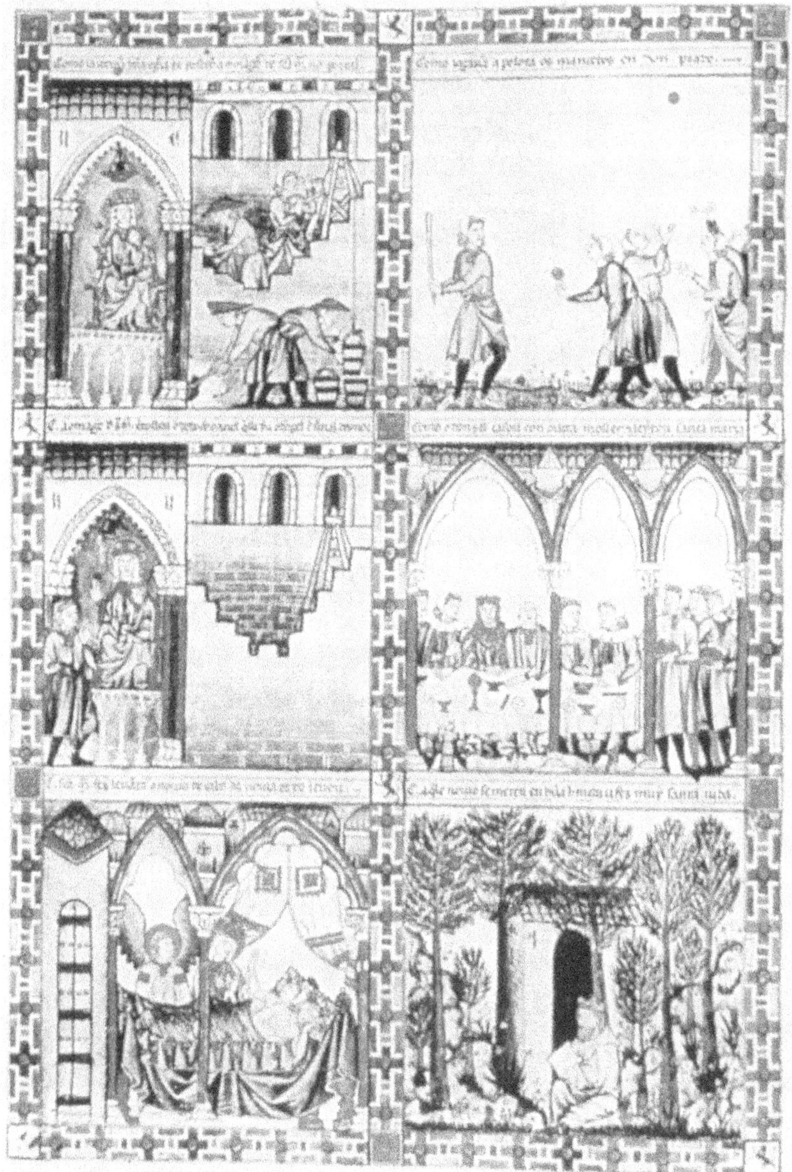

Plate 50: Cantiga 42. "This is about how the postulant put the ring on the finger of the image of Saint Mary and the image encircled it with its finger."

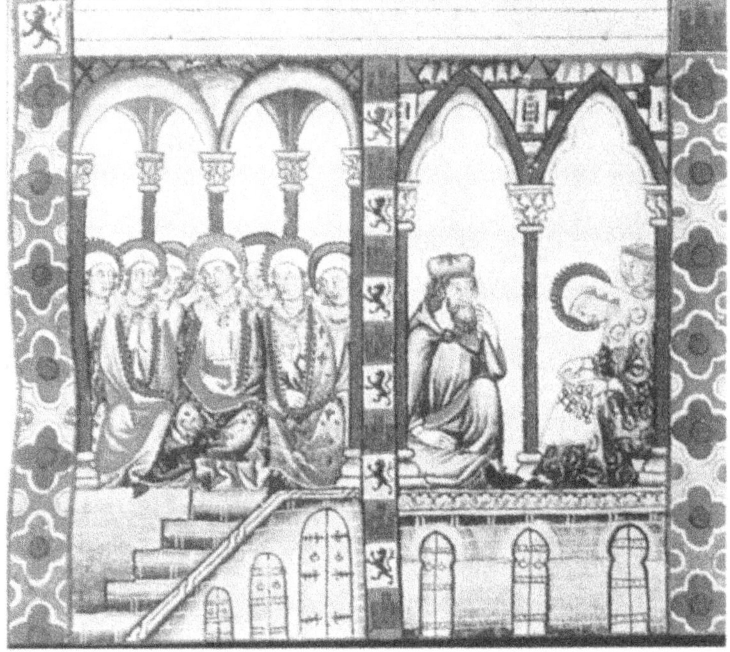

Plate 51: Cantiga 90, panel 3. What seems to be a stage for dramatization appears. No titles exist for this page.

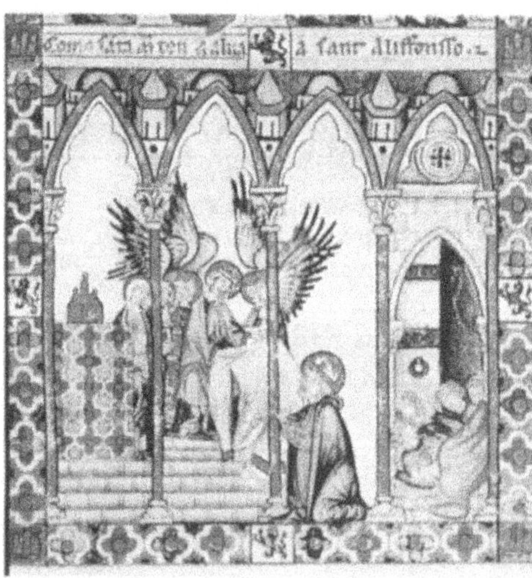

Plate 52: Cantiga 2, panel 5. "How Saint Mary gave the alb to Saint Ildefonso."

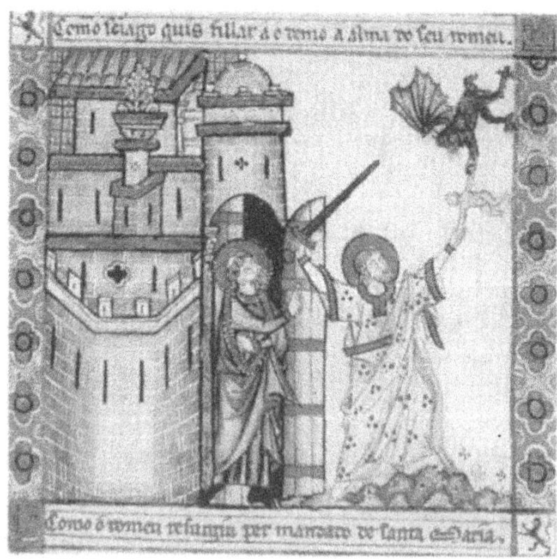

Plate 53: Cantiga 26, panel 4. "How Saint James wished to take the soul of his pilgrim from a devil."

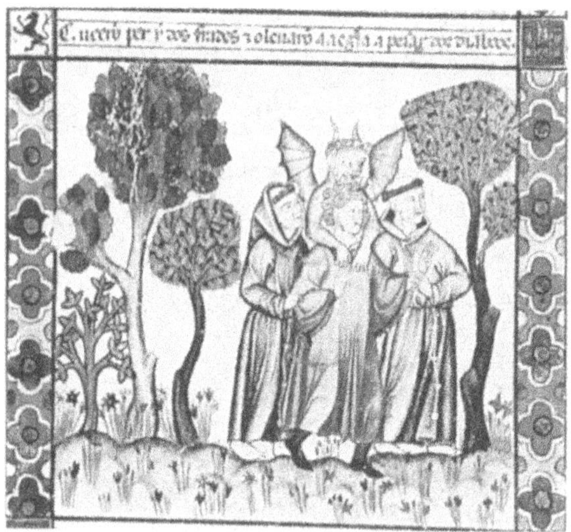

Plate 54: Cantiga 109, panel 3. "How two friars came by there and took him to the church in spite of the devil."

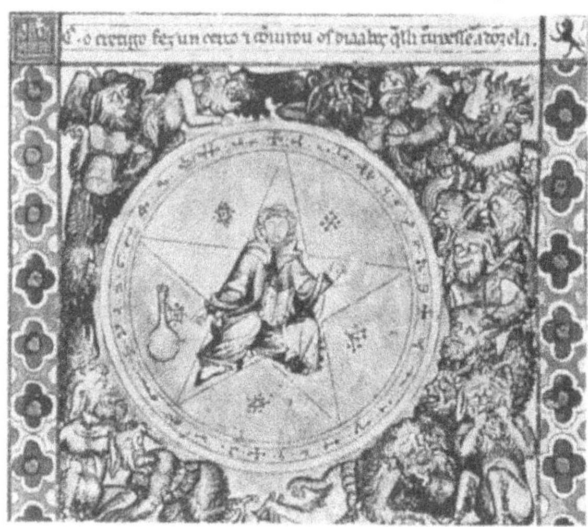

Plate 55: Cantiga 125A, panel 4. "How the priest made a circle and conjured the devils so that they might bring the damsel to him."

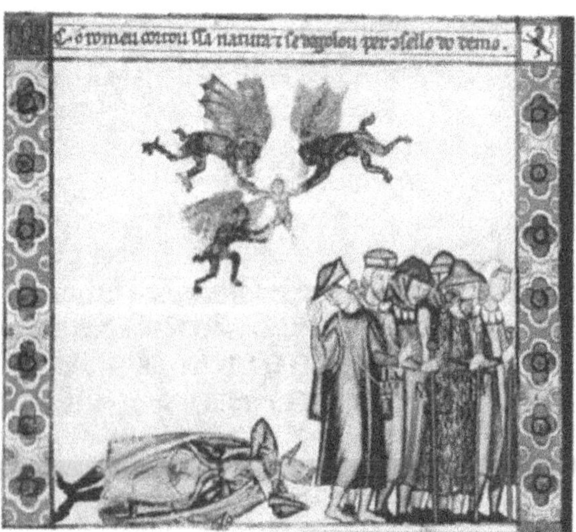

Plate 56: Cantiga 26, panel 3. "How the pilgrim cut off his private parts and slit his throat on the advice of the devil."

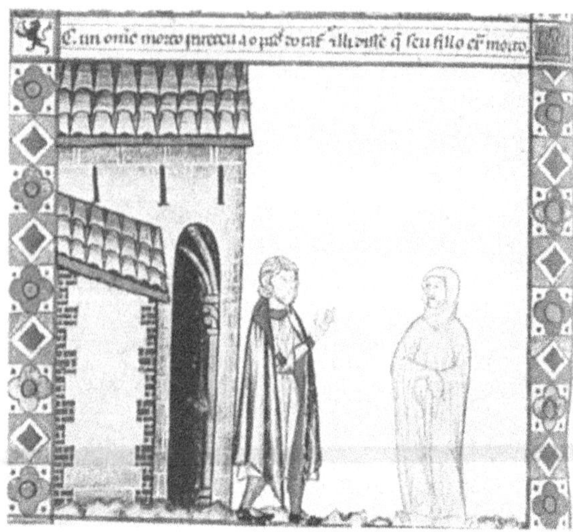

Plate 57: Cantiga 72, panel 4. "How a dead man appeared to the gambler's father to tell him his son was dead."

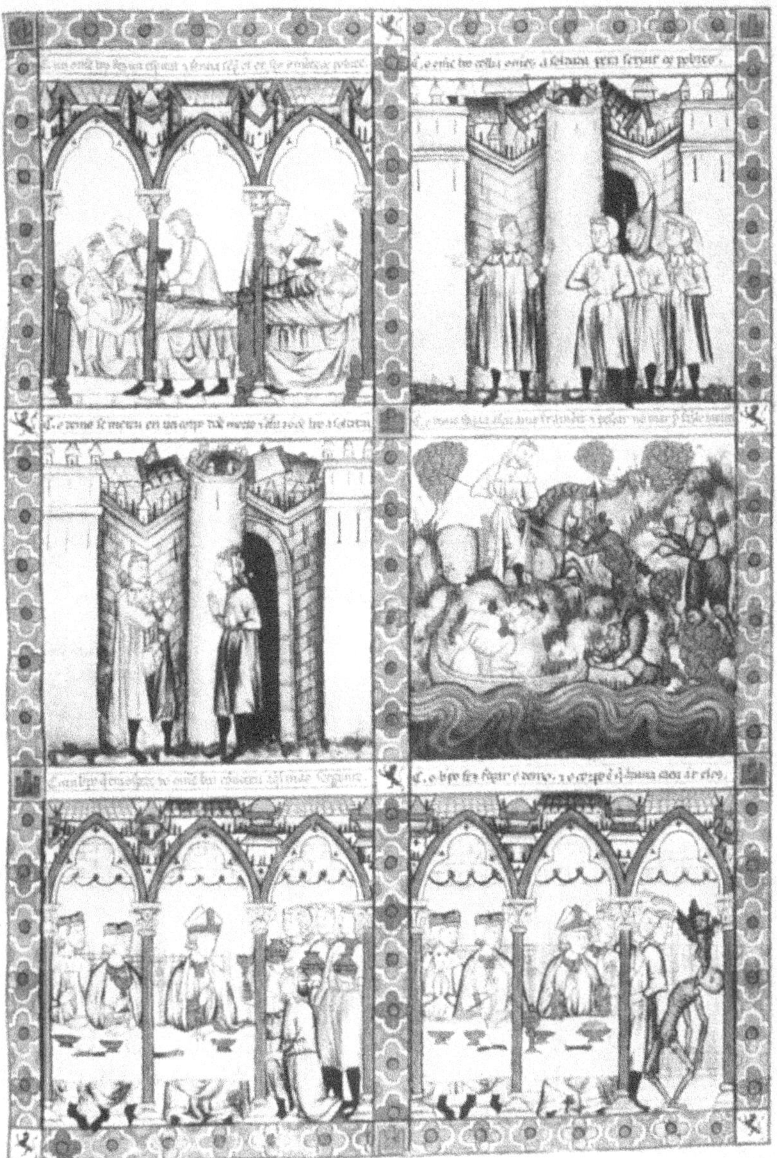

Plate 58: Cantiga 67. "This is how Saint Mary made the good man realize he had with him a demon for a servant and that he wanted to kill him, but for the prayer he said."

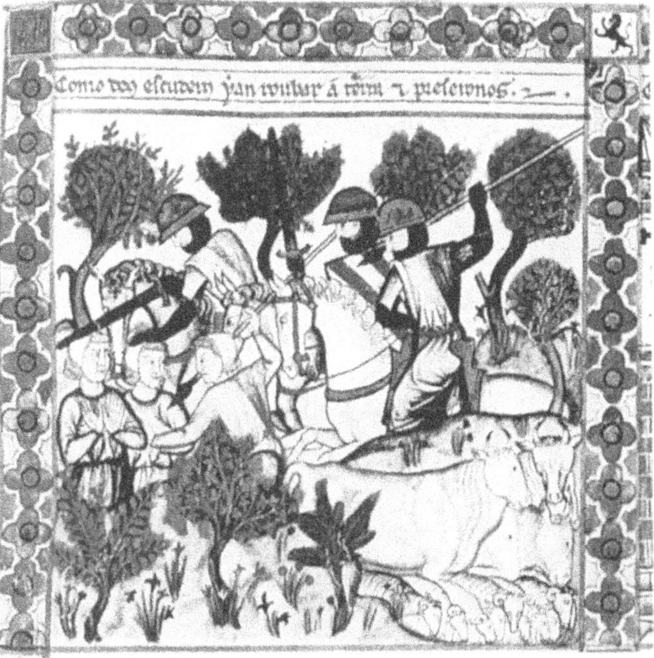

Plate 59: Cantiga 106, panel 1. "How two squires went out to rob the land and they captured them."

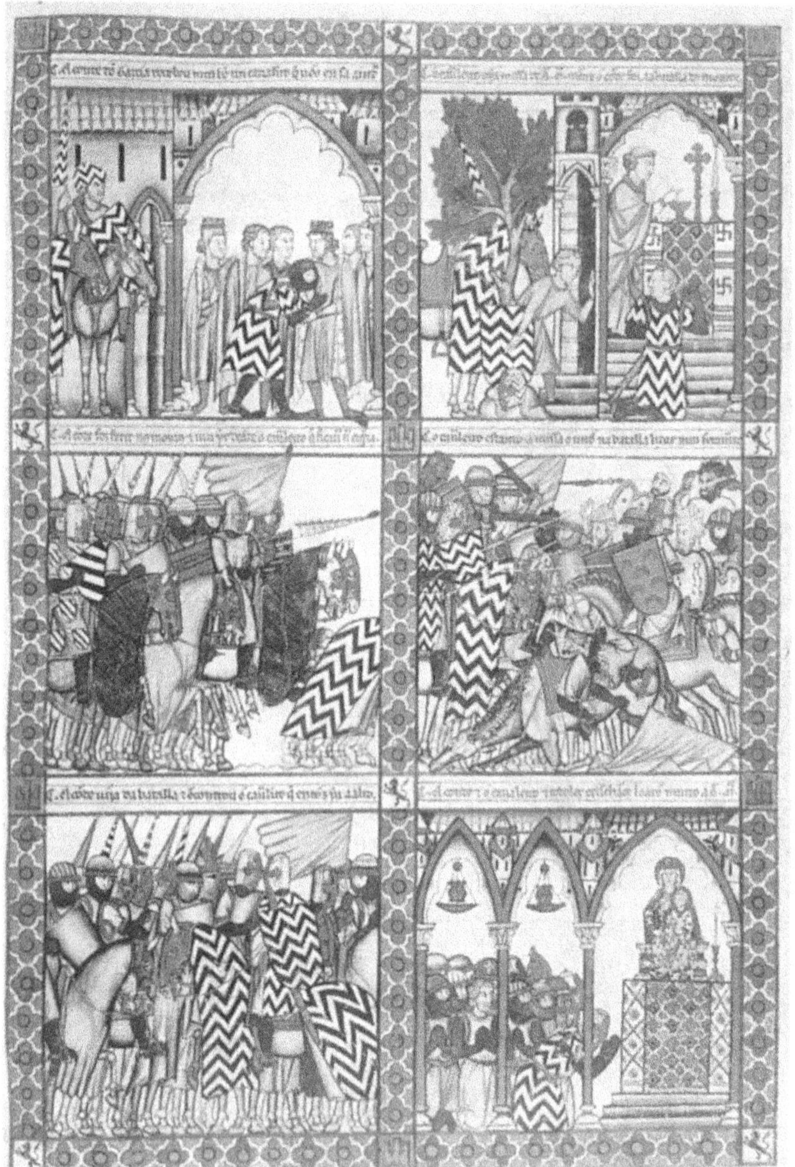

Plate 60: Cantiga 63. "This is how Saint Mary saved a knight from dishonor who ought to have been in battle . . ."

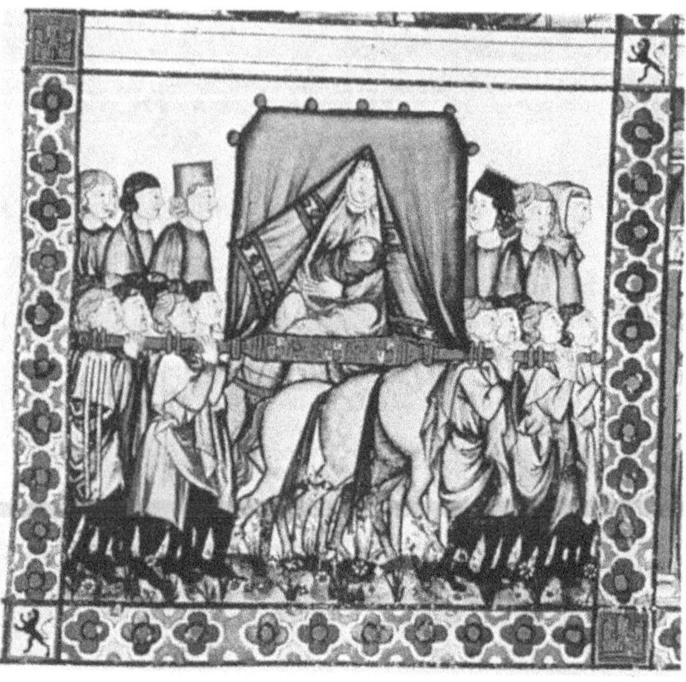

Plate 61: Cantiga 122, panel 5. Shows Queen Beatriz, Alfonso's mother, in a litter. There are no titles.

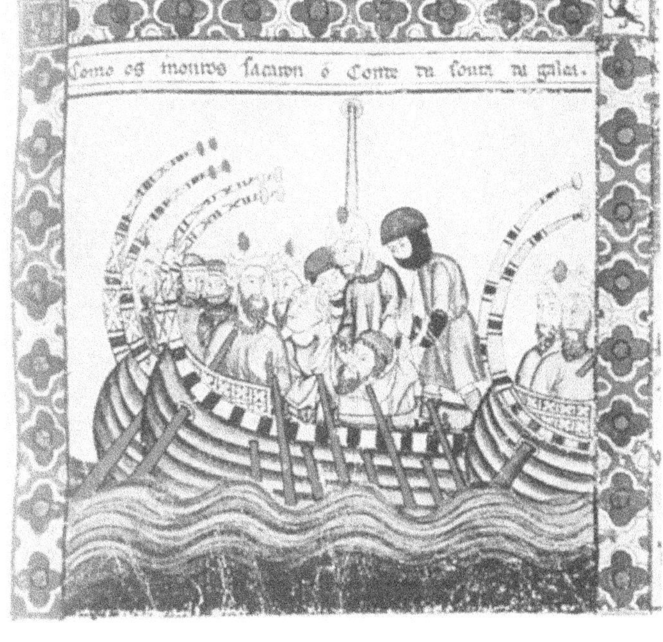

Plate 62: Cantiga 95B, panel 1. "How the Moors took the count out of the hold of the galley."

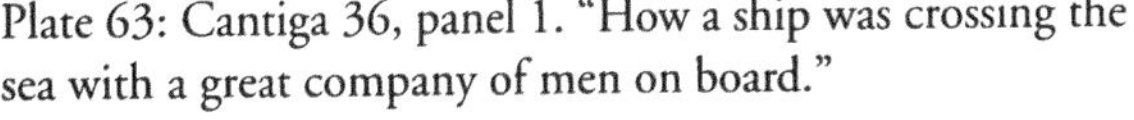

Plate 63: Cantiga 36, panel 1. "How a ship was crossing the sea with a great company of men on board."

Plate 64: Cantiga F 22, panel 4. "How Saint Mary restored to John Damascene the hand which had been cut off."

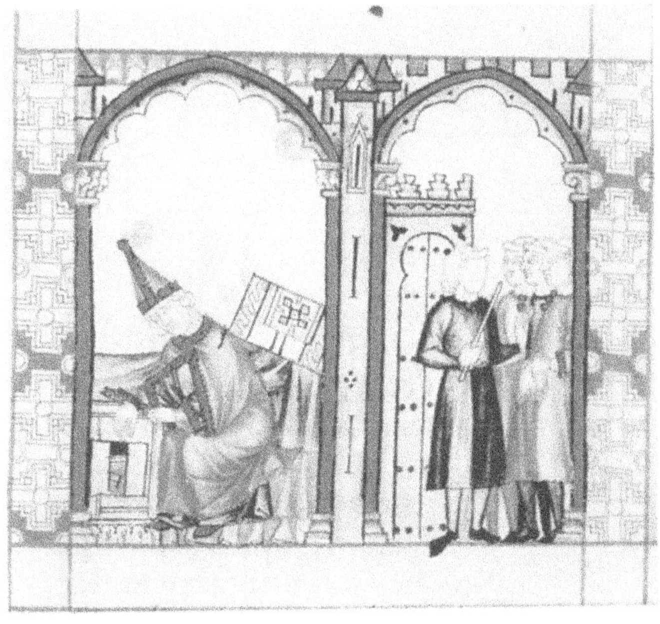

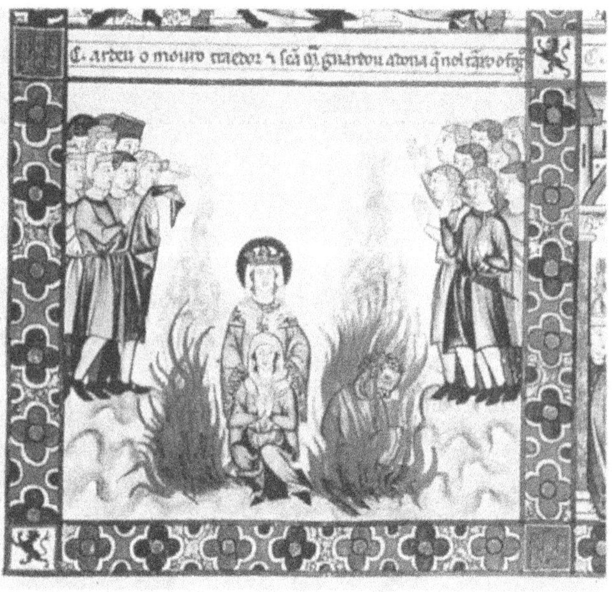

Plate 65: Cantiga 185, panel 6. "How the Moorish traitor burned and Saint Mary protected the lady so that the fire did not touch her."

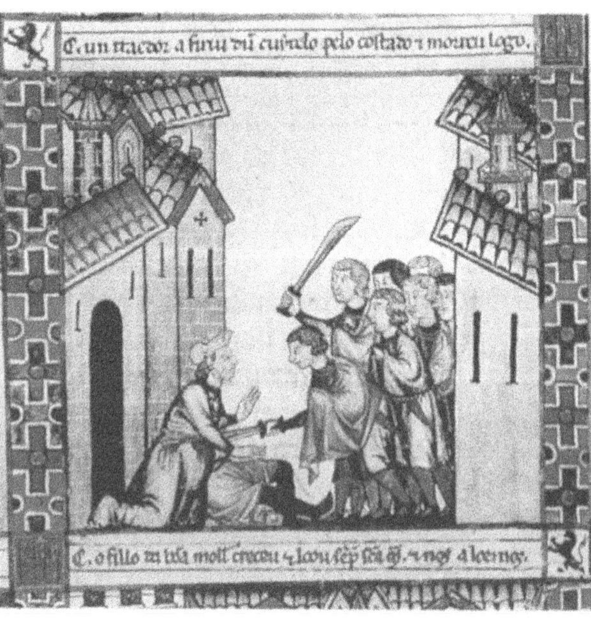

Plate 66: Cantiga 184, panel 4. "How a traitor struck her in the side with a knife and she died immediately."

Plate 67: Cantiga 107. "This is how Saint Mary saved from death a Jewess whom they cast down from a cliff in Segovia."

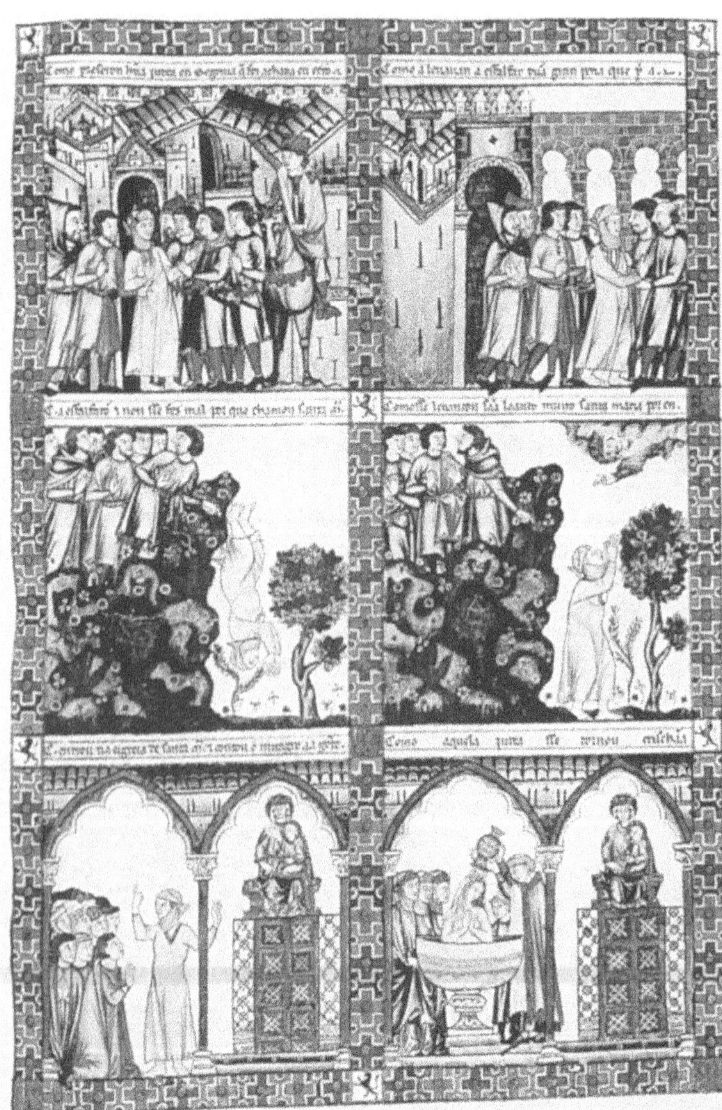

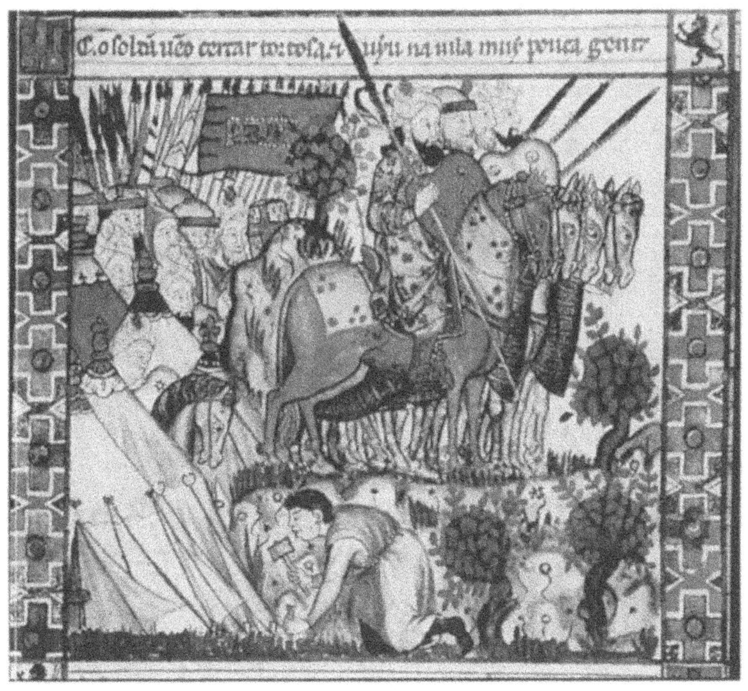

Plate 68: Cantiga 165A, panel 3. "How the sultan came to lay siege to Tartus and saw few people in the city."

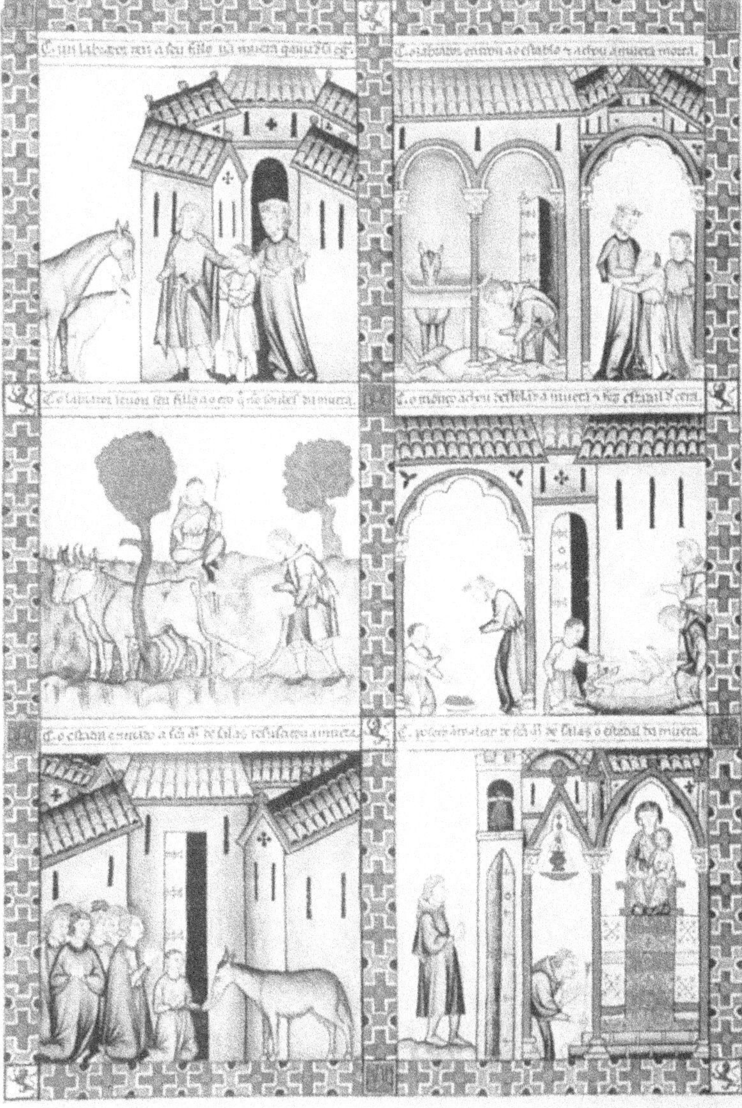

Plate 69: Cantiga 178. "How a farmer gave his son a little she-mule he had from his mare."

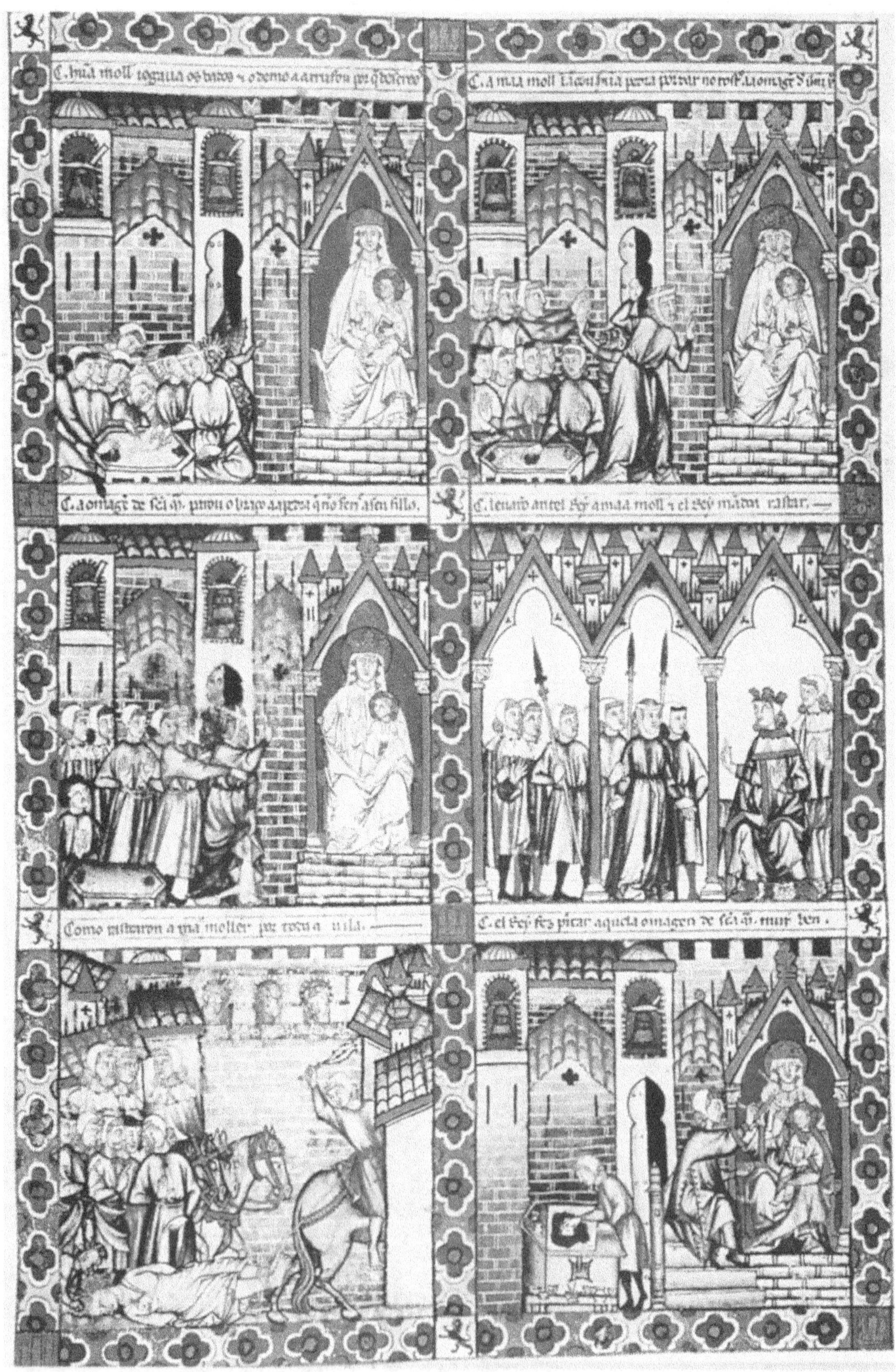

Plate 70: Cantiga 136. "Saint Mary displayed this miracle in the land of Apulia in a city called Foggia."

24
Travel

Land Travel

There are no surprises as concern travel on land. Horses of various sorts appear frequently: knights in battle rode heavy war horses, known in France as *destriers*. In 63, 3 and 4 (pl. 60) and in 129, 1 and 2, they are depicted wearing heavy leather body armor and protective head armor. Bridles and stirrups are also visible.

Palfreys were ridden by male and female civilians, as well as by knights and clergy for travel, as in 121, 2. In 175A, 4 (pl. 45), constabularies ride another variety of equine after a youth accused of theft; in 107 (pl. 67) a judge rides to take care of a legal matter; in 57, 1 and 171, 2, pilgrims travel on horseback to Montserrat; in 98, 1, appears a lady riding sidesaddle on a palfrey, and in 135B, 3 (pl. 36), a lady named Alys also rides sidesaddle and holds a small spaniel in her arms. In 59, 1 (pl. 39), a gentleman who comes to take a nun from her convent brings a palfrey for her to ride.

Hunters rode lighter mounts than the heavy war horses, palfreys, and mules: in 44 (pl. 44) a hunter rides a lighter horse as he launches a small raptor at partridges. In 67, 4 (pl. 58), a hunter rides a horse as he spears a bear. Spaniards brought to the New World both war horses and lighter breeds, and as we know from the varieties captured and bred by Indians, some resemble horses pictured in the miniatures, notably the gray mottled Appaloosa-type horses, bred by the Nez Percé Indians of our Southwest; compare 67, 4 (pl. 60).

Hunters and fowlers sometimes rode mules. Alfonso himself and his huntsmen in 142, 1, 3, and 5 (pl. 4), ride mules as the king looses a falcon at a heron. In 57, 4 and 5 and in 132, 2, monks also ride mules.

People of consequence, especially women, sometimes rode in litters, which could be carried by horses, mules, or human litter bearers: in 122, 5 (pl. 61), Queen Beatriz, Alfonso's mother, rides in a covered litter on the way to Burgos, and in 91, 2, sick people are carried in a litter. In 15B, 4 and 5 and in 91, 2, we see low carts used to convey sick people to hospitals; in 31, 5 (pl. 15), a laborer in a wain with large wheels and spiked metal tires drawn by bullocks hauls stone.

People who could not afford to use horses rode asses: an ass is shown as a beast of burden, for example, in 43, 5 and in 167, 3 (pl. 26), where the coffin containing the corpse of a child is strapped to the back of an ass; in 168, 3, a sick child is carried on the back of an ass. The poor, as well as pilgrims, who traveled for the glory of God, went on foot, as in 166, 4.

Travelers mounted and on foot faced many dangers, ranging from bad weather to attacks by brigands, robber nobles, and wild beasts. In 29, 4, to the left of the panel, a lion accosts a pilgrim while, on the right hand, robbers armed with hooks attack him. And in spite of laws and the obligations of the church and nobility to repair and protect the roads, many roads were difficult to travel. Regardless of dangers and discomforts, people traveled more widely than might be expected. For other examples of travel on land, see the appendix.

Travel by Water

The miniatures of the *Cantigas* provide very detailed illustrations of a wide variety of ships, dinghies, lifeboats, rowboats, and other small craft. Muslim war galleys can be seen in 95A, 4, 5, and 6 and in 95B, 1 (pl. 62), 2, and 4. They were large and could be propelled by oars or by the use of sails, or both. The two banks of oars are seen clearly, as are the large sails. The prows are ornate. Many passenger ships are also portrayed, for example in 33, 1 and 2 and 36, 1 (pl. 63). Merchant ships are numerous, as seen in 172, 1, 2, and 3. In 15B, 1, 2, and 3, a dinghy appears, in which sailors carry the empress of Rome to a rock, on which they maroon her. Rowboats are exemplified in 25B, 3 and 35B, 4. Fishermen in a small craft seine for fish in 183, 3, 5, and 6, as also in 67, 4 (pl. 58). Lifeboats are seen in 33, 2, 3, 4, and 5. See the appendix for more examples of such watercraft.

25
Violent Acts

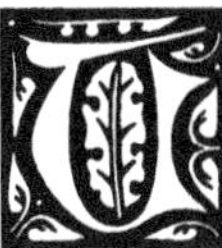
he Middle Ages, as we all know, was a period of physical violence, especially with regard to punishments for crimes. The *Cantigas* miniatures contain many miracles in which violence is seen. Even divine punishments were often violent. In *cantiga* 138, "How they put out the eyes of Saint John the Golden Mouthed and he was exiled and removed from the patriarchate," panel 1 shows pagans putting out the eyes of Saint John Chrysostom because he revered the Virgin. We see the saint clearly, stretched out on the ground as people gouge out his eyes. In panel 2, strangely enough, before exiling him they provide him with bread and a pilgrim's staff. In F 22, 3 (265) (pl. 64), Saint John Damascene's hand is cut off. Another blinding occurs in 177, "About the man whose eyes were put out," in which we see a man lying on the ground while his eyes are removed (panel 2). This atrocious act is committed after he falls into his master's disfavor because of calumny. He is given back his eyes, which he takes to a surgeon to have replaced in his head. His prayer to the Virgin leads her to restore his vision. Still a third blinding occurs, along with amputation of hands, in *Cantiga* 146, "How Holy Mary cured a young man, son of a good woman of Briançon, who was on a pilgrimage to Holy Mary of Albeza . . ." In this case (panel 3), the victim is the enemy of his attackers. When the young man's mother learns of this, she hastens to the Virgin's shrine to beg Holy Mary to restore her son to health, which, of course, Our Lady does.

Often, as in *Cantiga* 175, "How Holy Mary freed from death a young man whom they hanged unjustly, and they burned a heretic who was responsible for it," we see execution by burning (175B, 6). There are other instances of Jews and Muslims being burned alive: for ex-

ample, in *Cantiga* 4, 4, "How Holy Mary saved from burning the son of the Jew, whose father had thrown him into the furnace" (pl. 13), we see the Jewish father consigning his young son to be burned in his glass furnace because the Virgin has given the boy the communion wafer. The citizenry then forces the Jewish father (panel 6) into the furnace, where he is burned to death. In *Cantiga* 6, "How Holy Mary revived the little boy whom the Jew had killed because he sang 'Gaude Virgo Maria,'" a Jew splits open the head of a Christian boy, killing him, and buries him in his wine cellar (panel 3). When the child's mother seeks her son, she hears him from where he is interred singing *Gaude Maria*. Then many Christians go to the Jew's home, learn the truth, kill all the Jews, and burn the murderer to death. In *Cantiga* 185, 5, "How Holy Mary saved from the fire a woman whom they were trying to burn" (pl. 65), a black Muslim is burned for lying in bed with his master's wife. The Muslim did so at the order of his master's mother, who sought to alienate her son from his wife. They attempt to burn the innocent wife, but the Virgin protects her. Holy Mary does not save the Muslim, who did not refuse the mother-in-law's order to enter the bed of his master's wife. In 136 (pl. 70), a female gambler throws a stone at the image of the Christ Child and is dragged to death.

In two *Cantigas*, 156 and 174, tongues are cut out. In the former, "How Holy Mary performed a miracle in Cluny for a priest who sang his hymns very well in her praise," a Cluniac priest who sings for the Virgin has his tongue cut out by heretics (panel 2) who, according to Filgueira Valverde (1985, 262), were Albigensians. They prefer to make the priest suffer rather than to kill him. The Virgin restores his tongue, so that he can sing her praises as before. In *Cantiga* 174, "How a knight served Holy Mary, but it chanced that he played a game of dice and because he lost he denounced Holy Mary," a man cuts out his own tongue, because he denounced Holy Mary when he lost at dice (panel 3). For three days he begs the Virgin's pardon, and she restores his tongue.

Another mutilation occurs in 37, 2, "How Holy Mary restored the foot of the man who had cut it off because of the great pain he suffered," where a man suffers such pain in his foot because of disease that he has it amputated. Lying before Saint Mary's altar, he begs for a miracle to restore his foot, which she accomplishes.

A third mutilation is found in *Cantiga* 127, "How Holy Mary would not let a young man who had given his mother a kick enter her church of Puy" (panel 4). Here a young man who kicked his mother goes on a pilgrimage as penance. At the shrine, he cannot enter the church and is advised to cut off the offending limb. The miniature shows no self-mutilation, but rather the leg amputated by someone else. Here is a good example of the text and caption being at variance with the illustration, since in the text and the caption, he cuts off his own foot.

Decapitation occurs in *Cantiga* 96, "How Holy Mary saved the soul of a good man from being lost when thieves had beheaded him." A devotee of the Virgin, but even so a sinner, is robbed and beheaded by thieves (panel 2). She restores his head to his body. Later, two friars hear him crying out and confess him, after hearing his account of the miracle. His head is then again separated from his body, and he dies.

In 114, "About a young man who was mortally wounded by his enemies," a man is beaten and stabbed almost to death with spears and his head split open by his enemies (panel 2). His mother binds up his wounds and commends him to the Virgin, who heals the wounds overnight.

In 184, "How Holy Mary saved from death a little boy who still lay in the womb of his mother who had been struck in her side with a knife," great violence occurs (panel 2). A woman, none of whose children have lived, begs the Virgin to spare the child she is carrying. In a fight with enemies, her husband is stabbed to death. In the miniature, his enemies can be seen splitting open his head, revealing again a variance between text, caption, and visualization in the miniature. More violence occurs in panel 4 (pl. 66), when the husband's adversaries stab the pregnant woman in her abdomen with a sword. She dies, but her baby is delivered through the open wound.

In *Cantiga* 72, 3, "How the devil killed a gambler who cursed Holy Mary because he had lost," according to the text God kills a gambler who cursed Holy Mary be-cause he had lost at dice, but in the miniature, we see him split open from behind by a devil.

In 105, "How Holy Mary cured the woman whose husband had struck her because he could not have his way with her," we see this woman in Arras cruelly stabbed in her genitals by her abusive bridegroom (105A, 5 [pl. 42]). We see her being held hand and foot by her husband's servants. Because the spouse can never possess her, he performs this horrid deed. Nothing can heal her wound. Moreover, the bishop to whom she complains sends her back to her husband because he prefers not to cause trouble with him.

In *Cantiga* 84, "How Holy Mary revived the wife of a knight who had killed herself because the knight told her that he loved another more than her," we see a suicide (panel 3). A knight facetiously tells his wife that he loves another lady more, when she questions him. He is referring to the Virgin. On hearing this, she stabs herself and dies. The miniature graphically shows how she kills herself.

The motif of suicide appears in F2, 4 (201), "How Holy Mary freed from death a maiden who had promised to keep her virginity." A wife takes one of her godfathers as her lover. Each time she bears a child, she murders it. This occurs three times. Because she feels remorse and fears she can never be pardoned by God, she stabs herself. This suicide attempt fails, so she tries a strange method of killing herself: she swallows a spider, but its poison is not strong enough, so she swallows a huge spider; this almost kills her. In 136 (pl. 70) and in the same miracle in F 18 (294), a woman who throws a stone at an image of Saint Mary holding the Christ Child is dragged through the street until dead. In F 18, 5, she is also cast into a fire.

In 155A, 1, a man is scalped. *Cantiga* 124, "How Saint Mary protected a man because he had fasted on the eve of her feast days whom they stoned and he did not die until he confessed" (pl. 21), depicts a man stoned in panel 1, stabbed in the chest with a lance in panel 2, and his throat cut in panel 3. Since he has not been confessed, he survives until he has been. Then his body is left unburied in panel 5. In panel 6 vultures, ravens, magpies, and dogs cannot damage his corpse. The violence here is depicted in a grisly manner, and there is much blood.

In *Cantiga* 102, 4, "How Holy Mary freed a priest whom the thieves threw in a well," a priest devoted to Holy Mary is led by a deceitful lad to thieves who beat and rob him and throw him into a well or pit, closing the opening with stones and burying the priest alive. Shep-herds hear the priest crying out and rescue him.

In *Cantiga* 107, 3, "How Holy Mary saved from death the Jewish woman who was thrown over a cliff in Segovia" (pl. 67), we witness the plight of a Jewish woman cast down from a cliff by her coreligionists because of a crime she has committed. As she falls, she calls on the Virgin to save her and she lands safely at the foot of a fig tree. We know from an account in prose of the same century that the Jewish woman had sinned with a Christian, hence the reason for her violent punishment.

In 26 (pl. 56) a pilgrim who fornicated before he left his home castrates himself, cuts his own throat, and dies because the devil, disguised as Saint James, tells him to do so. The Virgin resuscitates him but does not restore the parts with which he has sinned. Berceo relates the same story in his *Miracle 8*. We record instances of other violent acts in our listing of categories in the appendix.

26
War

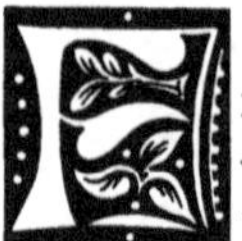

rom time immemorial Spain was never free from warfare. In Alfonso's thirteenth century, war constantly beset his kingdom. The Muslims still held considerable portions of the Peninsula. Christians fought Muslims, and both Muslims and Christians fought against their coreligionists. Knights in armor, armies on the march, sieges, battles in progress, engines of war, and other objects and activities associated with war are depicted in many miniatures.

In 28, 1, 3 (pl. 20), and 4, the artists depict a city under siege. Workers have pitched tents and are still doing so, allowing us to see tent stakes driven by hammers into the ground (panel 1). Shields, siege engines and a catapult appear in panels 3 and 4, as do crossbows, and on the city's walls are seen defenders wielding spears; 51, 1, 2, and 3, is rich in details of sieges; another siege is depicted in 99, 2 and 3, and in panel 4 we see workers demolishing a city wall with picks. In 165A a Muslim sultan raids Christian lands, and in its miniatures can be seen the details of his army in action (pl. 68); in 165B, 1 and 3, can be seen the sultan's campaign tent. In F 5 (205) another siege with tents is represented, with besieging army, cavalry, and banners; F 14, 1 and 2 (408), reveals two armies; F 26 (323) represents Muslim cavalry; F 46 (271) is unusual in that a stranded warship is attacked from a city. In 63, 3 and 4 (pl. 60), a cavalry battle rages, permitting the viewer to see knights in full armor carrying lances; horse accoutrements and armor are also depicted in great detail. In this miniature we see knights wearing suits of chain mail.

See also chapter 23, "Tools, Implements, and Weapons." Guerrero-Lovillo (1949, 112-62) has illustrations of military attire and arms, including, we believe, all of those seen in T.I.1 and F.

27
Women and Children

The importance of women in T.I.1 and F is manifested in the number of miracles that deal with women as protagonists or as secondary characters. Of the 195 *cantigas* in the *Códice Rico,* exclusive of *loores,* 44 treat women; of the 99, exclusive of *loores,* in F, 23 are concerned with women; that is, in toto 67 *cantigas* have female characters, or a little more than one-fourth in the two illustrated manuscripts. We include in this section women of high and low degree, from an empress and a few queens, through the middle class and down to prostitutes and gamblers. The 67 portrayals of women in the miniatures in T.I.1 and F reveal a veritable cross-section of the feminine part of Alfonso's own realm, as well as women in miracles that occurred abroad and in previous times. Most of the women portrayed are primary characters; others, who are represented as lesser characters because they are the sexual partners of men, play less important roles but must be included because they reveal certain functions of women in the *Cantigas.*

Although Alfonso X felt strong sexual attractions and therefore as a youth in Galicia probably engaged in sexual adventures with peasant girls (Brenan 1960, 51-68) and as an adult had mistresses and several illegitimate offspring, he respected womankind and wanted women to realize that his protection was present and that the Virgin was much concerned with their well-being and their everyday lives, even those of Jewish and Muslim women.

Beginning at the top of the social hierarchy, in *cantiga* 15 we find the empress of Rome in a miracle we discuss in chapter 1, "Classes and Masses"; in 122, 5 (pl. 61), Alfonso's own mother, Queen Beatriz, is the protagonist

of the miracle, in which she travels by litter to Las Huelgas with her infant daughter, Berenguela, who has been resuscitated by Saint Mary. She prays to the Virgin and sees the child become a novice; Queen Beatriz also appears in F 7 (256), a miracle in which the royal lady, beset by a deadly fever, is cured by the Virgin; in 17 (pl. 41) a noble lady in Rome, whose husband has died, commits incest with her son (treated in chap. 19, "Sins and Crimes"); in 23 a lady in whose house the king stops on his travels seats him at her table, only to find that her wine barrels are empty; they are refilled as soon as she prays to Saint Mary; in 64 (pl. 1) the wife of a knight is all but persuaded by a go-between to yield to a lover (treated in chapter 12, "Love, Lust and Marriage").

Women of the middle class frequently appear: in 68 Saint Mary urges a woman who has stolen a neighbor's husband—a merchant—to stop committing adultery; Saint Mary persuades the neighbor woman to forgive the first woman, and they become friends; in 18 (pl. 3) a middle-class woman is in the business of producing silk; a seamstress, in 117, works on the Sabbath and becomes crippled, but Saint Mary heals her; in 89 a Jewish housewife goes into labor and cannot bring forth her child until she calls upon the Virgin and the child is delivered; in 167 Saint Mary resuscitates the son of a Muslim woman after she carries the corpse to Salas.

Female religious also appear: a nun, in 94 (pl. 38), runs away with a gentleman, but her duties are carried out by the Virgin; another nun, in 55, becomes pregnant by a priest; a third nun, in *Cantiga* 59 (pl. 39), agrees to run away with a would-be lover, but a life-size crucifix strikes her with the nail in its hand; in 58 a fourth nun is showed a vision of hell, and this persuades her to remain chaste. Guerrero-Lovillo (1949, 98-111) describes feminine dress as seen in various *cantigas* and illustrates it with line drawings.

One interesting story about a woman gambler, a woman obviously of the lowest stratum of society, appears in *Cantiga* 136 (pl. 70). The page of miniatures is so brilliantly colored and the narrative so revealing of daily life that we will treat the illustrations with considerable detail. The title of 136 reads "This is how in the land of Apulia, in a city called Foggia, a woman was playing dice with some companions in front of a church. Because she lost, she threw a stone at the image of the Holy Child held by the Statue of Holy Mary, which raised its arm and received the blow."

In panel 1, "How a woman played dice and the devil incited her to disbelieve," some eight men and one woman sit in front of the church, around a low hexagonal dicing table. The woman, who according to the text is a German, a rogue, and a fool, is seen dressed in a simple *brial*, with headgear composed of straps of white cloth to hold her hair in place and a chin strap to hold the headpiece firm (Guerrero-Lovillo 1949, 211), and is pointing at the game being played on the table. Behind her stands a hideous black devil, who points at the beautiful statue of the Madonna and the Child. These statues merit close attention, because they are of pure white stone, which indicates that they had not been painted, as all such statues eventually were. However, the Virgin's and the Child's halos are red, and she wears a golden crown. The infant Jesus holds a small red book bound in silver. In panel 2, "How the evil woman threw a stone so as to hit the face of the statue of Jesus Christ," she stands in front of the statues, raising her left had, in which she holds the stone. An expression of anger suffuses her face. Behind her the dice players raise their hands in protest at her action, and one has reached out as though to prevent the act, but a black and ugly devil pushes back the player's hand.

In panel 3, "How the statue of Holy Mary fended off the stone with her arm so that it would not strike her Son," the miniaturists have presented a scene of lively action: all but one of the dicers now stand, hands open in rejection, and one actually has his arms around her waist to hold her back, but the ugly demon thrusts him back. Having transferred the stone to her right hand, she has thrown it and it can be seen striking the arm of Saint Mary's statue, which can clearly be seen raised to catch the blow. The narrative of this miracle relates that the stone chips the statue's arm and the damage remains forever.

In panel 4, "How they took the evil woman to the king and the king ordered her dragged through the streets," three golden arches encapsulate the action: in the one to

the far left stand five of the king's ministers, clad in the basic tunics and wearing the usual head kerchiefs. One carries a spear. The central panel reveals the woman, whose hands are held by two soldiers, each holding a spear. The king, in the right-hand arch, sits on a covered chair or couch. He wears a golden crown and a luxurious and colorful mantle. His shoes are gilded and pointed (see Guerrero-Lovillo's line drawing, 1949, 225).

In panel 5, "How they dragged the evil woman throughout the city," the artists have almost outdone themselves in their portrayal of violent action. At the right, a man mounted on a gray horse holds a cat-o'-nine-tails, here with only three tails of leather, all of which are barbed. The woman, now stripped to her shift, is being pulled along the street, her feet tied with ropes attached to the horse's saddle. Her legs, bosom, and face are bloodsplotched. Behind her we see a group of men standing and three mounted men gesticulating. People stare from the upper story of the building, before which this scene unfolds, making it clear that all is taking place in a street.

In panel 6, "How the king had that statue of Holy Mary painted very properly," we see, to the left, that the painter stands at a workbench, on which he is grinding and mixing colors needed for painting the statues. At the foot of the bench are seen a half dozen small paint pots. In the right-hand action, he sits beside the two images. He is just completing the final touches of his task, since both images now appear in brilliant colors. In these scenes he wears a mantle with a side opening, to enable him to work freely. We can only speculate why he appears so well-dressed while engaged in such a task.

Few pages of miniatures reveal so many aspects of daily life: gamblers male and female, their game in front of a church, their gambling table, the unpainted and painted statues, the emotions of all concerned, the building overlooking some of the action, the attire of the gamblers, the king, the horseman with the scourge, the graphic portrayal of the devil or demon, the painter's materials. We believe that this page reveals the only unpainted statues, giving the artists the opportunity to show how they were painted.

The same miracle in F 18 (294), although of artistic merit, differs slightly from the one in T.I.1: instead of Saint Mary's statue deflecting the thrown stone, in F an angel deflects it in panel 4, and a monk, also in 4, tries to prevent the woman from throwing the stone. The listing of women in *Cantigas* appears in the appendix under "Women."

Children

Children across the centuries have been cherished by Spaniards. In the *Cantigas de Santa Maria* they are the subject of the Virgin's special affection and protection. The following cases come from T.I.1. In *Cantiga* 4, 2 (pl. 13), a Jewish lad receives communion from an image of Saint Mary, reports it to his father, and is cast into a glass furnace, where she protects him. In 6 she resuscitates a lad who sings *Gaude Maria* and who is killed by Jews. In 21 a child given to a barren mother has died, and when the child is laid upon Saint Mary's altar, she resuscitates him. Number 43 relates that Saint Mary resuscitates a couple's son even though they failed to give her the wax they have promised. *Cantiga* 53 relates how Saint Mary resuscitates a child who has suffered from Saint Martial's fire and died. In 7, 4, the child of an abbess is taken away from her as soon as he is born. *Cantiga* 62 relates the story of a boy given to merchants as security for a debt. When the mother prays, Saint Mary redeems him. In 79 we read that the damsel named Musa is cured of her frivolity and taken to heaven. In 86 a pregnant woman with Saint Mary's assistance gives birth to a baby under water in the sea. Saint Mary protects mother and child. In 89 a pregnant Jewish woman cannot give birth to her child, but when she appeals to Saint Mary, the birth takes place. *Cantiga* 94 (pl. 38) tells how a nun flees her convent with a knight and later returns, confesses, and summons her lover and her three children to verify her story. *Cantiga* 108 (pl. 19) tells of a Jewish boy born with his head on backward. He is used to convert Jews, but his head remains looking behind him. In the lengthy *cantiga* 115, a boy travels far and is threatened by devils but is saved by Saint Mary. *Cantiga* 118 tells of a mother whose children are stillborn. At last, she calls on Saint Mary, and the recently stillborn babe comes to life. In 122 (pl. 61) "a queen," who we are certain was Queen Beatriz, Alfonso's

mother, carries her recently resuscitated daughter to Burgos, where she becomes a novice. In 123 a boy enters the order of friars minor. Later, as a man, he dies and the Virgin resuscitates him. Number 133 relates that a girl falls into a ditch and drowns. When her father places her before Saint Mary's altar, she revives. Two children in 135A (pl. 35), a lad and a girl, swear everlasting love. *Cantiga* 139 relates that a little boy who offers a bite to eat to an image of Jesus the Child is taken to heaven. In 167 a Muslim boy dies, but when his corpse is carried to Saint Mary's shrine at Salas (pl. 26), she resuscitates him. Number 171 tells that a couple's son falls into a river and, presumably, drowns. When his parents reach Saint Mary's shrine at Salas, the boy greets them. In 178 (pl. 69) a farmer gives his son a she-mule colt, and after the little mule dies, the little boy takes a wax candle to Saint Mary of Salas and she resuscitates the animal. In 184 (pl. 66) a pregnant woman is killed by a sword thrust into her abdomen. When women rescue the baby, he lives.

There are children in MS F also. We index only those miracles that are illustrated, in accordance with our demands for visualized elements of daily life. In F 3 (224) Saint Mary resuscitates a dead girl; in F 5 (286) she saves a Muslim baby and her mother as they fall from a tower; in F 88 (228) (pl. 25) she makes a boy happy by curing his sick mule, whose legs are swollen; and in F 98 (269) she gives hearing and speech to a deaf-mute boy. Not all children are kind. In F 104 a deceitful lad lures a pilgrim to robbers who throw him into a pit, and in F 127 a youth kicks his mother.

We add that in the unillustrated miracles the following treat children: F 24 (321), F 29 (303), and F 58 (319).

Concluding Remarks

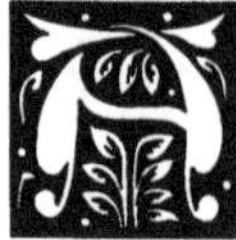 s we planned, researched, and wrote this volume, we believed that it could be valuable to many scholars and to the general educated public interested in the medieval world. Having completed it, we found we had underestimated its impact. Scores of unexpected items, even some discoveries, came to light. The two codices are indeed a world of exceeding varieties of information. Who would have expected a crossbow to be used to extract a missile shot into a man's face from another crossbow? Or that bullfighting, better called bull-baiting, would be carried out with all the human participants attacking the bull from the safety of the roof? Who would have thought we would be able to study the treatments physicians would employ to heal Alfonso, dying in his own bed? Or that other incidences of the king's own life would teach us so much?

Given the exceedingly great financial cost of the two facsimile volumes, the color plates herein will bring the beauty of the *Cantigas* to the attention of a much wider audience than hitherto.

Appendix
Index of Daily Life Categories
in the *Cantigas de Santa Maria*
T.I.1. AND F

Children
In T.I.1

Accomplice of robbers, 102, 2

Baby born under water, 86, 4

Baby delivered through fatal wound inflicted on mother, 184

Bastard child of abbess saved, 55B, 2

Boy enters religious order, 76, 6

Boy offers Christ a bite to eat and is taken into heaven, 139

Boy redeemed from slavery, 62, 5

Boy saved from devils, 115B, 5, 6

Child lost in river appears, 171, 5

Child sees Virgin in vision, 53

Child sings, 6, 2

Children betroth each other, 135A, 1

Children of runaway nun revealed, 94, 6

Girl taken to heaven, 79, 6

Jewish baby born with head on backward, 108, 3

Jewish child born with Virgin's help, 89, 4

Jewish lad saved from death, 4, 5

Mule cured for boy, 178, 5

Resuscitation, 6, 5 (of murdered boy); 21, 5 (of sick boy); 43, 6 (of a lad); 53, 5 (of a diseased boy); 118, 4 (stillborn baby); 122, 4 (dead daughter of queen); 133 (drowned girl); 167, 5 (Moorish boy); 168 (dead boy from Lérida)

Son on pilgrimage hanged but supported on gallows by Holy Mary, 175A, 6

In F

Boy pushed out of window by devil resuscitated 52, 3 (241)

Child falls from high bridge, F 102 (337)

Dead girl resuscitated, 3, 3 (224)

Moorish baby and mother saved, 5, 4 (286)

Mule cured for boy, 88, 4 (228)

Speech and hearing restored to deaf-mute, 98, 2 (269)

Church Hierarchy

Abbess, 7; 55; 61, 4

Abbot, 4, 2; 14, 2; 36, 4; 85B, 2; 141, 2, 6; 151; 164, 2, 4, 5 (prince); 187, 5 (186 in Filgueira Valverde 1985)

Acolytes, 2, 3; 92, 5; 149, 1; 172, 6

Archbishop, 2 (Ildefonso and Siagrio); 12 (of Toledo)

Bishops, 2; 7; 19, 5, 6; 30; 32, 2-5; 33; 65A, 2, 3; 66; 67; 77, 5; 87, 2, 6; 101, 6; 105A, 6; 105B, 1; 125B, 6; 162, 2, 3; 164, 5; 190, 6; F 36, 1 (261); F 43, 5 (259)

Canons, 35A, 2-5

Chaplain, 75 A and B; 125B, 2; 128, 3; 162, 3-6; F 49, 2 (238)

Dean, 35A, 3

Eastern Patriarchs, 115B, 1 (Syria); 131, 4; 145 A and B (Alexandria)

Guardian, 119, 5

Pope, 15B, 5, 6; 65A, 3; 115A, 5; F 54, 1 (206)

Prior, 57, 4; 115A, 5; 164, 1-4

Saint Basil, 5 A and B

Saint Catherine of Alexandria, 54 T

Saint Dominic, F 32 T (204)

Saint German, 28, 2

Saint Ildefonso, 2

Saint James, 26, 4, 5

Saint Joseph, 66, 2; 90, 3

Saint Leocadia, 2, 4

Saint Mercurio, 5A, 4

Saint Peter, 14, 2-4; 27; 66, 4

Treasurer, 187, 5 (186 in Filgueira Valverde 1985)

Religious Orders

Cistercian monks (white habits), 13, 6; 39; 45A, 5; 45B, 6; 48; 52; 54; 56; 57; 69; 73; 82; 85B, 2; 88; 109; 141

Cistercian nuns, 7, 3; 6; 55 A and B; 58; 59; 61; 71; 83, 6; 94

Dominican friars (black habits), 8; 9; 11; 14, 1, 6; 18, 5, 6;

Commoners and Occupations

Admiral, 35B, 1; 95B, 1
Bailiff, 175A; 175B, 4, 5
Beekeeper, 128, 3; F 28 (285); F 94, 2 (208)
Beggar, 35A, 1; F 92, 6 (317)
Blacksmith, 19, 6
Butcher, 159, 1
Caballero, 22; 44, 1; 45A; 48; 57, 2; 58, 1, 6; 59, 1; 63 (armor); 84; 94, 2, 6; 121; 137; 148, 3-6; 152; 155; 158; 162, 1; 174, 1; 194, 1, 2; F 12 (314); F 62 (233); F 65 (232)
Carpenter, F 55, 3 (223) (coffin)
Castellan, 185A, 2, 3, 5; 185B, 1, 2; 191, 1, 2
Castellan's wife, 191, 1, 3, 4-6
Concubine/prostitute *(barragana)*, 104, 2-5; 137, 4, 5; 151, 1
Doctor, 88; 157, 3; 173, 1; 177, 4, 5 (surgeon); F 95, 2 (209)
Falconer, 44
Farmer, 22; 31; 178, 3 (plowing)
Fiddler, 8; 120, 1; 194, 2; F 43 (259)
Fisherman, 67, 4; 95A, 4; 183, 6
Furrier *(pellejero)*, 199
Gambler, 72, 1-3; 76, 1; 174; F 49, 1 (238)
Go-between *(alcahueta)*, 64, 4, 5; F 45A, 6 (312)
Goldsmith, F 42, 1 (362)
Gospeler, 75 A and B
Guide for blind person, 92, 2-4; F 12, 2 (314); F 74, 5 (278)
Harlot, 68, 2
Honey producers, 128, 3
Hunter, 15A, 4; 44, 1; 67, 4; 142, 1; F 80 (276)
Innkeeper, 9, 1; 157; 175A, 2
Jewish sage *(alfaqui)*, 108, 1, 2, 4
Judge, 119
King's guards, 136, 4
Lime burner, 78
Madman, 65A, 6; 65B, 1, 2, 4
Magistrate, 13, 2, 3, 5 *(merino)*; 76, 2; 175A, 4, 5; 175B, 4, 5; 186, 3, 4
Maidservant, 43, 4; 153, 1; 159; F 61, 2 (215)
Manservant, 67, 3, 5; 116, 3-5; 186, 1-5; F 95 (209) (to Alfonso X)
Mason, 42.1
Merchant, 35A, 4; 35B, 3, 4; 62, 1, 2; 68, 2; 116, 1; 172, 4 (with wares); 193; F 53 (267)
Messenger, 64, 2
Midwife, 108, 3; 184, 5
Minstrel *(juglar)*, 8, 5; 194; F 37 (293); F 43, 1 (259); F49 (238)
Money changer, 25A, 1; 41, 1; 62; F 35B, 4 (305)
Mule skinning, 178, 4
Musician, 100, 6; 120, 1; 165B, 5; 194, 2; F 43 (259)
Nobleman, 44
Nurse, 67, 1 (male)
Painter, 74 (scaffolding, paint box, tools); 136, 5, 6 (of statues with work bench and paint pots); F 45 (312)
Peasant, 128
Pharmacist, 108, 1, 2, 173, 1
Pirate, 35B, 1; F 65 (232)

Poet, F 33, 1 (202); F 47 (291); F 79, 5 (307); F 85, 1 (316)
Pregnant woman, 55, 3; 86, 2-4; 89, 1-3; 184, 1-5
Princess (king's sister), 122
Prior, 164, 1-4
Privy counselor, 78, 1, 3, 6 (of a count); 97 (of a king)
Prostitute, 137, 5
Reaper of wheat, F 12, 1 (314)
Retainer, 97, 2
Rich person, 19; 75 A and B; 88, 2; 135A, 3-6; 135B, 1-3
Robber, 9, 4; 13; 24, 1; 85A, 1, 2; 96, 1, 2; 106; 155A, 2; 182; F 51, 1 (245) (noble)
Sage, 17, 3
Sailor, 15B, 1
Scholar, F 47, 3 (291) (writes song)
Scribe, 83, 5; 156, 1
Sculptor, F 45A, 1 (312)
Seamstress, 117, 2; 148, 3
Sheepshearing, 147, 5
Shepherd, 1, 3; 102, 5; 147, 2
Silk producer, 18, 3, 4
Sorcerer/sorceress, 3, 1; 128, 1
Spy, 165A, 2; 165B, 1, 3
Squire, 63, 2; 106; 148; 185A, 6; 185B, 1; 191; F 14 (408); F 87 (227); F 82 (301); F 92 (317)
Stevedore, 35B, 4
Steward, 7, 2
Stonemason, 42, 1; F 68, 3 (242); F 69 (249)
Surgeon, 177, 4, 5
Tax collector for king *(almojarife)*, F 3 (224)
Teacher, 4, 1; F 22A, 5 (265)
Treasurer of Ferdinand III, F 10, 1 (292)
Trobador, F 37, 1 (293); F 59, 3 (363); F 85, 1 (316)
Usurer (moneylender), 25A, 1 (Jewish); 62, 1; 75A; 75B
Vineyard worker, F 13, 3 (226)
Wagoner, 31, 5; F 65, 1, 2 (232)

Death

14, 1; 16, 6; 21, 3; 41, 5; 45A, 6; 54, 3; 65B, 6; 110, 2

Deathbed, 56, 4; 71, 6; 75; 79, 6; 87, 2 (bishop); 119, 6; 138, 6; 139, 6; F 11, (296)
Observances, 75
 Burials, 24, 3, 6; 43, 5
 Caskets, 113; child's coffin, 43, 5; 167, 3
 Dead child placed at altar, 122, 3; F 3, 4 (224)
 Face of dead person covered, 54, 3; 123, 4; 154, 6
 Funerals, 24, 4; 72, 6; F 50, 4 (311)
Signs of grief, 21, 3; 41, 5; 43, 4; 75B, 4; 98, 3; 122 T; 139, 6 T; 171, 4; F 95, 2 (209)

Disasters and Accidents

Disasters

Boat sinks, 111, 3
Church burns, 35A, 1; 39, 3
Church swallowed up by earth, F 13 (226)

Falling boulder threatens Monserrat, 113
Lightning strikes, 35B, 5 (wool in a ship); 39 (church); F 50,
    1 (311) (kills person)
Mine caves in, 131, 2
Sand collapses, F 63 (252)
Sea engulfs pregnant woman, 86, 3
Ship sinks, 112, 3; F 65, 2 (232)
Storm at sea, 172, 1 (mast breaks); F 16 (313); F 53, 2 (267)
Volcano erupts, F 79, 2 (307)

Accidents

Beam falls in church in Castrogeriz; 266 (miniature; no text
    in F)
Bell falls on man's head, F 80, 2 (276)
Child falls from high bridge, F 102 (337)
Child falls in river, 171, 3
Drowning, 11, 3; 133, 2
Falling from height, 191, 4; F 52, 3 (241)
Loss of way, 49, 2; 102, 2
Man chokes on rabbit bone, F25, 3 (322)
Man hit by strong wave falls overboard, F 53, 3 (267)
Man swept under river, 142, 4
Mast falls on head of ship's admiral, 35B, 1
Sailor falls overboard, 33, 2
Swallowing a poisonous spider, F 67 (225); F 93 (222)

Education

Instruction in praise of the Virgin by the Virgin, 71, 3
John of Damascus teaches penmanship, F 22A, 5 (265)
Man "instructs" woman in the art of making love, 111, 1
School (in church), 4, 1
Small boy explains Scripture and how to repair a church, 53, 5

Fauna and Flora
Fauna

Ass, 43, 5; 167, 3; 179, 2
Barn animals, 148, 5
Bear, 67, 4
Bees, 128, 2, 3; 326 (F miniature, no text); F 94, 2 (208); F
    97, 4 (211) (swarm)
Boars, 82, 1-4
Bull, 46, 2; 47, 2; 144, 3-6
Bullocks, 31, 5
Camel, 29, 5
Cattle, 46, 2
Cow, 1, 2; 31
Dog, 1, 3; 44; 124, 6; 135B, 3; 142; F 4, 4 (286)
Dove, 2, 1
Dragon-like beast, 189, 2
Elephant, 29, 5
Fish, 67, 4; 95A, 4
Frog, 69, 4
Geese, 148, 5
Giraffe, 29, 5
Goats, 46, 2; 48, 2
Goldfinch, 93, 3

Hawk, 44; 142, 2, 4, 6
Hen, 148, 5
Heron, 110, 6; 142, 2, 4, 6
Hippopotamus, 29, 5
Hoopoe (bird), 93, 4; 168, 3
Horse, 22, 1-4; 135B, 3; 148, 4; 171, 2, 4
Lion, 9, 4; 46, 2; 47, 4
Magpies, 124, 6; 175, 3
Mountain goats, 52, 1, 2, 5, 6
Mule, 43, 5; 142, 1; 178, 5; 179, 2; F 88 (228)
Owl, 93, 4; 135A, 6; 168, 4
Oxen, 1, 2; 48, 5; 178, 3
Partridge, 44, 1; 153, 2
Pigeon, 148, 5
Rabbit, 135A, 6; 155 A and B; F 25 (322); F 38 (274)
Ravens, 124, 6
Rooster, 69, 4; 148, 5
Sheep, 46, 2; 102, 5; 147, 1-5
Snake, 60, 2; F 40, 3 (320)
Swine, 148, 5
Vultures, 124, 6
Zebra, 29, 5

Flora

Date palm, 41, 6; 60, 2-4; 100, 6
Fig tree, 107, 3, 4
Grapevines, 132, 2; 161, 4, 5; F 13, 1, 2 (226)
Ivy, 65B
Lilies, 10, 2; 24, 5; 140, 3; 160, 3
Mulberry leaves, 18, 3
Mulberry tree, 148, 6
Pine grove, 9, 4; 42, 6
Roses, 10, 1; 56, 5
Wheat, 187, 2 (186 in Filgueira Valverde 1985); F 12, 1
    (314)

Food and Drink, Preparation and Presentation

Beef chops, 159, 1, 3-6
Bread, 5A, 1; 23, 3; 42, 4; 52, 3; 55; 65; 67, 5, 6; 84, 3, 88,
    4; 115B, 3; 119, 1
Broth with grape juice, 105 T
Chest, 25A, 4-6; 159, 4, 5
Dinners/banquets, 23, 3, 6; 42, 4 (wedding feast); 45A, 4; 67,
    5, 6; 132, 5 (wedding feast)
Dough, F 67[1] (258)
Electuaries, 88, 5, 6
Fritters, 157, 1, 2
Kitchen, 105A, 2
Milk, 52, 2
Rabbit, F 25 (322)
Scales, 105A, 2; F 35B, 1, 3 (305)
Tablecloths, 95A, 3
Utensils, 67, 5, 6 (table knife); 115B, 3 (bowl); 119, 1
    (serving dishes); 119, 4 (cauldron); 155B, 1 (pitcher);
    157, 1, 2 (skillet with tripod, cauldron, kitchen knife);
    159, 3 (iron oven, serving bowls); F 9, 2 (298) (brazier)

Wild greens without salt, 88, 4
Wine, 45A, 4; 47, 1; 73, 2; 132, 5
Wineskins, 38, 1, 2; 72, 1, 2

Furniture and Furnishings

Armoire, 2, 1; 56, 2; 156, 1; F 22B, 2 (265); F 33, 1 (202)
Banquet table, 42, 4
Beds, 24, 4; 25B, 2; 42, 5; 56, 4; 64, 6; 75A; 77, 2-5; 84, 2; 114, 3, 4; 118, 1, 3-5; 132, 6; 135A, 5; 135B, 6 (canopy); 173; F 71, 1 (218); F 95 (209) (royal beds)
Candles and lamps, 8; 116, 2, 4-6
Chairs, 153, 1-5; F 98, 5 (269) (child's chair)
Chest, 25A, 4-6; 159, 4, 5
Child's table, F 98, 5 (269)
Cot, 75A, 2
Curtains, 108, 3; 174, 4
Deathbed, 24, 3, 4; 56, 4
Desks, 2, 1; F 33, 1 (202)
Dicing table, 136, 1; F 18, 1 (294)
Dining table, 42, 4; 45A, 4; 52, 3; 67, 5, 6; 88, 2; 95A, 3; 115B, 3; 119, 1; 159, 3; F 25, 2 (322)
Footstool, 2, 1
Lectern, 94, 1, 3, 5
Litter, 91, 2; 122, 5 (royal)
Mattress or sleeping pad on floor, 166; 173, 2-4; 174, 4
Moorish divan, 165B, 1, 3
Nuptial bed, 42, 5; 135B, 6
Painter's workbench, 136, 6
Pillow, 165B, 1, 3
Refectory table, 88, 4
Sconces, 135B, 6 (lighting); 164, 6
Sickbed, 173, 2-4
Thrones, 97, 3-6; 155A, 3 (papal throne)
Window, 134, 3-6; 144, 4; 151
Writing tables, 2, 1; 56, 2; 138, 1, 6; 156, 1; F 33, 1 (202)

Geographic Place Names

Acre, 9 T; 15 T; 33 T; 172 T and C
Africa, 95 T
Agualdalfaja[ra], 142
Albarracin, 191 T
Albesa, 146 T and C
Alcala de Guadaira, 124 T
Alcarraz, 178 T
Alcazar de San Juan, F 1 T (246)
Alenquer, F 46 T (271); F 85 T (316)
Aleppo, 165 T
Alexandria, 65 T and C; 145 T and C; 155 T and C
Algarve, 183 T
Alicante, F 100 T (339)
Almeria, 192 T
Andalusia, 83 T; F 73 T (221)
Apulia, 136 T (villa de Foggia); F 18 T (294)
Aragon, 44 T; 64 T; 161 T; 173 T; 177 T
Arcila, 169 T
Armenia, 115 T

Armenteira, 22 T
Arras, 68 T; 105 T; 122 T; F 43 T (259)
Arreixaca (section of Murcia), 169 T and C
Auvergne, 66 T and C; 125 T
Ayamonte, F 39 T(273)
Azemmour (River), F 46 T (271)
Badajoz, F 89 T (213)
Barcelona, F 50 T (311)
Barcena de Cudón, F 70 T (263)
Beja, F 3 T (224)
Belmez, 185 T and C
Berrie (Viviers), 37 T
Bethlehem, 1 T; 111 T and C; 142 T
Black Mountain, 65 T and C
Bologna, 7 T
Borgogne, 146 T
Borja, 167 T and C
Bourges, 4 T
Bretaña, 23 T; 36 T
Briançon, 146 T
Brittany, 86 T; 135 T
Burgos, 122 T; F 10 T (292); F 38 T (274); F 73 T (221); F 83 T (361)
Byzantium, 25 T
Calatrava, F 5 T (205)
Cañete , 97 T; 162 T and C
Canterbury (Conturbel), 82 T; F 11 T (296); F 19 T (288)
Capilla, F 7 T (256)
Carmelo, 165 T
Carrion de los Condes, 31 T; F 71 T (218); F 74 T (278); F 82 T (301)
Cartagena, F 100 T (339)
Castilla, F 73 T (221); 235 T (F miniature, no text)
Castrogeriz, F 63 T (252); F 68 T (242); F 69 T (249)
Catalonia, 48 T; 154 T; 194 T and C; F 45 T (312)
Cesaria, 5 T
Ceuta, 169 T
Chartres, 24 T; 117 T and C; 148 T; F 42 T (362)
Chateauroux Monastery, 38 T
Chelas Monastery, F 93 T(222)
Chincolla, 185 T and C
Ciudad Rodrigo, F 67A T (225)
Claraval, 88 T
Cluny, 156 T
Clusa, 73 T
Coira, F 26 T (323)
Colliure, 112 T
Cologne, 7 T
Colonia, 14 T
Constantinople, 9 T; 28 T and C; 34 T; 131 T and C
Consuegra, 192 T
Conturbel, F 11 T (296)
Cordoba, F 24 T (321) (no miniature)
Cuenca, 162 T; F 7 T (256)
Daconada, F 57 T (351)
Damascus, 9 T; 165 T; F 22A T (265)
Damieta (Egypt), 182 T

Health
Abnormalities

Cures, 46, 5; F 2, 5 (201); F 9, 4 (298); F 22B, 6 (265)

Diseases

Institutions and Items Associated with Health

Medical Procedures and Practices

Pregnancy, Childbirth, and Child Care

Wounds and Mutilations

Legal Matters

Love, Lust, and Marriage

Punishments

Recreation and Entertainment

Religion

Vestments, 66, 3; 73, 2-4
Virgin appears on stones, 29
Virgin's milk, 46, 5; 54, 4
Visions, 4, 2; 24, 4; 32, 4; 36, 5; 42, 5; 47, 4; 53, 4; 58, 2-5;
Visions *continued*, 63, 3; 65B, 3; 66, 2; 68, 3; 71; 72, 4; 75 A
    and B; 79, 2, 5, 6; 84, 4; 85A, 3; 87, 3; 91, 4; 92, 4;
    105A, 1; 105B, 5; 123, 5; 125B, 5; 132, 4; 138, 5; 149,
    4; 152, 4; 174, 5; 176, 2; F 10, 1 (292); F 11 (296); F
    43, 2 (259); F 78, 2 (299)
Vows, 42, 2; 105A, 1; 135A, 1; 173, 2
Waxen images, 44, 4; 118, 2; 167, 2; 176, 6; 177, 6
Wax for candles, 166, 4
Wedding ceremonies, 15; 42; 64, 1 (nobles); 104, 1; 105A, 3;
    125B, 3; 132, 3; 135A, 4; 135B, 5; F 45 (312); F 65
    (232)
Wimple, 18, 4
Witnessing, 25B, 5; 31, 6; 34, 6; 39, 5; 44, 6; 75B, 6; 85B, 5;
    93, 6; 95B, 5; 96, 5; 107, 5; 114, 6; 121, 6; 129, 6; 155B,
    6; 158, 6; 159, 5; 162, 6; 171, 6; 175B, 4; 178, 6; 191, 6

Sins and Crimes

Adultery, 68; 104
Arson, F 85, 3 (316)
Blasphemy, 7; 19, 1; 34, 1, 2; 45; 55; 58; 59; 72, 2; 94; 108;
    136, 2; 174, 2; F 18, 3 (294); F 37, 2 (293); F 49, 1, 4
    (238)
Calumny, 78; 97 (slander); 177
Counterfeiting, 164
Deceiver *(engañador)*, 152
Drunkenness, 47
False witness, 175B, 6
Gambling, 38, 2; 72, 1, 2; 136, 1; F 18, 2 (294)
Gourmandise (gluttony), 88, 2
Greed, 75
Homosexuality, F 71 T (235)
Incest, 17, 1
Lust, 11; 26; 68; 93; 111; 137, 4; 151 (concubine); 152; F 2,
    2 (201); F 89, 3 (213); F 101 (336)
Murder, 6, 3; 19, 1; F 2, 3 (201) (of children)
Pride, 152
Rape (or attempted rape), 15A, 4; F 47, 1 (291); F 92, 2
    (317)
Stealing, F 48 (318); 326 (F miniature, no text)
Suicide (or attempted suicide), 84, 3; F 2, 4 (201) (by
    stabbing oneself and swallowing spiders)
Treason, 124

Structures and Streets

Aqueduct, 107, 2
Battlements, 183, 1-5; 185A, 1, 2; 185B, 1, 3, 5
Castle, 28, 1-4; 187; 191, 1, 3-5
Choir, 25A 4-6; 25B, 1, 4; 55B, 4, 5; 73, 1-4
City walls, 26, 4; 34, 1; 35A , 3; 44, 3; 62, 5; 65A, 6; 67, 2,
    3; 83, 3, 4; 101, 1; 111, 1, 3, 5; 126, 1; 129, 4; 133
    (Elche), 1-3; 134, 1, 2; 143, 1, 6; 148, 5; 155A, 1; 158,
    1-4; 165A, 4, 6; 165B, 2, 4, 6; 169, 1, 6 (Murcia); 176,
    1-4; 183, 1-5 (Faro)

Convent, 55 A and B; 58, 1; 59, 6
Facades, 9, 3 (open-air shop); 27, 1 (synagogue); 41, 1 (house
    of money changer); 59, 1 (of a convent); 108, 1, 2
    (pharmacy); 173, 1 (pharmacy)
Glass furnace, 4, 3-6
House exteriors, 79, 1; 136; 192, 2, 3; 194, 1, 3; F 18 (294)
House interiors, 4, 3-6; 25B, 2; 34, 2-6; 46, 4, 5; 64, 2-6; 75
    A and B; 84, 1-3; 108, 3, 4; 192, 1, 4; 194, 3
Jerez de la Frontera, 143, 1, 6
Lime kiln, 78, 3
Monastery, 103; 113, 5
Plaza, 144
Portico, 42, 1, 3
Straw hut, 75 A and B
Streets, 12, 3, 4; 25, 1, 4; 28, 1, 3, 4; 51; 64, 4; 68, 5, 6; 76,
    2; 91, 1-4; 104, 4; 107, 1, 2; 119, 2; 136, 1-3, 5, 6; 137,
    2-4; 145, 2, 3, 6; 154, 1-4; 155A, 1; 184, 2-5; F4, 2
    (286); F 18 (294)

Supernatural Beings

Angels, 1, 3; 2, 5; 3, 3; 7, 4; 10, 5; 11, 3-5; 13, 4; 16, 6; 20,
    4, 6; 23, 6; 24, 4; 26, 1; 32, 4; 41, 4; 42, 5; 43, 6; 45B,
    1, 4, 5; 54, 4; 55B, 3, 4; 58, 3-5; 60, 6; 65B, 3, 4; 66, 2;
    75B, 2; 77, 1; 79, 6; 81, 3, 6; 82, 4-6; 85A, 3-6; 85B, 1;
    88, 5; 90, 2, 6; 93, 5; 100, 1-5; 101, 3, 4; 105A, 4;
    105B, 4, 5; 111, 4; 113, 5; 115B, 3, 5; 116, 6; 118, 4;
    119, 6; 120, 3, 5; 121, 4; 125A, 5, 125B, 5; 126, 6; 130,
    2, 6; 131, 4; 132, 4, 6; 134, 5, 6; 137, 5; 138, 4-6; 140,
    3; 141, 4; 145A, 4; 149, 6; 152, 3, 4, 6; 154, 6; 158, 5;
    167, 5; 168, 5; 170, 2, 3, 5; 174, 5; 175B, 2; 189, 5;
    190, 4; F 18 (294) F 47, 6 (291); F 65A, 4 (232); F 70,
    2 (263); F 84, 4 (302)
Devils, 3, 2, 3; 10, 6; 11, 3, 4; 14, 1, 2; 26, 2-5; 34, 2, 3; 38,
    3-5; 39; 41, 2; 45A, 6; 45B, 1, 4; 58, 2-4; 65B, 5; 67, 6;
    70, 6; 71, 1; 72, 3; 74, 2, 4, 5; 75B, 1, 3-5; 81, 3, 6; 82,
    2-5; 85A, 3-6; 85B, 1; 88, 5; 90, 4, 6; 93, 5; 109, 1-3, 5;
    111, 4; 115A, 1, 3; 115B, 4, 5; 116, 6, 117, 2; 118, 3;
    119, 2-4; 121, 4; 123, 2, 3; 125A, 4-6, 125B, 1-3; 126,
    6; 130, 3, 4; 135A, 4-6; 136, 1; 138, 4-6; 152, 3; 154, 3;
    168, 5; 182, 4; 190, 5; 192, 2, 3; F 9, 1 (298); F 18
    (294); F 34, 2 (216)
Souls and Spirits, 11, 4; 14, 1; 16, 6; 26, 3, 4; 45B, 4; 53, 4;
    71, 6; 72, 4; 75B, 2, 5; 111, 4; 119, 6; 138, 6; 149, 6;
    152, 6; 154, 6; F 66, 6 (284)

Thieves, Gamblers, Highwaymen, and Counterfeiters

6, 1; 9, 4; 13; 24, 1; 38; 45; 57, 2; 72, 2 ; 76; 85; 96, 1; 102,
3, 4; 106, 1; 154, 1-4; 155A, 2; 163, 1-5; 182, 2; 194, 3, 4; F
    18 (294); F 49, 1 (238); F 99 (214)

Gambling house, 140, 6; 174,1
Robbers, F 51, 1 (245)
Steals silver from cross, F 48, 2 (318)
Thieves rob purse, F 84 (302)
Woman gambler, 136, 1
Woman innkeeper steals flour, 157

Tools, Implements, and Weapons

Travel by Water and Storms at Sea or on Water

Passenger ship, 25B, 3; 33, 1, 2; 35A, 4-6; 35B, 1, 2, 4, 5; 36,
    1-5; 65A, 4; 112, 1-3, 5; 115A, 6; F 16, 1, 3, 5 (313)
Pirate ship, F 65[1], 1, 2 (236)
Sails, 33, 4, 5; 95A, 6; 115A, 6; 172, 1
Warships, 95A, 4-6; 95B, 1, 2, 4

Travel on Land

Asses, 43, 5; 167, 3; 168, 3; 179, 2; F 3, 2 (224)
Carts, 15B, 4, 5; 31, 5; 91, 2, 3
Lighter horses, 22, 1-4; 48, 1, 2; 57, 1; 67, 4; 136, 5; 148, 4;
    171, 2
Litters, 85, 3; 91, 2; 122, 5; 163, 4
Mules, 43, 5; 57, 4, 5; 132, 2; 142, 1, 3, 5
Palfreys, 15A, 3; 59, 1; 62, 6; 97, 2; 98, 1; 106, 1; 116, 1;
    121, 2; 135B, 3
Sidesaddles, 98, 1; 135; F 3, 2 (224)
Warhorses, 19, 1; 63, 3-5; 129, 1, 2
    Muslim warhorses, 99, 6; 165B, 5; 181, 6; 185, 3-6

Violent Acts

Blinding, 138, 1; 177, 2
Blinding and amputation of hands, 146, 3
Burning alive, 175B, 6; 185, 5; F 18 (294)
Castration, 26
Child thrown into glass furnace, 4, 4
Cut throat, 15A, 6; 26, 3; 124, 3; F 90, 1 (237)
Cutting off hand, F 22B, 3 (265); F 54 (206)
Cutting out tongue, 156, 2; 174, 3
Decapitation, 96, 2
Dragging through streets, 136, 5; F 18, 5 (294)
Eye gouged out, 138, 1; 146, 3
Flagellation, 50, 3; 83, 2; 85A, 2; 136, 5; 152, 1
Foot mutilation, 37, 2; 62, 2; 127, 4
Kicking mother, 127, 1
Lance piercing, 114, 2; 124, 2
Rape, 15A, 4 (attempted rape); F 47, 1 (291); F 90 (237); F
    92, 2 (317) (attempted rape)
Rip open back and split heart, 72, 5
Scalping, 155, 1
Shooting at heaven, 154, 3
Split head, 6, 3 (of young boy); 114, 2; 184, 2
Stabbing, 84, 3; 105A, 5 (of woman in genitals); 124, 2; 184,
    4 (pregnant woman)
Stoning, 124, 1
Suicide, 84, 3; F 2, 4 (201) (attempted)
Thrown into a deep pit (hole) and covered entrance, 102, 4
Thrown over a cliff, 107, 3
Thrown overboard, 193, 2
Wife abuse, 105A, 5

War

Army on march and armor, 129, 1, 2; 165A, 3; 181, 3, 4;
    185A, 3, 4; 185B, 3, 6; F 14, 1, 2 (408); F 26, 3 (323)
Banner, 63, 3; 99, 1-3, 6; 181, 4, 5; 185
Battle, 15A, 5; 28, 1, 3, 4; 63, 3, 4; 181, 5
Cavalry, 181

Pennants, 99, 1-3, 6; 181, 3-5; 187A, 4
Retreat of army, 99, 6; 165B, 5; 181, 6; 185B, 6
River battle with city, F 46 (271)
Sea battle with pirates, 35 A and B
Shields, 99 (Moorish); 181, 4-6
Siege, 28, 1, 3, 4; 51, 1-3; 99, 3; 165A, 1 (Muslim); F 5, 1
    (205)
War drums, 165B, 5

Women
In T.I.1

Alis helped by Saint Mary to marry, 135, 5
Concubine of priest, 151
Empress of Rome, 15
Fickle young woman, 79
Gascon woman, 153
Harlot visited by monk, 11
Jewish woman saved from defenestration, 107
Lady courted illegally by knight, 16
Maiden marries cleric, 132
Man and wife vow chastity, 115
Marital rape, 105
Nun who said only 'Ave,' 71
Paralyzed woman, 77
Pregnant abbess, 7
Pregnant Jewish woman delivered, 89, 4
Pregnant woman saved from sea, 86
Princess resuscitated, 122
Roman noblewoman, 17
Runaway nuns, 55; 58; 59; 94
Seamstress crippled, then cured, 117
Silk producer, 18
Two women made friends, 68
Wife deserted by husband, 42
Wife kept chaste by Virgin, 64
Woman can't open church door, 98
Woman cured of Saint Martial's fire, 81
Woman falls from peak, 191
Woman given son by Virgin, 62
Woman hides communion wafer, 104
Woman instructed by Virgin, 71, 3
Woman "instructed" in sex by priest, 111
Woman pilgrim, 57
Woman resuscitated after stabbing herself, 84
Woman saved from fire, 186 (185 in Filgueira Valverde 1985)
Woman's love conjured up by cleric, 125
Woman's sheep guarded, 147
Woman's son resuscitated, 21; 76; 114; 118; 168
Woman's twisted limbs cured, 179
Woman's wine casks filled, 23
Young girl resuscitated, 133

In F

Blind girl cured, 62 (1) (247)
Eve, 40 (320)

Plates

Frontispiece: Alfonso with his scribes and musicians in the prologue of the *Cantigas de Santa Maria.* MS T.I.1.

Plate 1: *Cantiga* 64. "This is how the wife whose husband had left her under Saint Mary's protection could not put on or take off the shoes her suitor had given her."

Plate 2: *Cantiga* 120, panel 1. Untitled. A song of praise to Saint Mary, showing musicians, singers, and dancers

Plate 3: *Cantiga* 18. "This is how Saint Mary made the silkworms spin two veils . . ."

Plate 4: *Cantiga* 142. "This is how Saint Mary wished to save a king's man from death . . ."

Plate 5: *Cantiga* 9. "This is how . . . Saint Mary made her image painted on a wooden tablet exude oil."

Plate 6: *Cantiga* 52. "This is how Saint Mary made the mountain goats come to Monsarraz . . ."

Plate 7: *Cantiga* 103. "This is how Saint Mary made a monk remain three hundred years [listening] to the song of a bird . . ."

Plate 8: *Cantiga* 47. "This is how Saint Mary saved the monk whom the devil tried to frighten in order to destroy him."

Plate 9: *Cantiga* 75A, panel 2. "How an old woman sent a girl to call the priest to give her communion."

Plate 10: *Cantiga* 157. "This is about some pilgrims who were going to Rocamadour . . ."

Plate 11: *Cantiga* 8. "This is how Saint Mary made a candle descend on the fiddle of a minstrel who sang before her."

Plate 12: *Cantiga* F 79, panel 4. "This is how Saint Mary took away a great fire storm in the land of Sicily." Authorized by the Biblioteca Nazionale, Florence, and Edilán

Plate 13: *Cantiga* 4. "This is how Saint Mary kept the Jew's son from burning . . ."

Plate 14: *Cantiga* 74. "This is how Saint Mary protected the painter whom the devil tried to kill because he was painting him ugly."

Plate 15: *Cantiga* 31, panel 5. "How they hitched the bullock to the cart to carry stone for the building of a church."

Plate 16: *Cantiga* 1, panel 2. "How Saint Mary gave birth to Jesus Christ and laid him in a manger."

Plate 17: *Cantiga* 147, panel 5. "How the old woman sheared the sheep . . ."

Plate 18: *Cantiga* 34. "How Saint Mary got the better of a Jew for the dishonor he had done Her image."

Plate 19: *Cantiga* 108. "This is how Saint Mary made the son of a Jew be born with his head on backwards . . ."

Plate 20: *Cantiga* 28, panel 3. "How the sultan ordered siege engines set up."

Plate 21: *Cantiga* 124. "This is how Saint Mary saved a man whom they stoned . . ."

Plate 22: *Cantiga* 113, panel 5. "How Saint Mary made the rock change course so that it would not strike the monastery."

Plate 23: *Cantiga* 148, panel 5. "How the knight's men went to some villages to ask them to help him."

Plate 24: *Cantiga* 22, panel 4. "How Saint Mary protected the farmer so that he would not die from the wounds a knight and his men gave him."

Plate 25: *Cantiga* F 88, panel 2. "How a good man had a mule which was swollen in all four legs." Authorized by the Biblioteca Nazionale, Florence, and Edilán.

Plate 26: *Cantiga* 167, panel 3. Untitled, showing a child's coffin carried on the back of a donkey

Plate 27: *Cantiga* 128, panel 3. "How the peasant went to call a priest and showed him Saint Mary in the beehive."

Plate 28: *Cantiga* F 4, panel 4. "How a huge dog passed by there . . . and attacked a good man." Authorized by the Biblioteca Nazionale, Florence, and Edilán

Plate 29: *Cantiga* 29, panel 5. Untitled, reveals exotic beasts, birds, and fishes adoring the Virgin

Plate 30: *Cantiga* 189. "How a man went out to Salas on a pilgrimage and met a dragon which came to kill him."

Plate 31: *Cantiga* 56, panel 5. "How five roses bloomed from the mouth of the monk because of five psalms he recited."

Plate 32: *Cantiga* 153, panel 5. "How the woman lay down before the altar and the chair did not let go of her."

Plate 33: *Cantiga* F 95. "How King Alfonso fell ill in Vitoria . . ." Authorized by the Biblioteca Nazionale, Florence, and Edilán

Plate 34: *Cantiga* F 71, panel 5. "How Saint Mary cured King Alfonso in Valladolid who was judged to be dying." Authorized by the Biblioteca Nazionale, Florence, and Edilán

Plate 35: *Cantiga* 135A. "This is how Saint Mary confirmed the marriage of a boy and a girl."

Plate 36: *Cantiga* 135B. Untitled. Further adventures of the two young lovers.

Plate 37: *Cantiga* 115A, panel 1. "How a man and his wife vowed chastity and how the devil made them break it."

Plate 38: *Cantiga* 94. "How Saint Mary served in place of the nun who left the convent."

Plate 39: *Cantiga* 59. "This is how the crucifix for the honor of His Mother slapped the nun who had promised to go away with her lover."

Plate 40: *Cantiga* 7, panel 6. "How the abbess disrobed before the bishop and was cleared of the accusation."

Plate 41: *Cantiga* 17, panel 1. "This is how Saint Mary saved from death the honorable lady of Rome whom the devil accused in order to have her burned."

Plate 42: *Cantiga* 105A, panel 5. "How the wicked bridegroom planned to do something and committed a shameful deed."

Plate 43: *Cantiga* 5A, panel 1. "How Emperor Julian ordered hay given to St. Basil."

Plate 44: *Cantiga* 44. "This is how the gentleman lost his goshawk . . ."

Plate 45: *Cantiga* 175A, panel 4. "How the magistrate went after the pilgrims and told them to halt."

Plate 46: *Cantiga* 186, panel 2. "How the next day the monks found the storage bins filled with very good wheat."

Plate 47: *Cantiga* F 37. "This is how a minstrel wanted to mimic the image of Saint Mary . . ." Authorized by the Biblioteca Nazionale, Florence, and Edilán

Plate 48: *Cantiga* 38, panel 3. "How the rogue struck the arm of the image of Jesus Christ with a stone and the devil killed him."

Plate 49: *Cantiga* 144. "This is how Saint Mary saved a good man in Plasencia from a bull which charged him to kill him."

Plate 50: *Cantiga* 42. "This is about how the postulant put the ring on the finger of the image of Saint Mary and the image encircled it with its finger."

Plate 51: *Cantiga* 90, panel 3. Untitled. What seems to be a stage for dramatization.

Plate 52: *Cantiga* 2, panel 5. "How Saint Mary gave the alb to St. Ildefonso."

Plate 53: *Cantiga* 26, panel 4. "How St. James wished to take the soul of his pilgrim from a devil."

Plate 54: *Cantiga* 109, panel 3. "How two friars came by there and took him to the church in spite of the devil."

Plate 55: *Cantiga* 125A, panel 4. "How the priest made a circle and conjured the devils so that they might bring the damsel to him."

Plate 56: *Cantiga* 26, panel 3. "How the pilgrim cut off his private parts and slit his throat on the advice of the devil."

Plate 57: *Cantiga* 72, panel 4. "How a dead man appeared to the gambler's father to tell him his son was dead." Authorized by the Patrimonio Nacional, reproduced from the facsimile of Edilán

Plate 58: *Cantiga* 67. "This is how Saint Mary made the good man realize he had with him a demon for a servant and that he wanted to kill him, but for the prayer he said."

Plate 59: *Cantiga* 106, panel 1. "How two squires went out to rob the land and they captured them."

Plate 60: *Cantiga* 63. "This is how Saint Mary saved a knight from dishonor who ought to have been in battle . . ."

Plate 61: *Cantiga* 122, panel 5. Untitled, showing Queen Beatriz, Alfonso's mother, in a litter

Plate 62: *Cantiga* 95B, panel 1. "How the Moors took the count out of the galley."

Plate 63: *Cantiga* 36, panel 1. "How a ship was crossing the sea with a great company of men on board."

Plate 64: *Cantiga* F 22, panel 4. "How Saint Mary restored to John Damascene the hand which had been cut off." Authorized by the Biblioteca Nazionale, Florence, and Edilán

Plate 65: *Cantiga* 185, panel 5. "How the Moorish traitor burned and Saint Mary protected the lady so that the fire did not touch her."

Plate 66: *Cantiga* 184, panel 4. "How a traitor struck her in the side with a knife and she died immediately."

Plate 67: *Cantiga* 107. "This is how Saint Mary saved from death a Jewess whom they cast down from a cliff in Segovia."

Plate 68: *Cantiga* 165A, panel 3. "How the sultan came to lay siege to Tartus and saw few people in the city."

Plate 69: *Cantiga* 178. "How a farmer gave his son a little she-mule he had from his mare."

Plate 70: *Cantiga* 136. "Saint Mary displayed this miracle in the land of Apulia in a city called Foggia."

Selected Bibliography

Ackerlind, Sheila. 1992. "The Relationship of Alfonso X of Castile and Dinis of Portugal." Ph.D. diss., Yale Univ.

Aguado Bleye, Pedro. 1916. *Santa María de Salas en el siglo XIII: Estudio sobre* Las Cantigas *de Alfonso X el Sabio.* Bilbao, Spain: Garmendía.

Aita, Nella. 1919. "Miniature spagnuole en un codice fiorentino." *Rassegna d'Arte* 19:149-55.

———. 1921. "O códice florentino de *Cantigas* de Alfonso, o Sábio." *Revista de Lingua Portuguesa* 13:187-205; 14:105-28.

———. 1922. "*O códice florentino das* Cantigas *de Alfonso o Sábio. Revista de Língua Portuguesa* 15:169-76; 16:181-88; 18:153-60.

Alemparte, Jaime Ferreiro. 1971. "Fuentes Germánicos en las *CSM* de Alfonso X el Sabio." *Grial* 30:31-62.

Alfau de Solalinde, Jesusa. 1969. *Nomenclatura de los tejidos del siglo XIII.* Anejo 19 of the *Boletín de la Real Academia Española.* Madrid: Real Academia Española.

Alfonso X el Sabio. 1979. *Cantigas de Santa María. Edición facsímil del Códice Rico T.I.1 de la Biblioteca de San Lorenzo el Real de El Escorial, Siglo XIII.* With *Volumen Complementario.* Madrid: Edilán.

———. 1989. *Cantigas de Santa María. Edición facsímil del Códice B.R. 20 de la Biblioteca Nazionale de Florencia, Siglo XIII.* With *Volumen Complementario.* Madrid: Edilán.

.Anglés, Higinio. 1943. *La música de las* Cantigas de Santa María *del Rey Alfonso el Sabio: Facsímil, transcripción y estudio crítico II.* Barcelona: Diputación Provincial de Barcelona, Biblioteca Central.

Bagby, Albert I., Jr. 1970. "Alfonso X, el Sabio compara moros y judíos." *Romanische Forschungen* 82:578-83.

———. 1971. "The Jew in the *Cantigas* of Alfonso el Sabio." *Speculum* 46:670-88.

———. 1973. "The Moslems in the *Cantigas* of Alfonso X, el Sabio." *Kentucky Romance Quarterly* 20:173-207.

Bagley, John J. 1960. *Life in Medieval England.* London: B.T. Batsford.

Ballesteros y Beretta, Antonio. 1963. *Alfonso X el Sabio.* Barcelona: Salvat; Murcia: Consejo Superior de Investigaciones Científicas.

Baraut, Cebrià. 1949-50. "Les *Cantigues* d'Alfons el Savi i el primitu *Liber Miraculorum de Nostra Dona de Montserrat.*" *Estudis Romànics* 2:79-92.

Beaulieu, Michèle. 1951. *Le costume antique et médiéval.* Paris: Presses Universitaires de France.

Beltrán, Luis. 1990. *Las cantigas de loor de Alfonso X el Sabio.* Bilingual ed. Madrid: Los Poetas—Serie Mayor. Ediciones Júcar.

Bernis Madrazo, Carmen. 1956. *Indumentaria medieval española.* Madrid: C.S.I.C.

Boissonnade, Prosper 1927. *Life and Work in Medieval Europe (Fifth to Fifteenth Centuries).* Translated by and with an introduction by Eileen Power. New York: Alfred A. Knopf.

———. 1972. "The Medieval Crossbow as a Surgical Instrument: An Illustrated Case History." *Bulletin of the New York Academy of Medicine* 48:983-89.

Boswell, John. 1980. *Christianity, Social Tolerance, and Homosexuality.* Chicago: Univ. of Chicago Press.

Braga, Theophilo. 1878. *Camciomero portuguez da Vaticana. Edição crítica.* Lisbon: Imprensa Nacional.

Brenan, Gerald. 1960. *The Literature of the Spanish People.* New York: Meridan.

Burckhardt, Titus. 1972. *Moorish Art in Spain.* New York: McGraw Hill.

Burns, Robert I., S.J. 1987. "The *Cantigas de Santa María* as a Research Opportunity in History." *Bulletin of the Cantigueiros* 1, no. 1 (fall): 17-22.

———, ed. 1990. *Emperor of Culture: Alfonso X the Learned of Castile and His Thirteenth-Century Renaissance.* Philadelphia: Univ. of Pennsylvania Press.

Calcott, Frank. 1923. *The Supernatural in Early Spanish Literature.* New York: Instituto de las Españas en los Estados Unidos.

Calkins, Robert G. 1979. *Monuments of Medieval Art.* New York: E.P. Dutton.

Cano Ballesta, Juan. 1986. "Los 'cantares caçurros' como género juglaresco." La juglaresca, *Actas del I Congreso Internacional sobre la Juglaresca,* ed. M. Criado de Val. Madrid: Edi-6.

Cárdenas, Anthony J. 1987. "A Study of Alfonso's Role in Selected *Cantigas* and the Castilian Prosifications of Escorial Codex T.I.1." In Katz and Keller 1987b, 253-68.

———. 1988-89. "'De una maravilla que acaecio . . .': Miracles in the Prose and Poetry of Alfonso X's Royal Scriptorium." *Bulletin of the Cantigueiros* 2 (fall/spring): 13-30.

Carpenter, Dwayne. 1986. *Alfonso X and the Jews: An Edition and Commentary on Siete Partidas "De los judíos."* Berkeley: Univ. of California Press.

———. 1993. "A Sorcerer Defends the Virgin: Merlin in the *Cantigas de Santa María.*" *Bulletin of the Cantigueiros* 5 (spring): 3-24.

Castro, Américo. 1954. *The Structure of Spanish History.* Trans. Edmund L. King. Princeton, N.J.: Princeton Univ. Press.

———. 1959. *Santiago de España.* Buenos Aires: Emecé.

Chatham, James. 1976. "A Paleographic Edition of the Alfonsine Collection of Prose Miracles of the Virgin." In *Oelschläger Festschrift,* ed. James Chatham. *Estudios de Hispanófila* 36:73-111.

Chisman, Anna. 1974. "Enjambement in *Las Cantigas de Santa María* of Alfonso X, el Sabio." Ph.D. diss., Univ. of Toronto.

Clarke, Dorothy Clotelle. 1955. "Versification in Alfonso el Sabio's *Cantigas.*" *Hispanic Review* 23:83-98.

Cómez Ramón, Rafael. 1975. "La arquitectura en las miniaturas." In *Arquitectura Alfonsí* 103-34.

Davis, William R., Jr. 1969. "The Role of the Virgin in the *Cantigas de Santa María.*" Ph.D. diss., Univ. of Kentucky.

———. 1972. "Mary and Merlin: An Unusual Alliance." *Romance Notes* 14:207-12.

Defourneaux, Marcelin. 1971. *Daily Life in Spain in the Golden Age.* Trans. Newton Branch. New York: Praeger.

Dexter, Elise. 1926. "Sources of the *Cantigas* of Alfonso el Sabio." Ph.D. diss., Univ. of Wisconsin, Madison.

Diz, Ana. 1993. "Berceo and Alfonso: La historia de la abadesa encinta." *Bulletin of the Cantigueiros* 5 (spring): 85-96.

Domínguez Bordona, Jesús. 1929. *Exposición de códices miniados españoles: Catálogo.* Madrid: Sociedad Española de Amigos del Arte.

———. 1929. *Spanish Illumination.* 2 vols. Florence: Pantheon Casa Editrice. Reprint, New York: Hacker Art Books, 1969.

———. 1932. *El arte de la miniatura española.* Madrid: Plutarco.

Domínguez Rodríguez, Ana. 1976. "Imágenes de presentación de la miniatura alfonsí." *Goya* 131 (March-April): 287-91.

———. 1987. "Iconografía evangélica en las *Cantigas de Santa Maria.*" In Katz and Keller 1987b, 53-80.

Dunn, Maryjane, and Linda K. Davidson. 1996. *The Pilgrimage to Compostela in the Middle Ages: A Case Book on the Medieval Pilgrimage to Santiago de Compostela.* New York: Garland.

Durrieu, Paul. 1893. "Manuscrites d'Espagne remarquables par leurs peintures o par la beauté de leurs executions á la Bibliothèque de l'Escurial." *Extraite de la Bibliothèque de l'Ecole de Chartres* 54:251-326.

Egbert, Virginia Wylie. 1967. *The Medieval Artist at Work.* Princeton, N.J.: Princeton Univ. Press.

———. 1974. *On the Bridges of Medieval Paris: A Record of Early Fourteenth-Century Life.* Princeton, N.J.: Princeton Univ. Press.

Escobar, José. 1992. "The Practice of Necromancy as Depicted in the *Cantigas de Santa María.*" *Bulletin of the Cantigueiros* 4 (spring): 33-43.

Evans, Joan. 1969. *Life in Medieval France.* 3d ed. New York: Phaidon.

Fernández Pousa, Ramón. 1956. "Menéndez y Pelayo y el códice florentino de las *Cantigas de Santa María* de Alfonso X el Sabio." *Revista de Archivos, Bibliotecas y Museos* 62:235-55.

Filgueira Valverde, José, trans. 1985. *Cantigas de Santa María. Códice Rico de El Escorial, Ms. Escurialense T.I.1.* Madrid: Castalia.

García Cuadrado, Amparo. 1993. *Las Cantigas: El Códice de Florencia.* Murcia, Spain: Universidad de Murcia.

García Varela, Jesús. 1992. "La función ejemplar de Alfonso X en las cantigas personales." *Bulletin of the Cantigueiros* 4 (spring): 3-16.

Gies, Frances, and Joseph Gies. 1978. *Women in the Middle Ages.* New York: Harper and Row.

Gies, Joseph, and Frances Gies. 1969. *Life in a Medieval City.* New York: Crowel.

———. 1979. *Life in a Medieval Castle.* New York: Harper and Row.

González, Juan, Jr. 1969. "La sociedad medieval española reflejada en la obra de Alfonso el Sabio." Ph.D. diss., Univ. of Texas.

González-Casanovas, Roberto J. 1992. "Marian Devotion as Gendered Discourse in Berceo and Alfonso X: Popular Reception of the *Milagros* and *Cantigas.*" *Bulletin of the Cantigueiros* 4 (spring): 17-31.

Greenia, George. 1988-89. "A New Manuscript Illuminated in the Alfonsine Scriptorium." *Bulletin of the Cantigueiros* 2 (fall/spring): 31-42.

———. 1990. "The Court of Alfonso X in Words and Pictures: Las Cantigas." In *Courtly Literature: Culture and Context,* 227-37. Acts of the Fifth Triennial Congress of the International Courtly Literature Society. Dalfsen, The Netherlands, August 9-16, 1986. Amsterdam: Benjamins.

———. 1993. "The Politics of Piety: Manuscript Illumination and Narration in the *Cantigas de Santa María.*" *Hispanic Review* 61 (summer): 325-44.

Guerrero-Lovillo, José. 1949. *Las Cantigas: Estudio*

arqueológico de sus miniaturas. Madrid: Consejo Superior de Investigaciones Científicas.

———. 1956. *Miniatura gótica castellana: Siglos XIII a XIV.* Madrid: Consejo Superior de Investigaciones Científicas.

Gurevich, Aron. 1992. *Medieval Popular Culture: Problems of Belief and Perception.* Trans. János M. Bak and Paul A. Hollingsworth. Cambridge: Cambridge Univ. Press.

Hardison, Osborne B. 1965. *Christian Rite and Christian Drama in the Middle Ages: Essays in the Origin and History of Modern Drama.* Baltimore: Johns Hopkins Univ. Press.

Hatton, Vikki, and Angus Mackay. 1983. "Anti-Semitism in the *Cantigas de Santa María.*" *Bulletin of Hispanic Studies* 60:189-99.

Hauser, Arnold. 1951. *The Social History of Art--Prehistoric, Ancient-Oriental, Greece and Rome, Middle Ages.* New York: Vantage.

Hernández Serna, Joaquín. 1980. "La Orden de la Estrella, o de Santa María de España, en la *Cantiga 78* del Códice de la Biblioteca Nacional de Florencia." *Miscelánea Medieval Murciana* 6:147-68.

Holmes, Urban T., Jr. 1952. *Daily Living in the Twelfth Century Based on the Observations of Alexander Neckam in London and Paris.* Madison: Univ. of Wisconsin Press.

———. 1980. *Medieval Man: His Understanding of Himself, and the World.* Chapel Hill, N.C.: North Carolina Studies in the Romance Languages and Literatures.

Jayne, Cynthia. 1990. "The Virgin's Cures for Lust." *Estudios Alfonsinos y otros escritos.* New York: National Hispanic Foundation for the Humanities.

Jensen, Frede, ed. and trans. 1992. *Medieval Galician-Portuguese Poetry: An Anthology.* London: Garland.

Kassier, Theodore L. 1990. "The 'Salas' Miracles of the *Cantigas de Santa María.*" *Bulletin of the Cantigueiros* 3 (fall): 31-37.

Katz, Israel J., and John E. Keller. 1987a. "The Study and Performance of the *Cantigas de Santa María:* A Glance at Recent Musicological Literature." *Bulletin of the Cantigueiros* 1, no. 1 (fall): 51-60.

Katz, Israel J., and John E. Keller, eds. 1987b. *Studies on the* Cantigas de Santa María: *Art, Music, and Poetry. Proceedings of the International Symposium on the* Cantigas de Santa María of *Alfonso X, el Sabio (1221-1284) in Commemoration of Its 700th Anniversary Year--1981.* Madison, Wis.: Hispanic Seminary of Medieval Studies.

Keller, John E. 1954. "A Note on King Alfonso's Use of Popular Themes in His *Cantigas de Santa María.*" *Kentucky Foreign Language Quarterly* 1, no. 1: 26-31.

———. 1958. "Daily Living as Presented in the *Canticles* of Alfonso the Learned." *Speculum* 33, no. 4: 484-89.

———. 1959a. "Folklore in the *Cantigas* of Alfonso el Sabio." *Southern Folklore Quarterly* 23, no. 3: 175-83.

———. 1959b. "King Alfonso's Virgin of Villa-Sirga, Rival of St. James of Compostela." In *Middle Ages-Reformation-Volkskunde: Festschrift for John G. Kunstman,* ed. Victor Rudolph Bernhardt, 95-102. Chapel Hill: Univ. of North Carolina Press.

———. 1959c. "The Motif of the Statue Bride in the *Cantigas* of Alfonso the Learned." *Studies in Philology* 56, no. 4: 453-58.

———. 1965. "A Medieval Folklorist." In *Folklore Studies in Honor of Arthur Palmer Hudson,* ed. Daniel Patterson, 19-24. Chapel Hill, N.C.

———. 1967. *Alfonso X, el Sabio.* New York: Twayne.

———. 1972a. "*Cantiga 135:* The Blessed Virgin as a Matchmaker." In *Florilegium Hispanicum: Medieval and Golden Age Studies Presented to Dorothy Clotelle Clarke,* ed. John S. Geary, 103-18. Madison, Wis.: Hispanic Seminary of Medieval Studies.

———. 1972b. "The Depiction of Exotic Animals in *Cantiga XXIX* of the *Cantigas de Santa María.*" In *Studies in Honor of Tatiana Fotitch,* ed. Josep M. Sola-Solé, Alessandro S. Crisafulli, and Siegfried A. Schultz, 247-53. Washington, D.C.: Catholic Univ. Press.

———. 1975. "An Unknown Castilian Lyric Poem: The Alfonsine Translation of *Cantiga X* of the *Cantigas de Santa María.*" *Hispanic Review* 45:43-47.

———. 1976. "Verbalization and Visualization in the *Cantigas de Santa María.*" In *Oelschläger Festschrift,* ed. James Chatham. *Estudios de Hispanófila* 36:221-26.

———. 1979a. "More on the Rivalry between Santa María and Santiago." *Crítica Hispánica* 1, no. 1: 37-43.

———. 1979b. *Pious Brief Narrative in Medieval Castilian and Galician Verse: From Berceo to Alfonso X.* Lexington: Univ. Press of Kentucky.

———. 1984. "The Miracle of the Divinely Motivated Silkworms: *Cantiga 18* of the *Cantigas de Santa María.*" *Hispanófila* 28, no. 1: 1-9.

———. 1990. "Drama, Ritual and Incipient Opera in Alfonso's *Cantigas.*" In *Emperor of Culture,* ed. Robert I. Burns, 73-89. Philadelphia: Univ. of Pennsylvania Press.

Keller, John E., Clark L. Keating, and Eric M. Furr. 1992. *The Book of Tales by A.B.C.* Bern: Peter Lang.

Keller, John E., and Richard P. Kinkade. 1984. *Iconography in Medieval Spanish Literature.* Lexington: Univ. Press of Kentucky.

Keller, John E., and Robert W. Linker. 1974. "Las traducciones castellanas de las *CSM.*" *Boletín de la Real Academia Española* 54:221-93.

Keller, John E., and Charles L. Nelson. 1974. "Some Remarks on Visualization in the *Cantigas de Santa María.*" *Ariel* 3 (April): 7-12.

Keller, John E., with Albert Gier. 1985. *Les formes narratives brèves en Espagne et au Portugal.* In *Grundriss der Romanischen Literaturen des Mittelalters,* vol. 5. Heidelberg: Carl Winter Universitätsverlag.

King, Georgiana G. 1920. *The Way of St. James.* New York: G.P. Putnam.

King, Sharon D. 1988. "Wicked Laughter: The Devil as a Source of Humor in the *CSM.*" *Bulletin of the Cantigueiros* 1, no. 2: 129-38.

Kinkade, Richard P. 1986. "Sermons in the Round: The *Mester de Clercía* as Dramatic Art." In *Studies in Honor of Gustavo Correa,* ed. Charles Faulhaber and Richard P. Kinkade, 27-36. Potomac, Md.: Scripta Humanistica.

Kulp-Hill, Kathleen. 1985. "Sidelights on Daily Life of the Iberian Peninsula in the Thirteenth Century as Seen in the *Cantigas de Santa María*." Paper presented at the Kentucky Foreign Language Conference, Lexington, April.

———. 1987a. "Clothing in the *Cantigas de Santa María*." Paper presented at the American Association of Teachers of Spanish and Portuguese, San Francisco, August.

———. 1987b. "A World in Words in the *Cantigas de Santa María*." *Bulletin of the Cantigueiros* 1, no. 1 (fall): 33-39.

———. 1995. "Captions of Miniatures in the *Códice Rico* of the *Cantigas de Santa María*: A Translation." *Bulletin of the Cantigueiros* 6 (spring): 3-62.

Le Goff, Jacques. 1977. *Pour un autre Moyen Age: Temps, travail et culture en Occident: 18 essais.* Paris: Gaillamard.

———. 1982. *Time, Work, and Culture in the Middle Ages.* Trans. Arthur Goldhammer. Chicago: Univ. of Chicago Press.

Lloréns Cisteró, José María. 1979. Cantigas de Santa María, *del rey Alfonso el Sabio. La música, datos, transcripción y notas, con un apéndice descriptivo de la grabación discográfica que acompaña este volumen.* Edilán, II.

London, Gardiner. 1960. "Bibliografía de estudios sobre la vida y obra de Alfonso X el Sabio." *Boletín de Filología Española* 6 (April): 18-31.

López Estrada, Francisco, and John E. Keller. 1964. *El Abencerraje.* University of North Carolina Studies in Comparative Literature, no. 3. Chapel Hill, N.C.

Mackay, Angus, and Geraldine McKendrick. 1979. "Confession in the *CSM*." *Reading Medieval Studies* 5:71-88.

Madrigal, José Antonio. 1980. "'El ome muy feo'" ¿primera aparición del salvaje en la iconografía española?" In *Medieval, Renaissance and Folklore Studies in Honor of John Esten Keller,* ed. Joseph R. Jones, 67-76. Newark, Del.: Juan de la Cuesta.

Madriguera, Enric. 1991. "Guitarras moriscas and latinas in the *Cantigas de Santa María*." In *Estudios Alfonsinos y otros escritos,* ed. Nicolás Toscano Liria, 129-39. New York: National Hispanic Foundation for the Humanities.

Mâle, Emile. 1922. *L'Art religieux du XIIe siècle en France.* 4th ed. Paris: Armand Celin.

———. 1972. *The Gothic Image: Religious Art in France in the Thirteenth Century.* Trans. Dora Nussey. New York: Harper and Row.

Marchand, James. 1988. "The Adynata in Alfonso X's *Cantiga* 110." *Bulletin of the Cantigueiros* 1, no. 2 (spring): 83-90.

Martínez Diez, Gonzalo, in collaboration with José M. Ruiz Asencio. 1985. *Leyes de Alfonso X.* Vol. 1, *Espéculo.* Avila, Spain: Fundación Sánchez Albornoz.

Menéndez Pidal, Gonzalo. 1951. "Como trabajaron las escuelas alfonsíes." *Nueva Revista de Filología Hispánica* 5, no. 4: 363-80.

———. 1962. "Los manuscritos de las *Cantigas de Santa María*: Cómo se elaboró la miniatura alfonsí." *Boletín de la Real Academia Española* 150:23-51.

Menéndez Pidal, Marcelino. 1895. "Las *Cantigas* del Rey Sabio." *La Ilustración Española y Americana* 39:127-31, 143-46, 159-63. Reprinted in Marcelino Menéndez Pidal, *Obras Completas,* vol. 1, *Estudios y discursos de crítica histórica y literaria,* 161-89 (Madrid: Consejo Superior de Investigaciones Científicas, 1941).

Mettmann, Walter, ed. 1959-72. *Cantigas de Santa Maria.* 4 vols. Coimbra, Portugal: Acta Universitatis Conimbrigensis.

———. 1986-89. *Cantigas de Santa María.* 3 vols. Madrid: Editorial Castalia.

———. 1988. "A Collection of Miracles from Italy as a Possible Source of the *Cantigas de Santa María*." *Bulletin of the Cantigueiros* 1, no. 2 (spring): 75-82.

Montoya, Isabel. 1993. "La caza in las *Cantigas de Santa María*." *Bulletin of the Cantigueiros* 5 (spring): 35-48.

Montoya Martínez, Jesús. 1974. "Criterio agrupador de las *Cantigas de Santa María*." In *Estudios literarios dedicados al profesor Mariano Baguero Goyanes,* ed. Manuel Soler, 289-96. Murcia, Spain: Artes Gráficas Soler.

———. 1986. "El códice de Florencia: Una nueva hipótesis de trabajo 'Alfonsine Essays.'" *Romance Quarterly* 33:323-89.

———. 1990. "La 'gran vingança' de Dios y de Alfonso X." *Bulletin of the Cantigueiros* 3 (fall): 53-59.

Mount, Richard Terry. 1991. "The Treatment of the Miracle of the Devout Thief in Berceo and Alfonso el Sabio." In *Estudios alfonsinos y otros escritos,* ed. Nicolás Toscano Liria, 165-71. New York: National Hispanic Foundation for the Humanities.

———. 1993. "Levels of Meaning: Grains, Bread, and Bread Making as Informative Images in Berceo." *Hispania* 76, no. 3: 49-54.

Mount, Richard Terry, and Annette Grant Cash. 1997. *The Miracles of Our Lady.* Lexington: Univ. Press of Kentucky.

Nelson, Charles L. 1964. "Literary and Pictorial Treatment of the Devil in the *Cantigas de Santa María*." Master's thesis, Univ. of North Carolina, Chapel Hill.

Noticiero Alfonsí. Ed. Anthony J. Cárdenas. A bibliography-newsletter dealing with all materials devoted to Alfonsine studies.

O'Callaghan, Joseph. F. 1975. *A History of Medieval Spain.* Ithaca, N.Y.: Cornell Univ. Press.

———. 1987. "The *Cantigas de Santa María* as an Historical Source: Two Examples (nos. 321 and 386)." In Katz and Keller 1987b, 387-402.

———. 1993. *The Learned King: The Reign of Alfonso X of Castile.* Philadelphia: Univ. of Pennsylvania Press.

Oliveira Marques, António H. 1971. *Daily Life in Portugal in the Late Middle Ages.* Madison: Univ. of Wisconsin Press.

Pächt, Otto. 1962. *The Rise of Pictorial Narrative Art in Twelfth-Centry England.* Oxford: Clarendon Press.

Parker, Rowland. 1975. *The Common Stream: Two Thousand Years of the English Village.* Chicago: Academy Chicago Publishers.

Parkinson, Stephen. 1988. "The First Reorganization of the *Cantigas de Santa María*." *Bulletin of the Cantigueiros* 1, no. 2 (spring): 83-97.

Pelican, Jaroslav. 1996. *Mary Through the Centuries: Her Place in the Hisotry of Culture.* New Haven: Yale Univeristy.

Powers, James F. 1988. *A Society Organized for War: The Iberian Municipal Militias in the Central Middle Ages.* Berkeley: Univ. of California Press.

Presilla, Maricel. 1989. "The Image of Death in the *Cantigas de Santa María* of Alfonso X (1252-84): The Politics of Death and Salvation." Ph.D. diss., New York Univ.

Procter, Evelyn S. 1951. *Alfonso X of Castile, Patron of Literature and Learning.* Oxford: Clarendon Press.

Rey, Agapito. 1927. "Indice de nombres propios y de asuntos importantes de las *Cantigas de Santa María.*" *Boletín de la Real Academia Española* 14:327-55.

———. 1928. "Correspondence of the Spanish Miracles of the Virgin." *Romanic Review* 19:151-53.

Riché, Pierre. 1978. *Daily Life in the World of Charlemagne.* Trans. Jo Ann Mcamara. Philadelphia: Univ. of Pennsylvania Press.

Robb, David M. 1973. *The Art of the Illuminated Manuscript.* New York: A.S. Barnes.

Rogers, Donna. 1991. "*Cantigas de Santa María* 2-25 and their Castilian Prose Versions." In *Estudios alfonsinos y otros escritos,* ed. Nicolás Toscano Liria, 196-204. New York: National Hispanic Foundation for the Humanities.

Rowling, Marjorie. 1961. *Everyday Life in Medieval Times.* New York: Dorset Press.

Rubio y Balaguer, Jordi. 1943. *Vida española en la época gótica.* Barcelona: Editorial Alberto Martín.

Salzman, Louis F. 1929. *English Life in the Middle Ages.* London: Oxford Univ. Press.

Sánchez Cantón, Francisco J. 1940. "Seis estampas de la vida segoviana del siglo XIII." *Correo Erudito* 1:332-34.

Scarborough, Connie. 1982. "Verbalization and Visualization in Ms. T.I.1 of the *Cantigas de Santa María.*" Ph.D. diss., Univ. of Kentucky.

———. 1986. "Alfonso X: A Monarch in Search of a Miracle." *Romance Quarterly* 33, no. 4: 349-54.

———. 1987a. "A Summary of Research on the Miniatures of the *Cantigas de Santa María.*" *Bulletin of the Cantigueiros* 1, no. 1 (fall): 41-50.

———. 1987b. "Verbalization and Visualization in MS. T.I.1. of the *Cantigas de Santa María:* The Theme of the Runaway Nun." In Katz and Keller 1987b, 135-45.

———. 1993. *Women in Thirteenth-Century Spain as Portrayed by Alfonso X's* Cantigas de Santa María. Lewiston, N.Y.: Edwin Mellen.

———. 1994. "La voces de las mujeres en las *Cantigas de Santa María* de Alfonso X." In *Discursos de mujeres/Mujeres en el discurso,* ed. Juan Villegas, 16-24, vol. 2 of *Actas del Congreso de la Asociación Internacional de Hispanistas, Irvine 1992.* Irvine, Calif.: Asociación Internacional de Hispanistas.

———. 1996. "The Pilgrimage to Santiago de Compostela." In Dunn and Davidson 1996.

Scholberg, Kenneth. 1965. *Spanish Life in the Late Middle Ages.* University of North Carolina Studies in the Romance Languages and Literatures, no. 57. Chapel Hill.

Scott, Samuel Parsons. 1931. *Las Siete Partidas.* New York: Commercial Publishing.

Seniff, Dennis P. 1986. "Letter from Doña J. Alfau de Solalinde to R. Menéndez Pidal on Her Projected Study of the *CSM.*" *Romance Quarterly* 33, no. 3: 355-64.

———. 1992. "Falconry, Venery, and Fishing in the *Cantigas de Santa María.*" In *Noble Pursuits: Literature and the Hunt,* ed. Diane M. Wright and Connie L. Scarborough, 15-32. Newark, Del.: Juan de la Cuesta.

Smith, Bradley. 1966. *Spain: A History in Art.* Introduction by the Marqués de Lozano. New York: Simon and Schuster.

Snow, Joseph T. 1972. "The *Loor* to the Virgin and Its Appearance in the *Cantigas de Santa María* of Alfonso el Sabio." Ph.D. diss., Univ. of Wisconsin.

———. 1975. "Alfonso X y la *Cantiga* 409: Un nexo posible con la tradición de la Danza de la Muerte." In *Studies in Honor of Lloyd A. Kasten,* ed. John Nitti, 261-73. Madison, Wis.: Hispanic Seminary of Medieval Studies.

———. 1977. *The Poetry of Alfonso X, el Sabio: A Critical Bibliography.* London: Grant and Cutler.

———. 1987. "An Overview of Recent Studies Devoted to the *Cantigas de Santa María.*" *Bulletin of the Cantigueiros* 1, no. 1 (fall): 5-10.

Solalinde, Antonio G. 1918. "El códice florentino de *Las Cantigas de Santa María* y su relación sobre los demás manuscritos." *Revista de Filología Española* 5:143-79.

Stone, Marilyn. 1986. "Parents and Children in the *Quarta Partida* of Alfonso X." *Romance Quarterly* 33, no. 3: 365-71.

Sturm, Sara. 1970. "The Presentations of the Virgin in the *Cantigas de Santa María.*" *Philological Quarterly* 49, no. 1 (Jan.): 1-7.

Suárez, José I. 1997. "Titillation in the *Cantigas de Santa María.*" *Bulletin of the Cantigueiros,* 9, 60-70.

Tavini, Giuseppe. 1967. *Reporterio metrico della lirica galego-portoghese. Officina Romanica,* 7. Rome: Edizione dell'Ateneo.

Tinnell, Roger. 1990. *An Annotated Discography of Music in Spain before 1650.* 2d ed. Madison, Wis.: Hispanic Seminary of Medieval Studies.

Torres Balbás, Leopoldo. 1950. "Miniaturas españolas medievales." *Al-Andaluz* 15:191-202.

Trens, Manuel. 1946. *María: Iconografía de la Virgen en el arte español.* Madrid: Plus-Ultra.

Trevison, Mary Louise, S.N.D. 1988. "Pride and Prejudice in the *Cantigas de Santa María.*" *Bulletin of the Cantigueiros* 1, no. 2 (spring): 119-27.

Ward, Benedicta. 1982. *Miracles and the Medieval Mind: Theory, Record and Event 1000-1215.* Philadelphia: Univ. of Pennsylvania Press.

Warner, Marina L. 1976. *Alone of All Her Sex: The Myth and Cult of the Virgin Mary.* New York: Alfred A. Knopf.

Waverly Consort. 1972. *Las Cantigas de Santa María: Medieval Music and Verse in the Court of Alfonso X, el Sabio.* Vanguard Recording Society.

Werner, Alfred. 1951. *Medieval Miniatures.* New York: A.A. Wyn.

Wright, Diane. 1988. "Folk-Motifs in the Prose Miracles of the *CSM.*" *Bulletin of the Cantigueiros* 1, no. 2 (spring): 99-109.

Index of Front Matter